Archives & Manuscripts: Law

Gary M. Peterson
Trudy Huskamp Peterson

BASIC MANUAL SERIES

Society of American Archivists   Chicago, 1985

The opinions expressed are those of the authors and do not necessarily represent those of the federal agencies with which they are associated.

Foreword

In 1977, the Society of American Archivists published a series of five manuals dealing with basic archival functions: *Appraisal & Accessioning, Arrangement & Description, Reference & Access, Security*, and *Surveys*. The reaction to this series was so enthusiastic that a second series, also supported by the National Historical Publications and Records Commission, was begun. Included in this series are *Exhibits, An Introduction to Automated Access, Maps and Architectural Drawings, Public Programs,* and *Reprography*. In 1983 and 1984, the Basic Manual Series expanded further, to include *Conservation, Administration of Photographic Collections*, both supported by the National Endowment for the Humanities, as well as the manual, *Machine-Readable Records*. Taken together the manuals in this series represent an important step in a transition within the archival profession from an oral tradition to a body of literature that can be accumulated, revised, and criticized.

The Society of American Archivists is pleased to add *Archives & Manuscripts: Law* to the list of titles in the Basic Manual Series and wishes to thank its authors, Gary Peterson and Trudy Huskamp Peterson, for their important contribution to the literature on archives.

Andrea Hinding, *President*
Society of American Archivists

CONTENTS

Preface

Law. The very word sounds somber. Say it, and the voice drops, the vowel sounding in the back of the throat. And the mental images it prompts run to black, like a judge's robe or, at best, to the blue serge of a policeman's uniform. Or the image is row upon row of thick books, expensively bound, sitting on shelves in an office, waiting to be willing accomplices to getting you into trouble.

For most of us, the law means power. Gilbert and Sullivan, who satirized the law whenever they could, have the Lord High Chancellor in *Iolanthe* sing:

> The Law is the embodiment
> Of everything that's excellent.
> It has no kind of fault or flaw,
> And I, my Lords, embody the Law.

Americans are notoriously litigious. De Tocqueville wrote of an earlier generation that "scarcely any question arises in the United States which does not become, sooner or later, a subject of judicial debate." This generation is no less likely to turn to the law than were the men and women of de Tocqueville's time. Archivists are swept along in this general social attitude. A New Zealand reviewer of the SAA's *Archival Forms Manual* noticed this tendency, saying, "Legal considerations are obviously of greater importance to American archives than to the New Zealand scene," adding that these concerns seemed "a little foreign" to New Zealand archivists.

Archives & Manuscripts: Law is an attempt to sort out the legal issues that confront archivists in the United States. There is no doubt that the matters we are discussing in this volume are complex; if they were easy, there would probably not be a legal angle to them. They are practical matters with important consequences, whether for the institution or the user or the donor or the archivist. This manual focuses on basic legal questions in archives. It cannot answer all questions, consider all possibilities, or provide all answers. Its aim is to present the legal questions that confront archivists in the performance of their professional duties, to point to the major types of laws governing archives, and to discuss some reasonable means of analyzing and resolving legal issues.

We do not intend this volume to be frightening; we most emphatically do not want it read as suggesting that all problems have a legal component and that archivists should routinely seek legal help. Far from it. In fact, we believe that the tendency of most people is to use lawyers too often for too many problems. Many so-called legal problems are really just knotty ethical or procedural problems that can be solved by anyone willing to think carefully about them and to outline the alternatives and assess the risks. Of course a lawyer will be willing to talk with an archives about such problems; some lawyers even specialize in something called "conflict resolution." But there are several reasons to think twice before calling a lawyer. In the first place, a consultation with a lawyer will cost money, and the archives will pay. Second, the archives will be attempting to transfer a decision that is logically its responsibility to the lawyer, perhaps undercutting its own authority to make such decisions independently in the future. Third, the archives may not get the answer it wants, whereupon it is hard to ignore the advice and take the course the archives instinctively prefers. Use lawyers, but use them judiciously.

Several areas of law are not covered in this volume. First, we have omitted any topic that seemed not directly archival, such as equal employment opportunity laws or laws covering the rights of the handicapped. This is not to suggest that these are not laws of importance to archival institutions; they surely are. We have, however, limited this volume to laws that affect the holdings of the archival institution and the use of those holdings. We have tried to focus on topics unique to the archival profession or topics shared with other professions whose business it is to provide information and trusteeship services to the public. Readers interested in general problems in administrative law will find many other sources providing such information. Second, state and local laws are not covered in any comprehensive fashion. In a nation with so many governments creating laws about records it is simply impossible to review all the pertinent legislation in one volume. Consequently, most discussions of law and legal process use federal laws and practices as a basis and most examples are drawn from federal experience.

The volume is also unbalanced in another way. We are very conscious that our friends who are users of archives will notice that the volume stresses closure of records, worries about security in research rooms, describes litigation, and so forth. In all things, it is the problem areas that create the legal issues that give rise to litigation and thereby give people signposts to follow. Naturally, a manual looks to the problems and the potential solutions to them, not to the areas where everything runs smoothly. Like the purity of the famous soap, 99.44 percent of all records are open and 99.44 percent of all working relationships between archivists and users are noncontroversial. Unfortunately this volume must focus largely on the other half of one percent.

As this manual evolved we relied on many people for

information, advice, and encouragement. Several people wrote or telephoned to us with legal issues they wanted us to address, and we learned from all the very practical problems they presented to us. We gained insights from the reviewers of this volume in draft, and the final product is better for their comments and criticism. We particularly want to thank three people: Maygene F. Daniels, Richard A. Jacobs, and Ann M. Campbell. Over the years these three have challenged us to think deeply and critically about central archival issues, and this book reflects those hours of friendly debate.

The core of American law is the idea of resolution through vigorous controversy in a controlled setting, and we hope this book will provoke the reader to confront the issues we describe. The more of us who contest the concepts, the better will our understanding become of the relationship of law to archives.

Introduction: The Context of Law

There is no one law for archives. The United States, with its federal system of government, has multiple levels of law-making bodies, each with peculiar and specific responsibilities. Hierarchically, we live with federal law, state law, and local law. Laterally, at any one of these layers, we live with tax laws, property laws, sunshine and privacy and freedom of information laws, contractual and grant laws, and a full measure of other statutes affecting archives.

These laws, passed by government bodies, are known as statutory laws. In addition to this written law (sometimes called "black letter law") the United States judicial system operates on the principle of stare decisis, that is, the policy of courts to abide by the precedent of cases that have already been decided. Consequently, alongside the statutory law there is a body of case law formed by decisions made in courts on specific cases. For example, the federal Freedom of Information Act is a relatively short statute, but there are thousands of cases that have been decided interpreting it, leading to a very considerable body of case law.

This is the context of laws in which archivists, whether in public repositories or private institutions, must operate. Although each level of government principally makes laws affecting that level of government (for example, federal laws for federal agencies, state laws for state bodies), some overlap does occur. If laws at one level of government conflict with laws at another level of government, the courts ultimately will decide which laws will prevail.

Laws pertaining to archives can be found at all levels of government (see Figure 1). Two facts about federal records laws are important for all archivists. First, there are no general federal access laws that control non-federal records. There is, for example, no national privacy statute: the national Privacy Act applies only to federal records. There are two important exceptions to this general proposition, however: the Buckley Amendment governing access to student records and the executive order on national security information; they will be discussed in Chapter 1. Second, there are federal laws that affect the creation and disposition of nonfederal records that relate to federal grants and contracts; these also will be discussed in Chapter 1.

State laws, too, have a major impact on archival activity. Under the Constitution, powers not expressly granted to the federal government are reserved to the states. Most importantly, these reserved powers include maintaining the vital statistics of the people of the state and recording the transfer of real and personal proper-

ty. In her article, "Legal Aspects of Archives," Margaret Norton remarked that "an archivist from a country with a highly centralized government cannot understand why the records most important to individuals — title records, marriage registers, probate records, and vital statistics — should be left to the unsupervised custody of what to them appear petty officials of the lowest grade politically and professionally." She explained to her foreign visitors, she said, that "the origin of the custom of placing our most important records in the hands of county officials was to be able to watch over them and control them as officials of a remote central bureau could not be watched and controlled."[1] This does mean, however, that the different states will have different methods of documenting vital statistics and property transfers, that access provisions will vary by geography, and that a nationwide genealogical search will involve literally hundreds of records offices with different rules. And for archivists it means that any generalizations about state records laws must be tested in every individual case against the actual laws of the state.

Just as laws pertaining to archives can be found at different levels of government, at any one level the legislation affecting records can be found in a variety of statutes. The first and most obvious place is a specifically named records statute, for example, the Federal Records Act. This will probably cover such things as a definition of records, a statement of authority for retention and destruction of records, and perhaps a provision for the restriction of certain types of information. This is only the tent around the nose of the camel, however. Under the tent are almost surely specific legislative pronouncements about records creation, retention, and disclosure. Freedom of information acts, privacy acts, and sunshine acts are certainly places to look for such provisions, but so are acts directing specific government programs (such as laws regulating any sort of business or commerce, requiring the submission of information to the government, contracting for government services, providing social services, and the like). Another likely location for records law is in the general property statutes of the government; for example, the power of replevin (see Chapter 7) may be found there, as may prohibitions on removal of records by public officials unless certain conditions are met.

Because our legal system is based on a combination of statutory law and case law, archivists must also look to judicial decisions to understand the law governing archives. It was, after all, the Supreme Court that finally upheld the legality of the Presidential Recordings and

---

[1] Margaret Cross Norton, "Some Legal Aspects of Archives," *American Archivist* 8 (January 1945): 1.

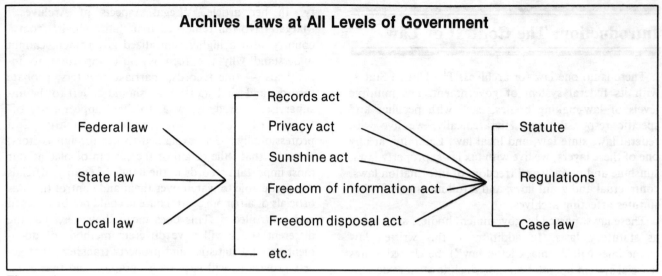

Figure 1

Materials Preservation Act governing the presidential papers of Richard Nixon, to name the most famous recent court case involving records,[2] but hundreds of less-heralded cases have also focused on records questions. Furthermore, it is within the jurisdiction of the courts to decide what records to admit as evidence, a point of special importance when the archivist is handling non-paper records.

The archivist must be aware of the context of laws in which the archival institution operates and must take prudent steps to understand the laws that affect records. When thinking about laws, the archivist must not hope for consistency. Laws are created by different people at different times in different places, and consistency and congruence are unusual. Especially when dealing with tax laws, it is important to remember that the logical answer may not be the legal one.

The discussion in this volume falls naturally into two parts. The first five chapters focus on the legal aspects of common archival functions: the accession, donation, and receipt of materials; the concepts and administration of access policy; and the legal implications of reference service. The last three chapters deal with special topics, including a discussion of copyright law, a review of the legal standards for admissibility of documents in evidence, a discussion of the problems of replevin, some advice on working with a lawyer, and a description of the process of litigation.

Sorting out which laws apply to records and archives in a specific instance and what the law really means is a common problem. Often there is no clear answer, but there are answers that are better than others. In the following chapters, some of the better answers will be explored.

---

[2]Nixon v. *Administrator of General Services*, 433 U.S. 425 (1977).

1 Law and the Three A's: Acquisition, Appraisal, Accessioning

The first question archivists ask about a newly arrived body of material is, "Are these records of an institution or personal papers of an individual?" From the answer flows a well-established set of procedures, from principles of arrangement to practices of description. For legal purposes, however, this distinction is not enough. The law needs to know who owns the materials and if and when the ownership changed hands, because from the basic property right of ownership come most other legal considerations for archival materials. And the time to determine ownership is when the materials are acquired.

With personal papers it is relatively easy to answer the law's questions. With only rare exceptions all personal papers originate outside the archival institution and thus must come to an archives as donated materials. Records are not so simple. Records in archival custody may be either the records of the institution of which the archives is a part or the records of another institution or organization. In the former case, the records will be transferred from one part of the institution (the operating office) to another (the archives) but the legal title does not change. In the latter case, records are transferred from the creating institution to the archival institution, and the transfer — a donation, just like the donation of personal papers — must be documented by an instrument of donation. Finally, a few archives acquire new bodies of material by purchase, and with these transfers there emerges yet a third set of legal problems to complement those questions of internal transfer and donation.

This chapter looks first at the legal questions involved in acquisition, appraisal, and accessioning when the records remain within the originating institution. The focus of the discussion is the records of public institutions, principally because the majority of legal problems aired publicly in courts or in the press have originated there. Following that review, some comparisons are drawn with legal problems of records that remain within a private institution. Chapter 2 considers donations of records and personal papers, including the problems associated with deeds of gift, deposit agreements, undocumented gifts, and the tax implications of donations. The chapter concludes with a brief discussion of the legal issues surrounding the purchase of historical materials.

Records that Remain in the Originating Institution

When the archives is part of the institution that created the records, the authorities for inspection, appraisal, accession, and transfer are wholly within the institution. There is a major distinction between public institutions and private institutions, however, for public institutions are governed by governmental statute and regulation, while private institutions are largely outside the ambit of government regulation on matters relating to recordkeeping. In both cases, though, the stages of records definition, inspection, appraisal, enforcement, and transfer must be negotiated successfully if the later processes of arrangement, description, access, and reference are to operate smoothly.

Records of Public Institutions

The records of public institutions are governed by statute, internal regulations, and judicial decisions (the last are often incorporated into regulations as well). Because the United States is a federal system, federal and state governments are independent of each other, and although there are some exceptions to this, it is generally safe to assume that authority is decentralized. This means that at each level of government there are statutes, regulations, and decisions pertaining to records that are unique to that level.

The relationship of state governments to local governments of counties and cities is more complex. Technically states create cities and counties, and state law governs them. Whether the state records law covers county and city records depends upon the language of the particular state statute.

For practical purposes we refer only to national, state, and local levels of government, but that simplicity is misleading. One recent estimate is that there are 81,000 governmental bodies in the United States, including such entities as water districts, regional public health facilities, and metropolitan area councils of governments, and they do not all fall neatly into the usual three levels.[1] Who, for example, is responsible for the records of a metropolitan area transit authority when the authority is created by an intergovernmental compact of the various independent cities within the metropolitan area? Probably no one of the cities, and the law creating the intergovernmental body is likely silent on the matter.

---

[1]H.G. Jones, *Local Government Records, An Introduction to Their Management, Preservation, and Use* (Nashville, Tenn.: American Association for State and Local History, 1980), p. x.

Yet as complex as the governmental system is, the problems for archivists at each level are remarkably similar. Most public archives encounter difficulties in defining records, obtaining access for purposes of records inspection, securing adequate appraisal authority, enforcing appraisal decisions, handling the transfer of records, and reappraising and disposing of records already in the holdings. While to some extent these are problems of archives everywhere, the nature of public records brings with it public controls and public scrutiny to a degree generally unknown to recordkeepers in private institutions.

Definition of Records

The definition of records is the first stage and a central issue at each governmental level. Normally the elected government body (Congress, legislature, city council) defines records through regulation. Following the model of the federal records statute, many governments have cast their records laws in such a fashion as to answer the questions, "What materials in what form?" (all documentary materials regardless of physical form) "That result from what action?" (made or received and maintained or appropriate for maintenance) "By whom?" (by the government) "For what purpose?" (in pursuance of its business and obligations).[2] A statement that the permanently valuable portion of the records will constitute the archives of the government is sometimes included in the definition.

Some archivists in public institutions will have the opportunity to write records legislation. More often, however, the public archivist will work with an existing statute that needs modification. Here the archivist will need to analyze the records law, identify gaps in its coverage, determine whether case law fills the gaps, and, perhaps, work to secure appropriate amendments.

It is important that the language of a records statute be carefully crafted to avoid ambiguity. In particular, the statutory language should define clearly the physical form of the materials; clarify the parts of government to which this definition will apply; distinguish between official, nonofficial, and personal materials; establish the applicability of the definition with respect to other parts of the legal code; and clearly identify who is responsible for determining what is a record within the scope of the definition. Each of these issues has recently been controversial, and a brief review of the questions raised in the controversies may clarify the reasons that such points should be covered in a records statute.

Physical Form. In the federal government it is well established in the eyes of the law and the minds of archivists that materials of any physical type can be agency records (it is not always so clear in the minds of agency personnel, especially with respect to nontextual materials). Some states, however, have found it necessary to define judicially the physical form of records, usually in the context of a freedom of information act lawsuit. For example, the Minnesota Supreme Court ruled in 1978 that data stored on computer tapes concerning payments to medical assistance vendors are public records, and in 1976 an Ohio court determined that microfilm is a public record.[3] While the temptation is great to list every physical type in the records statute, protracted debates on whether emerging records forms are or are not records within the statutory definition can only be avoided by using language of the broadest sort. Such language will, of course, ultimately be interpreted by a court if questions of the physical form of records arise in litigation, but if the statute has included expansive language at least the possibility of defining any physical type as falling within the definition has not been foreclosed.

Institutional Coverage. A second major issue is the application of the definition of records to agencies and official bodies. With a federal system of government, public records in the United States cannot be vertically integrated (that is, the National Archives cannot tell Texas State Archives or Portland City Archives what to do). It is, however, generally the goal of public archives to be integrated horizontally at each level of government, with the archives holding the records of all branches of government and associated public bodies. The unfortunate tendency has been for legislatures to pass records acts that apply only to agencies in the executive branch of government and only occasionally to extend those acts to cover legislative and judicial records. The status of the materials accumulated by the chief executives (president, governor, mayor) has undergone change in the post-Nixon years, and the trend is to define some portion of these records as public. But the legislative branches often have special provisions for their own records, and the records of the courts remain largely outside the purview of records statutes, probably reflecting the general legislative unwillingness to tangle with the judiciary.

Just as the application of the records statutes to the various branches of the government at a particular level is a problem, so it is that the definition of records is called into question by those bodies that lie at the edge of government: advisory committees, peer review groups, contractors, grantees, consultants, and so on.

---

[2]The federal statute is found at 44 U.S.C. §3301.

[3]*Minnesota Medical Association* v. *State*, 274 N.W. 2d 84, 89 (Minn. 1978); *Lorain County Title Co.* v. *Essex*, 53 Ohio App. 2d 274, 275, 373 N.E. 2d 1261 (Ohio 1975).

The records of many of these entities have been defined as records for freedom of information act (FOIA) cases if the documents were in the possession of an agency, but the abstract question of the nature of these records absent an FOIA request has not been resolved. Perhaps the most reasonable approach here is to ask a series of questions.

Are the records in the physical possession of the agency? Often records of advisory bodies, including peer review groups, are. Possession would tend to suggest records status.[4]

Were the funds provided to the individual or institution to support private work? This is most usually the case with grants, and in this situation the government has no interest in the product of the grant, aside from assurance that the work that the grant was to support was carried out.

What does the written agreement between the government and the contractor, consultant, or grantee say? The agreement may define what the government is to receive as a product; it may also say that the government can obtain from the contractor-consultant-grantee any further materials that are needed to make the required materials understandable or that may be needed in the future to replicate or continue the work. In those instances, the archives may be able to suggest to the agency which materials will have an enduring value for further research (for example, the computerized raw data from which a report was produced).

Is the function that the contractor-consultant is performing a central function of the agency? Increasingly governments employ private sector institutions to handle specified portions of the official duties of an agency. If the statutory authority establishing the agency mandates a programmatic function which has subsequently been performed by contractors, the government may specify that those records produced by the contractor in the course of carrying out that function are government records. This could, for instance, apply to a contractor who administers a city lottery, a consultant collecting and analyzing on a continuing basis the health care needs of the state population when such analysis is a statutory function of the state department of health, and so on.

Were the materials in the possession of the quasi-official body either used by or communicated to governmental personnel to assist them in their official duties?

If so, this tends to give them color of official records, for it implies that the information is necessary to carry out official duties.

Does the government plan to continue this program over time, and is possession of the materials necessary in order to carry out further work? This question is most often asked about statistical and analytical studies, and it may be argued that even though the government has no immediate plan to extend the study, it may do so in the future and thus will claim the materials as records. Because this argument is not based on present character and use but on probable future use, it would be best if such statements of claim were included in the contract itself. Lacking such a statement, the government would have to turn to a common-sense interpretation of the contractual language requiring the contractor to deliver the final product and all required backup information.[5]

Record and Nonrecord, Official and Personal. The distinction between record and nonrecord materials and the distinction between official records and personal papers are related but separate issues. In the case of official records and personal papers, the question is one of legal title. Does the public own the document or does the individual? In the case of record and nonrecord the question is one of maintenance. If records are documents that are created or received *and* maintained or appropriate for maintenance by the government, when is maintenance appropriate? To put it another way, personal papers are by definition nonrecord, but not all nonrecord materials are personal papers.[6] (See Figure 2.)

At present the federal government and some state governments define some documents as nonrecord by law. In the federal statute, three types of materials are defined as nonrecord: library and museum material made or acquired and preserved solely for reference or exhibition purposes, stocks of publications and of processed documents, and extra copies of documents preserved only for convenience of reference.[7] It is the last category that has been most at issue. Although the

[4]A Virginia Freedom of Information Act case makes the point. In an opinion issued January 31, 1979, the Virginia attorney general ruled that a report distributed to a public body becomes an official record if it pertains to the business of the public body, even though no action is taken on the document. The "mere possession of a document is sufficient to make it an official record," the attorney general wrote. Report of the Va. At. Gen. (1978-1979), p. 317.

[5]The National Archives has debated the contractor records problem; see "Appraisal and Disposition Policies in NARS: A Report and Recommendations to the Archivist of the United States on Performance of the Appraisal and Disposition Functions in the National Archives and Records Service," November 23, 1983, and "The Impact of the Federal Use of Modern Technology on Appraisal: A Report to the Appraisal Task Force," by Tom Brown, n.d. See also *Final Report of the Joint Committee on the Archives of Science and Technology: Understanding Progress as Process* (Chicago: Society of American Archivists, 1983).

[6]Maintenance in this instance does not necessarily mean permanent retention but instead means official retention by the government for the period of time required to fulfill its programmatic responsibilities. This question is particularly troublesome with electronic records. Note, too, that "nonrecord" is not the same as a record having no continuing value.

[7]44 U.S.C. §3301.

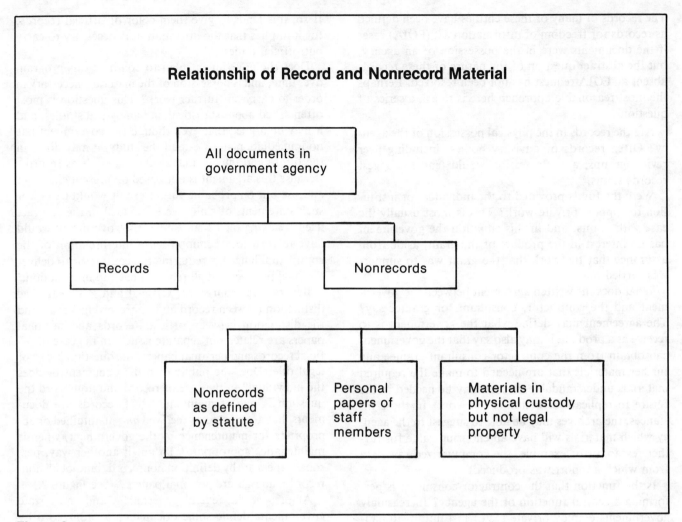

Relationship of Record and Nonrecord Material

All documents in government agency

Records

Nonrecords

Nonrecords as defined by statute

Personal papers of staff members

Materials in physical custody but not legal property

Figure 2

"convenience of reference" clause was probably conceived as a cover for the extra carbon copies that many offices create and give to the drafters of documents, it has become embroiled in the issue of working papers.

Defining "working papers" is difficult. Although archivists generally agree that some documents are ephemera with only momentary usefulness, many working papers are records because they clearly provide evidence of the activities of the government. Still others, perhaps most, fall between ephemera and records. Two conflicting state interpretations show the range of debate on the question. In Kentucky, the attorney general issued an opinion in 1976 that working papers prepared by members of the state auditor's staff in pursuit of their statutory duties are official records. In South Dakota, the attorney general decided that a county assessor's working papers and preparatory data sheets are not.[8]

While the difference between those two interpretations probably reflects South Dakota's narrower records statute, it is not dissimilar to a series of sometimes contradictory federal views on working papers. Again looking to freedom of information act cases, when judges have been asked to decide whether a document is a federal record, in general they have been extremely reluctant to accept arguments that documents in an agency's possession are not agency records.[9]

Most often the issue of working papers reflects the limbo world of scraps of paper with hieroglyphic notes, half completed and rejected drafts, and telephone numbers. In 1981 a National Archives task force considered the question of working papers. It recommended that archivists attempting to decide whether working papers are record or nonrecord ask five questions, with a "yes" to any one of them suggesting that the documents have record status:

[8]*Ky. Op. Att'y Gen.* 76-204 (1976); *1979-1980 S.D. A.G.R.,* Official Opinion No. 79-6.

[9]See discussion of the definition of "record" under the Freedom of Information Act in Chapter 4, p. 68.

(1) Do the papers form a unique part of an adequate record of an agency's organization, functions, policies, decisions, procedures, operations, or other activities?

(2) Were the papers controlled, maintained, preserved, processed, filed, or otherwise handled following usual agency methods and procedures?

(3) Were the papers produced by an individual in official capacity?

(4) Do the papers relate to official functions of the agency?

(5) Were the papers communicated or used or intended for communication or use by agency personnel other than the employee who generated them?[10]

Deciding that working papers are nonrecord does not mean that they are personal papers; it simply means that their disposition will fall outside the scope of records laws. (One possible disposition, of course, is to allow the creator of the documents to take them home.)

The larger question, however, is whether there is anything to be gained by defining some government documents as nonrecord. Such a definition creates a third category of document (other than records and personal papers) and in the process creates a grey area within records law. Perhaps the best approach is to define all agency documents as records and to deal with marginal types such as stocks of publications through the issuance of a general disposal authorization in a records schedule. Such an approach would also be more consistent with the emerging pattern of the courts as they proceed to define records under the freedom of information acts (see Chapter 4, page 68).

The distinction between official records and personal papers of public employees has been aired repeatedly over the last twenty years at all levels of government. Presidents considered their papers personal property until the passage of the Presidential Records Act in 1978. Many presidential appointees also removed records at the close of their days in office; the controversy over the record status of the Henry Kissinger telephone transcripts is only the most famous recent case (for a fuller discussion of the Kissinger case, see page 17). Questions have also been raised about the documents from congressional committees that find their way into the papers of the committee chairmen, the missing office files in the mayor's office in Bridgeport, Connecticut (they were subsequently returned), and so on.[11]

Several attempts have been made by the federal government to define personal papers. One, a property management "Bulletin" issued by the National Archives in the waning days of the Ford administration, opened by stating the statutory definition of federal records, then warned government officials that "correspondence designated as 'personal,' 'confidential,' or 'private,' etc., but relevant to the conduct of public business, is nonetheless an official record." Only material "pertaining solely to an individual's private affairs" was to be considered personal property that the official could take with him when he left government.[12] A second attempt to define the line between personal and official materials is found in the regulations implementing the Presidential Recordings and Materials Preservation Act of 1974 (also known as the Nixon Papers Act).[13] A third is the definition provided by Congress in the Presidential Records Act of 1978, which states:

> The term "personal records" means all documentary materials, or any reasonably segregable portion thereof, of a purely private or nonpublic character which do not relate to or have an effect upon the carrying out of the constitutional, statutory, or other official or ceremonial duties of the President. Such term includes —
> (A) diaries, journals, or other personal notes serving as the functional equivalent of a diary or journal which are not prepared or utilized for, or circulated or communicated in the course of, transacting Government business;
> (B) materials relating to private political associations, and having no relation to or direct effect upon the carrying out of constitutional, statutory, or other official or ceremonial duties of the President; and
> (C) materials relating exclusively to the President's own election to the office of the Presidency; and materials directly relating to the election of a particular individual or individuals to Federal, State, or local office, which have no relation to or direct effect upon the carrying out of constitutional, statutory, or other official or ceremonial duties of the President.[14]

A particular problem in both the Nixon papers regulations and the debates over the Presidential Records Act was what documents reflecting the political

[10]Richard A. Jacobs to Gary Brooks, Maygene Daniels, Jean Fraley, Steve Tilley, February 27, 1981, "Report on 'working papers.' " National Archives, unpublished.

[11]*Kissinger* v. *Reporters Committee for Freedom of the Press*, 445 U.S. 136 (1980); the Bridgeport case was reported in *New York Times*, November 20, 1981, A: 14.

[12]*Federal Register*, v. 41, November 19, 1976, p. 51149. The most recent issuance by the National Archives is a 1985 pamphlet titled "For the Record: Guidelines for Official Records and Personal Papers."

[13]Presidential Recordings and Materials Preservation Act, 44 U.S.C. §2111 *note*. (This section was previously codified as 44 U.S.C. §2107 *note*.) The most recent set of proposed implementing regulations, including citations to pertinent court decisions, is found in *Federal Register*, v. 50, March 29, 1985, p. 12575.

[14]Presidential Records Act of 1978, 44 U.S.C. §2201 *et. seq.* For a critical view of changes in the presidential papers law, see Alexandra K. and David Wigdor, "The Future of Presidential Papers," in Harold Relyea, ed., *The Presidency and Information Policy* (New York: Center for the Study of the Presidency, 1981), pp. 92-101.

activities of the president would be considered official and what personal. Although this issue is not completely resolved, there is general agreement that there are some "public political" functions, such as meeting with party leaders on strategy for legislation, and some "private political" ones, such as making monetary contributions. The distinctions are not easy to draw. Furthermore, whether or not documents reflecting a particular activity of the president as leader of the party are public or protected by privacy (as the courts at some time will probably have to decide), it is not at all clear that this distinction would apply to governors, mayors, city councilmen, aldermen, and so on. But a resolution of the issue at the national level will form a precedent that will have to be taken into account by courts, officials, and archivists at all other governmental levels.[15]

A fourth and the clearest distinction between official records and personal papers at the federal level is found in a court ruling in a recent freedom of information act case. The case arose when requesters sought copies of appointment calendars and telephone message slips from high-level officials in the Justice Department and the Office of Management and Budget. From this narrow focus, the circuit court of appeals turned to a general consideration of the criteria involved in determining whether items are properly official record material or personal property. Summarizing the court's findings, the Justice Department lists the following criteria to be used in making agency record determinations:

(1) *Creation*. Was the document created by an agency employee on agency time, with agency materials, at agency expense? (If not, then it very likely is not an "agency record," on that basis alone.)

(2) *Content*. Does the document contain "substantive" information? (If not, then it very likely is not an "agency record," on that basis alone.) Does it contain personal as well as official business information?

(3) *Purpose*. Was the document created solely for an individual employee's personal convenience? Alternatively, to what extent was it created to facilitate agency business?

(4) *Distribution*. Was the document distributed to anyone else for any reason, such as for a business purpose? How wide was the circulation?

(5) *Use*. To what extent did the document's author actually use it to conduct agency business? Did others use it?

(6) *Maintenance*. Was the document kept in the author's possession or was it placed in an official agency file?

(7) *Disposition*. Was the document's author free to dispose of it at his personal discretion? What was the actual disposal practice?

(8) *Control*. Has the agency attempted to exercise "institutional control" over the document through applicable maintenance or disposition regulations? Did it do so by requiring the document to be created in the first place?

(9) *Segregation*. Is there any practical way to segregate out any personal information in the document from official business information?

(10) *Revision*. Was the document revised or updated after the fact for record-keeping purposes?

These criteria are adaptable to distinctions between records and papers at other levels of government; in fact, with some modifications they may be applicable to private sector institutional records as well.[16]

A final type of nonrecord material is that which is in the physical custody but not the legal control of the agency, that is, legal custody is retained by a person or organization outside the agency. For example, a judicial agency may have records of a private party on loan; an agency may have legislative documents on loan; one agency may have documents that have been loaned to them by another agency. Legal problems involving these materials have surfaced in freedom of information act cases at the federal level, and they are discussed in Chapter 4, page 68.

Application of Definition to Other Laws. A fourth major area that must be considered in the definition of records is how broadly the definition is to be applied with respect to other parts of the legal code. In particular, will the definition of records for administrative and archival purposes also be used as the definition of records for freedom of information and privacy acts? To avoid confusion and to assure consistency in record-keeping practices, it is desirable that one definition of records exists. In the federal government, the Freedom of Information Act did not specifically refer to the definition of records in the Federal Records Act, and in an important freedom of information act case the judge decided that the definition of federal records in the Federal Records Act did not apply in FOIA cases. Congress, the judge pointed out, "had ample opportunities to make the [Federal Records Act] definition of 'records' applicable" in FOIA cases but had never done so. He concluded, and other courts have followed, that there is no definition of the records in the federal

---

[15]Determinations under the Presidential Records Act have yet to be tested, for the act applies for the first time to the Reagan presidency and the disposition of those materials at the close of the administration.

[16]U.S. Department of Justice, *FOIA Update*, v. 5, no. 4, Fall 1984, pp. 3-4.

government for FOIA cases and each court will make determinations as cases come before it.[17] The pattern in the states appears to be mixed, but it is probably fair to say that the more restrictive the general records law is, that is, the more narrowly the records that are public are defined, the more likely it is that incongruities will arise between the records act definition and definitions for public access purposes.

Authority to Define Records. A final consideration in defining public records is a clear statement of who is the official who has the authority to determine what is a record within the scope of the definition. Here again the federal problems are instructive. In the case of *Kissinger* v. *Reporters Committee for Freedom of the Press*, the committee sought access to transcripts of Kissinger's telephone conversations during the periods when he served as national security adviser and as secretary of state.[18] The Supreme Court ruled against the committee, saying that the records management statutes under which the plaintiffs sued did not create a private right of action for return of records for FOIA purposes. In other words, the case was decided on the question of the right (known as "standing") of the committee to bring the suit, not on the facts of the case.[19]

Following the Kissinger decision, the Office of Legal Counsel of the Department of Justice issued a legal opinion on the determination of records status. In it the counsel argued that only the head of the agency originating the document can determine what is a record of the agency and that GSA-National Archives had no independent authority to determine the records status of particular materials.[20] This leaves the archivist of the United States in an advisory role, and in practice it could mean dozens of different interpretations of what is a record. The difficulty with leaving the determination to the agency head is that if he determines that certain materials are not records, the archivist may have no authority to inspect, examine, and appraise them, no matter how significant the archivist may believe the materials to be. The result is a diminution of the archivist's ability to protect records of historical value.

The federal law did not specify who was to define records, leaving it open to judicial interpretation. Lacking such an interpretation, the legal advisers provided one. Archivists at all levels of government should seek legislative clarification of the central role of archivists in determining records status.

Inspection

Assuming that the determination has been made that the materials in question are records, the next stage of the archival process is inspection, whether for the purpose of preparing a records schedule or appraising a specific body of records for immediate transfer. If possible the right of the archives to inspect should be codified, in regulation if not in statute (if the governmental records statute has, in effect, a "necessary and proper" clause that allows the archives to do all those things that are necessary to implement the statute, a regulation may be all that is required). In a number of instances, public archivists have confronted an agency bar to examining records. The most usual case arises when an archives wants to inspect the records of an agency that is normally prohibited from opening its files, for example, a police agency, a health care institution, or a welfare office. (The problem is further complicated if the records management function of government is in an agency separate from that of the archives; in such cases it is possible to have a three-way negotiation over access for inspection.)

At the federal level, the problem of access for purposes of inspection had been well known for years, particularly with regard to the Internal Revenue Service's claim that archivists could not examine tax returns and tax return information because of certain provisions in the Tax Reform Act of 1976. The issue was most forcefully presented, however, during the inspection of the records of the Federal Bureau of Investigation in 1981. That appraisal was being made under the direction of the court in the lawsuit *American Friends Service*

---

[17]*Goland and Skidmore* v. *Central Intelligence Agency, et al.,* 607 F. 2d 339 (D.C. Cir. 1978). See also Trudy Huskamp Peterson, "After Five Years: An Assessment of the Amended U.S. Freedom of Information Act," *American Archivist* 43 (Spring 1980): 161-168.

[18]At the time Kissinger left the Department of State he removed the transcripts and deposited them with the Library of Congress, restricting access to them. The committee wanted the court to compel the return of the transcripts to the State Department so they could be evaluated for release under the provisions of the Freedom of Information Act. The committee argued that the transcripts were records under the terms of the Federal Records Act and the Records Disposal Act and should therefore be returned to the executive branch of government.

[19]*Kissinger* v. *Reporters Committee for Freedom of the Press,* 445 U.S. 136 (1980). It is important to understand what the court did **not** do. First, it did not decide whether the telephone notes were agency records. Second, it did not decide whether the telephone notes were wrongfully removed from the Department of State. Third, the court specifically said that it was not deciding whether the plaintiffs could have prevailed if instead of linking the return of the documents to an FOIA case they had instead lodged a complaint against the executive branch for breach of duty to enforce the Federal Records Act. This means that the question of private actions to compel the return of alienated records is still open. The court noted, "The Archivist did request return of the telephone notes from Kissinger on the basis of his belief that the documents may have been wrongfully removed under the Act. Despite Kissinger's refusal to comply with the Archivist's request, no suit has been instituted against Kissinger to retrieve the records under 44 U.S.C. §3106."

[20]Office of Legal Counsel, Department of Justice, to National Archives, January 13, 1981.

Committee v. *Webster*, and during the appraisal archivists were not permitted to review information from Internal Revenue Service tax returns, informants, grand juries, and electronic surveillance.[21] On appeal of the lower court decision, the plaintiffs raised the issue of archival access for purposes of inspection, challenging the adequacy of the appraisal determinations made on the basis of partial access. The circuit court ruled that access by the National Archives for purposes of inspection is contingent upon the approval of the "head of the agency concerned" or of the president of the United States. This decision clearly limited the ability of the National Archives to inspect records.[22] A subsequent event appeared to confirm the weakness of the Archives' position, for in early 1984 the United States Information Agency refused a formal request from the archivist of the United States to review transcripts of telephone conversations secretly recorded by the agency's director.[23]

It is reasonable that the archivists inspecting the sensitive records of an agency be subject to the same constraints to which the employees of that agency are subject; for example, the archivists should have the appropriate level of security clearances, may be required to sign any confidentiality pledges required of agency employees, and so forth. But the governmental policy must reflect the principle that archivists must be allowed to inspect all records of the government for purposes of appraisal and for monitoring the implementation of the appraisal decision (if the records management function is part of the archives, this declaration should also include inspection for the purposes of monitoring records creation and maintenance).[24] And because legislators continually create new laws prohibiting access to some type of information or body of records, it is useful to have statutory language confirming that inspection for the purpose of carrying out archival activities is not to be considered public access. A phrase in the legislation

covering archival access (for example, "archival access is permitted, all laws barring public access notwithstanding") would clarify archival authority.

Appraisal

With the right to inspect clarified, other legal problems may arise, focusing on the actual process of appraisal. Because appraisal is subjective, the legal issues surrounding it are often procedural. The FBI case mentioned above is surely the most famous appraisal case ever to be challenged in court, and thus far its issues have been largely whether the archivists had inspected the materials, had made a timely and comprehensive review of the records, and had adequately examined field office as well as central office files.

Archival appraisal judgments will always be arguable, and there are relatively few precautions archivists can take to deflect a challenge to a particular substantive decision. Where archivists can take prudent steps, however, is in the procedure employed in the appraisal process. Archives should have a clear set of written procedures and standards for general appraisal work. If a question is raised in the course of litigation about an appraisal decision, the archivist should be able to demonstrate that the appraisal in question followed the standard method and pattern and therefore was not arbitrary and capricious. If the appraisal deviates from the standard, the archivists must have an explicable reason for doing so and should have a justification written at the time of the appraisal explaining the deviations.

Documenting the appraisal decision in writing is standard archival practice, and for legal purposes the key is clarity. A clear and accurate description of the records, including physical type, office of origin, dates, volume, topics or functions reflected in the records, and retention period is fundamental. The description should be detailed enough to ensure that it applies to the records in question and not others, leaving no confusion in the reader's mind as to what was proposed for retention and what for destruction.

But description is only part of the documentation needed if an appraisal is challenged. Documenting the determination—why it was made and how it was arrived at—is equally important. Standard lists of questions or checklists setting out major appraisal criteria are one way to ensure that all pertinent issues are regularly and routinely considered.

Another procedural matter, but one that can have significant substantive consequences, is, quite simply, who has the final word. The records statute should state explicitly that the appraisal is the judgment of the archives and that its word is final. Many public archives are buried in the bureaucracies of larger departments in

[21]The Department of Justice, acting as a mediator between the demands of the National Archives for access and the demands of the Internal Revenue Service and the Federal Bureau of Investigation to protect information, sided with the IRS and FBI and barred NARS.

[22]*American Friends Service Committee* v. *Webster*, 720 F. 2d 29 (D.DC 1983). Curiously, the plaintiffs contested the access prohibitions on tax, grand jury, and electronic surveillance information but not on informant names; consequently, the appeals court ruled only on those three.

[23]"USIA Refused Wick Tapes to Archivist," *International Herald Tribune* February 29, 1984, p. 2; Robert M. Warner, National Archives, to Thomas E. Harvey, USIA, March 1, 1984.

[24]The law creating the National Archives contained strong language on inspection, giving the archivist "full power to inspect personally or by deputy the records of any agency of the United States Government whatsoever and wheresoever located, and the full cooperation of any and all persons in charge of such records in such inspection." Unfortunately, this language was dropped in a revision of the law in 1976.

the executive branch of government, and although in most instances higher levels within the government show no interest in becoming involved in appraisal questions, absent a specific statement the possibility exists.[25] And, of course, if partisan politics becomes involved, questions will be raised about the independence of archival judgment, particularly in matters of records destruction. Rarely does records *retention* cause controversy, although the court-ordered retention of the FBI records on Martin Luther King, Jr., is one example of it.[26]

A further issue is whether the public has standing to sue the government if the decisions embodied in a schedule or in an appraisal of a direct offer appear to be questionable.[27] The federal courts at both the district and the appeals levels held in the FBI case that the public did have the right to bring suit over appraisal decisions. That case, however, concerned mainly records where the plaintiffs claimed to have a direct personal interest (for example, the Meerpol brothers and the records of their parents, Julius and Ethel Rosenberg; historians and journalists who wanted particular records for their writing) and may not be controlling if a member of the public wants to challenge a decision in which there is no direct personal connection.[28]

Because, as mentioned above, the questions on which the courts have ruled have concerned procedural issues, it is not clear how often courts will want to intervene in substantive appraisal questions. Judges may certainly tell archivists, "Go back and follow correct procedures," and a judge may employ outside archivists as an arm of the court (known as "special masters") to do a second appraisal. It does seem unlikely, however, that judges in the already overburdened court system will often want to take responsibility for deciding whether to toss or retain particular bodies of material, thereby substituting judicial judgment for professional archival judgment. And if such judicial decision-making does occur, it is more likely to be at the federal than the state level, where no cases are known to have been brought.

Enforcement

Enforcing an appraisal determination raises the next set of potential legal problems. There are rarely difficulties when the appraisal is made on material directly prior to the transfer of the selected material to the archives (assuming that the appraisal is made relatively quickly after the creating office offers the records). Scheduling and the enforcement of schedules is another matter. A records statute may specify that all permanently valuable records are to be turned over to the archives at a specified time unless the archives and the agency make an agreement to amend the deadline. Schedules are then created within this time framework. Other statutes provide no time guidelines at all. In either case, scheduling raises several issues: What do the schedules cover? Is there a limit to their validity? How binding are they? If one party defaults, what is the recourse?

Coverage. Because schedules are implementing documents (that is, they are not statutory or regulatory but instead are made pursuant to statute or regulation) they must clearly define the nature and extent of their coverage. The most common problem is that of the partial schedule, covering only a part of the records of the agency: while all parties may understand it at the time of creation, at some time in the future someone will surely ask what is the status of the records not on the schedule. (This is a special problem if there is a standard general schedule of records common to all agencies and it is a practice not to list those general schedule items on the individual agency schedules.) It is important that at the beginning of the schedule it states unequivocally what it covers and warns the agency that unless records not on the schedule can be determined to be covered by the general schedule, if any, they must be considered unscheduled and cannot be destroyed without the permission of the archives.

Duration. A second issue, related to the question of coverage, is the duration of a schedule. It is usual to find that over time the character of the records arriving at the archives under a scheduled item changes: one day

[25]The best-known example of interference from a higher political level is the "Nixon-Sampson Agreement" in which, without the knowledge of the archivist of the United States, his boss, Arthur Sampson, administrator of general services, agreed with ex-president Nixon on the control and destruction of certain Nixon presidential materials. The resulting uproar led to congressional passage of the Presidential Recordings and Materials Preservation Act of 1974, which nullified the agreement. Notice, however, that the materials in question were not records but presidential papers. Nixon-Sampson Agreement, September 6, 1974, in *Weekly Compilation of Presidential Documents*, v. 10, September 16, 1974, pp. 1104-5.

[26]*Lee* v. *Kelly*, Civil Action No. 76-1185, decided January 31, 1977, *Southern Christian Leadership Conference* v. *Kelly*, Civil Action No. 76-1186, decided January 31, 1977, both D.DC. Editorial, "Garbage Disposal," (re retention of King materials), *Washington Post*, February 2, 1977, A: 14. Since the decision, questions have periodically been raised about the retention, most recently during the debates over a federal holiday in honor of King, when Senator Jesse Helms unsuccessfully sought access to the King files.

[27]The new law governing the National Archives and Records Administration, PL 98-497, provides that, prior to the archivist's authorizing disposal of records, a notice of the proposed disposal shall be printed in the *Federal Register* with a period for public comment.

[28]The court wrote, "The legislative history of the records acts supports a finding that Congress intended, expected, and positively desired private researchers and private parties whose rights may have been affected by government actions to have access to the documentary history of the federal government.... Various private parties and the public cannot review records that an agency has destroyed in violation of disposal laws. This appears to us to be a sufficient interest. ..." *Webster*, above.

the archivist realizes that these are supposed to be records on the manufacture of cordage and they seem to be about apple inspections. Normally the schedule will state in its opening paragraphs that these disposal authorities are valid only insofar as the character of the records remains constant and that if the nature of the records changes the schedule provision is to be considered void and the agency should return to the archives for a new appraisal determination. Unfortunately, agency personnel are usually in no position to make that judgment of the long-term shift in record types. Often it is the lowest level personnel who are assigned to the job of "cleaning out the files" for the annual files campaign. And subtle shifts over time do occur; in the example above the archivist should be asking both, "What happened to the cordage stuff?" and "Where was this apple documentation before?" The implication that schedule decisions are eternal exacerbates the problem.[29]

The possibility exists that a legal challenge to a schedule could be brought, alleging that records are being destroyed pursuant to an outdated, inaccurate, and hence invalid schedule item. (A challenge over retention under an outdated item is theoretically possible but seems unlikely.) Legally the government as a whole has a responsibility to protect records within the scope of the records statute. By placing caveats at the beginning of the schedule that explain the limits to the validity of the schedule, the archivist is merely clarifying responsibility within the government (that is, shifting it from the archives to the agency of origin). Recognizing the prevalence of change in records series over time, however, perhaps the more prudent approach would be to develop schedules with stated expiration dates. Such schedules could carry a warning that after the expiration date the agency could not destroy records until the archives reauthorizes the application of the schedule.

Compliance. Schedules may be revised with the consent of both agency and archives, but what if the agency refuses to turn over records scheduled to come to the archives? What if the archives refuses to accept scheduled records, pleading that it has no room to store them? Is there a legal mechanism that can be used by agency or archives to obtain compliance?

In general it is very difficult to enforce schedules. The problem is that both agency and archives are part of the same governmental entity and, as such, normally cannot sue each other for compliance. The only recourse for

either party is an appeal to a body with authority over both agency and archives; that may be a judicial agency within the government, the body of elective officials at the head of the government, or the chief executive. In these quasi-judicial determinations, the status and reputation of both agency and archives — rather than pure records considerations — are likely to be key factors.[30]

The role of the public in enforcing schedules by petition to the courts is untested; generally it may be assumed that if the decision in the FBI case on the right of citizens to sue is controlling, the public could sue to enforce a schedule. It is more likely, however, that the public would use publicity tactics rather than lawsuits to obtain transfer and disclosure; the recent publicity over the declassification and transfer of State Department records of the early 1950s is an example of this approach.

Transfer

The last stage of the appraisal and accessioning process is the physical transfer of the records. When records remain within the institution that created them, the transfer of the records does not transfer legal title but only transfers custody. The dominion of the records — that is, the institutional hegemony with final, absolute control of ownership — does not change. Custody — the immediate charge and control, implying responsibility for the protection and preservation of the thing in custody — does. Dominion, as a property right, is the superior right.[31]

While it might appear that there is no need to document transfer for legal purposes when title (dominion) remains constant, there are two important reasons to do so. First, a transfer document will clarify the responsibility for guarding against physical intrusion and damage to the records. Second, the transfer document will establish the rights and responsibilities of the new custodian for controlling intellectual access to the materials. These reasons are easily seen if the transfer of records to an archives is compared with transfer of records to a records center. In the latter there is a transfer of responsibility for the physical safety of the materials but no transfer of the control over intellectual disposition of the materials (that is, who can use them). Transfer of materials to an archives, on the other hand, includes transferring both the controls over the physical items and the intellectual content of them. This means

---

[29]One of the more uncomfortable parts of the FBI case for the government was explaining why a "laconic" schedule (as one judge characterized it) from 1946 had never been reviewed again by the National Archives for nearly thirty years, given the changes in government and the FBI during that period of time.

[30]If the archives refuses to take in scheduled records at the agreed time, it must ensure that the agency continues to fulfill all preservation and reference responsibilities. This is a very sticky problem, but not a purely legal one.

[31]*Black's Law Dictionary* 460, 573 (4th ed., 1951).

that the archivist is responsible both for preventing unwarranted physical access to the documents and for making the determination either to release or withhold the documents' information.

Documenting the transfer, then, requires agreement between the transferring office and the archives on several key points. First, a document of transfer must clearly identify what material is transferred; this can become critical if the transfer includes both documents that are open to research and documents that cannot be released to the public. If information from closed documents somehow shows up in the press, it is often necessary to determine when and how such information became available, and clear transfer agreements should show when the information passed into the control of the archives. Similarly, the creating agency may come to the archives in the future and ask to review or borrow certain files; if the archives does not locate all the files, the transfer documentation should be clear and sufficient evidence of whether the files were transferred in the first place. This requires that the description of the materials transferred be complete: "Four boxes of case files" will not help if in the future the archives must determine whether it ever had the case file on a particular individual.

A second area that must be detailed in transfer documents is the physical form of the items transferred. This is especially true if the archives is receiving a microform copy as the archival copy and the agency is retaining the paper records for its own use, to be destroyed whenever the agency has no need for the records. Legally the transfer document merely reports that the archives accepted the indicated format; in the case of a microform or other copy, it does not guarantee that this is a true copy of the original but only that this is the copy that the archives accepted. In Chapter 7 the legal sufficiency of various physical types is discussed; here it is only necessary to know that in the event that an archives is required to produce documents in court, it will be necessary to establish the form of the documents at the point of transfer.

A third feature of the transfer document should be a clear statement of access conditions, including a statement of the type of material to be restricted (if any); the authority (normally a provision of the freedom of information act, sometimes supplemented by another statute) for the restriction; the duration, stated either as a fixed period of years or as a contingency of an event; and the official responsible for making the determination to lift the restriction. The type of material can be defined explicitly ("all welfare case files less than seventy-five years old") or it may be stated subjectively ("those portions of the records of the Commissioner of Insurance that reflect the internal business decisions of the companies regulated"). The former is easier to administer, but the latter may enable the archives to make more information available to the public, albeit at the cost of archival time to review the files.

The authority for restricting public records must be found in statutes, whether explicit (such as the provision restricting the records of the U.S. decennial census for seventy-two years from the year of the census-taking) or general ("the archivist shall, in his judgment, restrict those records which would tend to invade the personal privacy of the citizens"). Often, as in the census statute, the duration of the restriction is found in the explicit statutes; this is not true with general restriction statutes such as the provisions of freedom of information acts.

Perhaps the most critical clarification in the restrictions section of a transfer document is who will be responsible for removing restrictions. Agency officials may want to retain either complete authority or veto power; archivists seek to avoid having custody and responsibility but not control. Again, if the public records statute is silent on the question of authority for administering restrictions and if the creating agency and the archives cannot agree, the dispute may be resolved by a superior office or officer within the government. If that occurs, the decision reached should be explicitly included in the transfer documentation. If subsequent transfers of the same type of material occur, each set of transfer documents should make reference to the decision, if only by reference to the initial transfer file. Archivists should not assume that their successors will read all transfer documentation before providing reference service on a single transfer, so each set must have complete information. Standard forms help reduce the burden of repetition, as does automated electronic storage of transfer information.

Fourth and finally, the transfer documents should reflect any unique agreements between the agency and the archives about loan of the documents back to the agency of origin or its successor agency. Again, disagreement between agency and archives will have to be resolved within the government, and in most instances an archives will seek to limit or prohibit the return of materials to the agency. Legally the return of documents does not matter, so long as the loan and return are clearly documented, because the dominion of the records does not change. But both because of the loss of access to the documents by potential users and because of the possibilities for deletion, addition, misfiling, and loss of the records while in agency custody, archivists are loath to loan them. In at least one instance, records returned to an agency by the National Archives were lost, in another instance the agency subsequently refused to return them, and in a third case the records were supplemented on a file-by-file basis with so much additional documentation that the prospect of the return raised questions as to whether these could be considered part of the original series at all.

Reappraisal and Disposal

A final issue in appraisal and accessioning of public records is reappraisal of records, leading to destruction of some or all of them. The decision to reappraise is usually that of the archives. As with initial appraisals, the greatest legal protection for an archives in reappraising records is to follow established patterns and procedures and to document the stages of the reappraisal. If the reappraisal leads to the destruction of records previously accessioned, the archives must document both the reasons for the destruction and the act of destruction itself.

The reason for controlling the actual destruction is quite simple: if items that appear to be official records from the archives subsequently surface on the manuscript market, the archives will have to spend time determining whether these items were stolen, were never transferred by the agency and were somehow removed without approval, or were reappraised records that were not destroyed. Not long ago the National Archives found itself in just this position: bound volumes of official records began turning up in antique dealers' shops, and questions were raised about the provenance of the items. After some detective work it became clear that these were items that had been reappraised, found to be lacking in sufficient value to warrant further retention, and transferred to a private concern for destruction. Someone in the firm apparently retained some of the items and sold them. The resulting investigation led to the press becoming interested in the items, some dealers claiming that the items were of significant historical value, and a general review of the adequacy of the appraisal. But who really owned the documents in the hands of the dealers? The legal answer is probably the government, for it turned the records over to the private company only for purposes of destruction, not for resale, and when resale occurred it voided the contractual arrangement and the property rights reverted to the government.[32] The question that follows, then, is whether the government should undertake a replevin action to retrieve these materials from the hands of private dealers, even though these are records that the government says have no lasting value. Conversely, should the government destroy records that would have some value to a private citizen, as the dealers clearly believed?

Here it is important to remember that the disposition of government property, of which records are a part, is governed by the general property rules of the government and as such is often outside the control of the archives. Some rules require a bidding process, some the use of firms with state contracts, and so forth. A request by the archives to use some means of disposal other than that normally used for government property will require the approval of the agency responsible for the disposition of government property or by the government lawyers or perhaps by the legislative body itself.

Disposal by gift to another institution or by sale brings other problems. Assuming that the archives has authority to give or sell records, the archives will need to develop clear procedures for these activities. Again, the possibility occurs that in the future some of these documents will surface on the manuscript market, and someone will approach the archives believing that the documents were purloined, necessitating an investigation. One way to solve the problem would be to mark the items as "deaccessioned" before sending them out of custody; that, however, involves an expenditure of labor that is probably unjustifiable. Once again, the best protection is a clear description of the items removed. If the items are destined for deposit in another institution, an agreement should be drawn up between the archives and the recipient stating what the disposition of the materials will be if the receiving institution should, at some time in the future, no longer want the records. The most important question in such a case is whether the records will revert to the public archives or whether the receiving institution has the right to dispose of them in any way it sees fit. Legally, as long as the transfer document is unambiguous, any means of subsequent disposal may be used; procedurally, the archives should consider what future controls it wants to assert.

Records of Private Institutions

Most of the foregoing issues applicable to the archives within public institutions apply to archives within private institutions as well. Legally, the type of private institution does not make much difference when discussing records. All private institutions hold legal title to their records and, with title, the other associated property rights. Corporations are fictive individuals for legal purposes; churches, which may or may not be incorporated, are recognized bodies in the eyes of the law; charitable and eleemosynary institutions are often incorporated, and so on.

An important difference between public and private archives is that the public scrutiny that is part of the life of the public institution is often missing in private institutions, at least with regard to their recordkeeping

---

[32]If the institution has no stated method of disposition and merely puts the records in the trash, a person taking items out of the trash may be able to claim them legally, citing abandonment by the institution.

practices. Controversies between the archives and a records-creating unit in a private institution or between the archives and an individual employee (such as a college dean who wants to claim the records of his office as personal papers) will be resolved internally, usually without any public intervention. And in a private institution the authority and prestige of the archives may relate more closely to the person and personality of the archivist and his or her superiors in the corporate and institutional structure than to the body of policy and written procedure that has grown up. Only if the institution is involved in litigation that includes a total or partial ban on institutional records destruction will outside forces intervene. For example, the lawsuit that led to the breakup of AT&T, included a broad, court-ordered ban on records destruction.

In other words, in a private institution there is no statute defining records, and the institution itself must decide the scope that it wants to claim as its own. The institution can decide what it wants to claim as institutional records and what it will allow officers and employees to remove as personal papers. In a private institution, archival inspection will not be helped or impeded by statutes, but the archives will have to succeed by persuasion and internal politicking. Appraisal determinations may be criticized by persons external to the institution, but unless some direct harm is sustained by that individual by the destruction of the institution's records (a private hospital destroying medical records of a living individual, perhaps) intervention by the public is unlikely to have a legal basis on which to proceed. Similarly, the enforcement of schedules and the reappraisal and disposal of records will nearly always proceed outside the reach of public legal claims. With regard to influencing the disposition of private records, the most potent weapon the general public has is publicity, not the law.

Law does have a direct effect on private archives, however. For certain types of business activities — for example, the construction of low-cost housing under a state contract — the state law may require that the records relating to the fulfillment of the contract be maintained by the contractor for a specific period of years. Normally such requirements will be specified in the contract. The contract may require retention of certain records and may include inspection rights for government officials, but it does not represent a determination about the permanent disposition of the records. Once the time period or particular event (such as an audit) has passed, the institution is free to dispose of the records in any manner it chooses. Similarly, for tax purposes, grant fulfillment, audits, and various government reports, institutions may be required to maintain records for specified periods, but again the permanent disposition of the records is normally reserved to the institution itself.

A special legal problem may arise with university records. The private college or university has a clear legal status; the public college or university raises some questions. As mentioned above, it is likely that the state records law was designed to control the records of agencies in the executive branch of the state government and may not fit very well if applied to state universities. If the state records law clearly excludes the state colleges and universities, then for most purposes the state school can act as a private institution (for the Buckley Amendment exception, see Chapter 3). The Colorado Supreme Court, for example, has ruled that the University of Colorado is not covered by the state's Open Records Act. If the state records law covers state university records, as the attorneys general in Tennessee and North Carolina have ruled, the university must administer records accordingly. But if the law is unclear, either the state archives and the university can reach a written agreement on the university's records status or the university can seek a legal opinion from the state attorney general. The latter will perhaps carry more weight, but it also involves raising the level of debate and decision beyond the level that may be necessary to resolve the issue. The point remains, however, that public colleges and universities must clarify their legal position on records control vis-a-vis the public records authority.

Conclusion

As the foregoing suggests, the acquisition, appraisal, and accessioning of records is a complex process affected by both laws and internal rules and procedures. Although law provides the framework within which the activities take place, it is often the rules that are decisive. To avoid as many later difficulties as possible, the archives should follow some simple general guidelines: write it down, be clear, and be consistent.

One final note of caution is necessary. Few laws or rules in the area of appraisal, particularly those attempting to define records, can be applied mechanically. They are usually more like criteria to be applied in the light of the facts in an individual case, in conjunction with a healthy dose of common sense. An understanding of the basic goals of the archives and the institution of which it is a part will greatly help the archivist administer these procedures.

2 Donations and Purchases

Throughout the preceding chapter, the subject was records that remain within the institution that created them. The custody of the records changed from creating unit to archives, but the legal title or dominion of the records remained the same. In the institutional archives, the archives has the right of possession or use, that is, "custody," while the institution itself has the right of property, that is, "dominion." When records move from one institution to another or when personal papers move from the person to the institution, however, dominion changes and legal title passes. And here a new set of legal issues arises.

Many of the problems of institutional records evaporate when dealing with donated materials. There are no arguments over the definition of records, no controversies over inspection rights, no internal battles over enforcement. Donations are arms-length transactions between equal parties, each with particular goals and objectives. The compromises agreed upon between the parties are normally embodied in some form of document. Donations are gifts, and in legal terms a gift means that title to property passes from the giver to the recipient. The legal characteristics of a gift are a clear offer, acceptance, and delivery.

The focus of this chapter is instruments of gift, principally deeds. It briefly considers deposit agreements and undocumented gifts, then reviews the tax implications of donations of documentary materials. Finally there is a short discussion of the legal issues that may arise when historical materials are purchased.

Instruments of Gift

Before entering into a gift agreement, the archival institution should make sure that the prospective donor is competent and has clear title to the materials. Take as an example a case in which a very elderly woman signed a deed. After her death the heirs demonstrated that she had not been competent at the time of the signing, thus the deed was void. In another case, an heir offered to donate some papers but investigation by the archives revealed that he was not the sole heir. The other heirs were not agreeable to the donation, and the negotiations foundered because the prospective donor did not have the capacity to convey a clear title. In a third case, the secretary of a corporate entity may offer the records of the corporation to the archives, but it is not clear that the secretary can act on behalf of the corporation, the entity that has legal title to the records. This does not mean that the archivist must hire a private detective to investigate prospective donors, but it does mean that some tactful questions should be asked early in the negotiations.

All transfers of private property to an archives should be documented in a clear, unambiguous fashion. As archival materials have both a physical and an intellectual component (that is, a medium and a message), it is important that the transfer document records the disposition of both the physical and the intellectual property. A number of instruments can be used to record the transfer of property; the three most common are letter, will, and deed.

An exchange of letters is probably the easiest of the written instruments to execute, and many important archival holdings have been acquired with an exchange of letters documenting the transfer of the title. The *exchange* of letters is not just common courtesy; the exchange serves also to indicate acceptance by the recipient, one of the keys to determining title. Exchange of letters does not solve all the problems. The archives often does not have the opportunity in an exchange of letters to advise the donor or to obtain from the donor the elements of information that are or will be needed, such as the restrictions to be applied (if any), whether the archives has disposal authority, and many other such matters. The lack of this information may require protracted subsequent correspondence, or it may lead to legal difficulties in the future. ("I know I didn't say you should withhold my correspondence with X, but I thought you would have known better.")

Transfers of property, primarily personal papers, by will is also common. Because a will is usually prepared by a lawyer, some of the elements such as restrictions, access, and disposition may be clearly defined, although the conditions may be more stringent than the archives would like. It is also probable that the donor or his lawyer will have discussed the gift with the archives before the provisions of the will are drawn up, giving the archives the opportunity to suggest language to use in the will's provision about the prospective donation.

There are, of course, a few cases in which an archivist opens the morning mail to find that the archives has been left the Jane Doe papers, papers which are entirely inappropriate to its holdings and which have severe restrictions on them; mercifully such cases are rare. The archives has the right to refuse to accept property transferred by will. In such a case, it would be up to the executor to decide, based on the provisions in the will, what to do with the items the archives renounced.

Deeds are the third common written instrument used to transfer property to an archives. A deed is an instrument in writing, purporting to effect some legal disposition, sealed and delivered by the disposing party or parties. It is usually prepared after consultation between the donor and the recipient and is usually signed by both to indicate offer and acceptance. It is the usual method to transfer materials of private persons and institutions to an archives.

There are a number of important or desirable elements in instruments of gift. Not all of these will be appropriate for every donation, but they are worth considering during the negotiations. Because the archivist generally has the most influence on preparation of deeds (as compared to letters and wills), the elements are discussed in terms of deeds. The elements include clear answers to the following questions.

Who is the donor? The creator of the materials? The heirs of the creator? A purchaser? A governing board acting for an institution? This information normally appears twice, once in the opening paragraph of the deed and again in the signature block at the end. If the relationship between the creator and the donor is complex and not self-evident (a child with power of attorney donating property of a living parent, an executive officer acting on behalf of a corporation), it should be spelled out in the deed. A cautious archivist may request that the donor have his or her signature notarized.

Who is the recipient? If, for example, the archives is part of a state university, is the formal recipient the state, the university, or the university archives? If the state is the recipient, the state may be able to remove the materials from the university archives and place them in the state archives. If the legal formalities require donation to the state (the university lawyer can provide that information), the donor may wish to specify that the donation is to the state *for purposes of deposit* in the archives of the state university. The same considerations would apply to a church-diocese-diocesan archives, corporate-conglomerate archives, or any archives in a multilevel bureaucracy.

Some public institutions, especially universities, have established private foundations that accept donations from private sources on behalf of the university. If private materials are to be donated to the foundation but deposited in the university archives, that should be specified in the deed. In addition, the archives should have a written agreement with the foundation spelling out the responsibilities of both parties. For example, can the foundation solicit papers on behalf of the archives? What if the archives doesn't want something the foundation has acquired? Could the foundation keep something in its offices and not turn it over to the archives, such as a restricted item? And so on. (Whether such an arrangement would place the material beyond the reach of a state freedom of information act that applies to a state university would be subject to an opinion by the state attorney general.)

What is the date of the transfer of title? This is important primarily for tax purposes. The deed should bear both the date when the donor signed it and the date when the recipient accepted it.

What is the material conveyed by the deed? Who created or collected the material? What is the volume? What are the inclusive dates? For a small donation this information can be incorporated into the introductory paragraphs of the deed (for example, "seven typed letters signed by Franklin D. Roosevelt, dated October 4, 8, 9, 14, and 22, and November 6 and 12, 1919, concerning the possible purchase of a sloop from the Mariner Boatworks"). For most donations, however, it is useful to attach to the deed an appendix containing a detailed archival description of the material donated. This is especially important in instances in which the donor plans to give, for example, a large collection of autographs but wants to spread the donation out over a period of years to take as much advantage of the tax deductions as possible. The donor may physically transfer the entire collection at one time, but donate the items over a period of years. In such cases, detailed descriptions appended to the deed are crucial to determining what of the materials are the property of the archives and what are still the property of the donor. If the material donated is from an ongoing institution, it is especially important to define the series accessioned; in this way the selection process is clearly documented.

Who holds the copyright? Here is where the distinction between physical property and intellectual property becomes important. It is entirely possible to transfer the physical property to the archives while reserving the copyright in the material for the donor. It is desirable to write into the deed the transfer of the copyright from the donor to the archives or to the public at large; failing that, the deed should clearly specify who holds the copyright and for how long. Of course, a donor cannot transfer copyright to intellectual property unless the donor created the property or had the copyright legally transferred to him; consequently, most deeds will convey only such copyright as the donor holds in the materials donated (See Chapter 6 for a full discussion of copyright).

What are the restrictions on use? Broadly speaking, restrictions normally specify either time or content or both. For example, a restriction might specify that the entire donation remain closed for twenty-five years or until the death of the donor (time). Or, a deed might require that materials relating to the donor's service on the ministerial commission for the review of candidates for the clergy be restricted (content). Or the deed might restrict correspondence between the donor and her husband until both are deceased (content and time).

While some archivists favor restrictions worded narrowly ("my letters from Jacqueline Kennedy") and others favor restrictions specifying general categories ("information the disclosure of which would be an unwarranted invasion of personal privacy"), both should strive for statements of restriction that are clear and unambiguous.

Who can impose restrictions? Here there are normally three options: the donor, the donor's designee, or the archivist. The donor usually establishes the restrictions through the deed, often in great detail, and the donor may also amend the deed with the concurrence of the archives if the donor believes that further categories of materials should be restricted. In other instances the donor frames the restrictions in general terms and then either gives the archivist the authority to determine what materials fall within the restriction categories or names a person to review the files and establish what can be made available at various times. In the latter case, the archives should make sure that the duration of review by the designee is limited (the designee could take a decade, with the papers completely closed during that time; the designee could die with the papers unreviewed) and that after such time the archives has the authority to make the access determinations.

To whom do the restrictions apply? Although it seems unlikely that problems would arise, it may be wise to indicate in the deed that the restrictions will not prevent the staff of the archives from performing normal archival work on the restricted materials and that any necessary preservation measures may be taken. Without a formal statement, it is possible that such steps could be barred by heirs or future officials of the donating institution.

Who can lift restrictions? There are two issues here, temporary waivers and permanent openings. In the category of temporary waivers, some donors want to be able to authorize select researchers to use restricted materials if the researchers obtain the permission of the donor or the donor's designee. Because this results in unequal access, archivists are usually reluctant to accept such conditions unless there is no other way to obtain the materials. If the archives will agree to such temporary waivers, it should be clearly stated in the deed.

In the category of permanent openings, restrictions that have a specific time period are relatively easy to administer, but if restrictions have no fixed time of expiration, trouble can arise. It is advisable to state clearly in the deed that all materials will eventually be opened and that the archivist has the authority to open materials at his or her discretion. Some donors want to review and approve materials selected by the archivist for opening; this is cumbersome but workable as long as it is understood that all materials will eventually be open. A fixed

duration for such review is preferable; the deed should specify the procedure in the event of the death of the donor or designee during the review period; and the deed should state the archivist's authority to open material after the time period for donor or designee review has expired. An archives should establish a policy on the length of time that donors, heirs, and designees can control access. Deeds have been proposed that would pass control from a donor to children and, at their deaths, to grandchildren. Such provisions could restrict materials for nearly a hundred years; this is almost always unacceptable.

Who has disposal authority? Donations often contain a certain amount of ephemera: multiple copies of the donor's Christmas cards from 1958, a broken transistor radio, boxes of duplicate copies of congressional hearings. The deed should indicate whether the archivist can dispose of such materials in any way seemly, whether the materials must be offered to the heirs first before other means of disposal are used (in such cases, there should be a time limit), and what the criteria for disposal are ("no significant historical value," "inappropriate to the collections of the State Historical Society," etc.).

In designing this part of the deed, the archivist should also consider whether the archives wants to obtain authority to dispose of the entire collection, not just those parts without historical value. For example, the donation might contain a collection of Confederate money, which clearly has historical value, but the archives subsequently obtains an outstanding set of Confederate currency. Consequently the archives wants to sell the money from the first collection or trade it to another institution in return for Confederate bonds. Legally, once the archives has title to the property, if the deed is silent on the matter of disposition the archives can do what it wants, but it may be neater to have a clause authorizing the disposition of any materials which, in the judgment of the archivist, are not required by the archives.

What provisions cover subsequent gifts? The nature of the highly competitive collecting business is such that young people who come to prominence are often asked to donate their materials to an archival institution. This means that the institution can look forward to acquiring increments of materials over a long period of time. This incremental acquisition is also almost always true of donations of records of ongoing institutions. Rather than write a new deed each time, it may be possible to include in the initial deed a provision saying that all subsequent donations will be made in accordance with the provisions of that deed. Then, at the transfer of each increment, the donor and the archives can sign a statement that the materials are transferred in accordance with that deed, and the archives can prepare a description of the material transferred and append to the deed both the statement and the description.

The foregoing is not meant to suggest that a lawyer must draw up a separate deed for each donation. Most archives have a standard deed form, often with blanks at the places where names and dates must be inserted. These forms can be mailed to prospective donors, handed to the drop-in visitor who presents a World War II diary to the archives, and used in most cases. A sample deed is found in Figure 3. In this sample, the deed is followed by a number of alternative paragraphs that might be used in certain cases. The donor specifies which substitutes, if any, are to be incorporated, and the final copy to be signed is then produced. (Word processing equipment makes these modifications a simple matter.) Only if there is a truly unusual donation does the archives need a specially drawn deed.

The sample deed gives all property rights to the archives immediately. There are no restrictions, except by reference to the general restriction policy of the archives (a topic covered in Chapter 3). The reference to the general restrictions is included to cover that World War II diary given with no restrictions but, upon archival review, found to contain information that would invade the privacy of living individuals. With the full transfer of property rights, the archives has the authority to restrict portions, even if the donor has imposed no explicit restrictions. It is neater and more explicable to users and donors, however, if a reference to the archives' authority to restrict is incorporated in the deed.

While developing a deed of gift, it is useful to remember that it is a contract in which both parties promise certain things: the donor to give, the archives to respect the conditions stipulated by the donor in the deed. And once the conditions are agreed upon, if the archives fails to meet its obligations (for instance, not restricting one category of restricted materials), the contract could be determined to be void and the donor could reclaim the property; alternatively, the donor could sue the archives for damages that resulted from the breach of the contract. Neither course, however, is likely to occur in the normal relations between donor and archives.

Archives have had to return items to donors and depositors. Generally returns come about either because the donor did not have clear title to the materials and later a person with better title appeared who did not want the material in the archives or because the donor became unhappy with the archives and changed his or her mind. In the latter case, if the deed does not give the donor revocation rights by which he can withdraw the donation, the only way the materials can be withdrawn is with the consent of the archives. Archives may agree

to a withdrawal to avoid unpleasantness, but if the deed is legally sound there is no legal reason to do so. Materials that are only on deposit and not deeded can, of course, be withdrawn at any time.

Deposit Agreements

One other legal instrument is common in archival circles: the deposit agreement. A deposit agreement is a statement of intent to transfer title at some future date, usually unspecified, but in the meantime the prospective donor deposits the physical property with the archives for safekeeping. Here many of the same elements must be incorporated as in a deed, but the deposit agreement should also contain a statement of the intent to donate, a statement regarding the archives' liability for accidental damage to the property, and a statement regarding the types of archival and preservation work that may be undertaken on the collection. In some cases, materials may even be made available for research use under deposit agreements, but the archives should consider very carefully how certain the donation is before agreeing to spend the money not only to store but also to process and provide reference service on materials that could be withdrawn.[1]

Most of the difficulties with deposit agreements center around the finale: the transfer of title. Sometimes the depositor does not have the authority to transfer title but wants to see the materials in safekeeping; other depositors simply will not specify a termination date. Generally these problem depositors are institutions or organizations (including governments). When the depositor is an individual, the deposit agreement should state that in the event of the death of the depositor, title passes to the archives. A sample deposit agreement is found in Figure 4.

Undocumented Gifts

It is likely that some materials will always be transferred to an archives through simple oral statement and delivery. For example, a senior citizen comes to the local historical society with an armload of local newspapers from the 1920s and says, "I've been cleaning out the attic. If you want these you can have them; if you don't want them, just throw them away." Such oral transactions may be perfectly sound, for they usually meet the three common legal tests for a gift: a clear offer ("you

---

[1]At least one archives that agrees to "permanent deposit" without the transfer of title includes in the deposit agreement a stipulation that if the records are withdrawn the archives will be repaid for the costs of materials and labor devoted to processing and preservation. The archives keeps careful accounts during processing and when the records are processed the owner is provided an itemized statement of costs, which is incorporated into the deposit agreement by reference.

Model Deed of Gift for Donation of Historical Materials

This deed of gift has been designed as a model that may be used in whole or in part, as appropriate, for donations of historical materials to an archives. Alternative paragraphs that could be substituted at the donor's request for paragraphs in the body of the model deed are placed together at its conclusion.

Gift of Papers and Other Historical Materials

of

_____

to the

_____ Archives

1. Subject to the terms and conditions hereinafter set forth, I, _____
_____ (hereinafter referred to as the Donor), hereby give, donate, and convey to _____ (hereinafter referred to as the Donee) for deposit in the _____ Archives, my papers and other historical materials (hereinafter referred to as the Materials) which are described in Appendix A, attached hereto.

2.   Title to the Materials shall pass to the Donee upon their delivery to the Donee.

3.   Following delivery, the Materials shall be maintained by the Donee in the _____ Archives. At any time after delivery and subject to the provisions of paragraph 5, the Donor shall be permitted freely to examine any of the Materials during the regular working hours of the _____ Archives.

4.   It is the Donor's wish that the Materials be made available for research as soon as possible, consistent with the General Restriction Policy of the _____ Archives, following their deposit in the _____ Archives. The Donee shall have the Materials reviewed and shall restrict access to those Materials the use of which should be restricted in accordance with the normal application of the General Restriction Policy of the _____ Archives.

5.   Following the completion of the review provided for above, materials so restricted shall not be made available for inspection, reading, or use by anyone, except regular employees of the Donee in the performance of normal archival work on such Materials, and the Donor, or persons authorized by him in writing to have access to such materials.

6.   Notwithstanding the provisions of paragraph 5, Materials covered by this instrument shall be subject to subpoena or other lawful process, subject further to any rights, privileges or defenses that the Donor, the Donee or any other person may invoke to prevent compliance with said subpoena or other lawful process. To insure Donor the opportunity to raise such rights, privileges, or defenses, the Donee shall notify the Donor or his representative, so long as the Donor lives, as expeditiously as possible of the receipt of such subpoena or other lawful process.

Figure 3

7.   Materials which have been restricted from access as herein provided shall be reviewed by the Donee from time to time and any Materials which, because of the passage of time or other circumstances, no longer require such restrictions shall be opened to public access.

8.   Subject to the restrictions imposed herein, the Donee may dispose of any of the Materials which the Donee determines are not required by the _____ Archives.

9.   The Donor hereby gives and assigns to the Donee all rights of copyright which the Donor has in (a) the Materials and (b) in such of his works as may be found among any collections of Materials received by the Donee from others.

10.   In the event that the Donor may from time to time hereafter give, donate, and convey to the Donee, for deposit in the _____ Archives, additional papers and other historical Materials, title to such additional papers and other historical Materials shall pass to the Donee upon their delivery, and all of the provisions of this instrument of gift shall be applicable to such additional papers and other historical Materials. A description of the additonal papers and other historical Materials so donated and delivered shall be prepared and attached hereto.

Signed: _____
Donor

Date: _____

The foregoing gift of the papers and other historical Materials of the Donor is accepted on behalf of the _____ Archives, subject to the terms and conditions heretofore set forth.

Signed: _____
Donee

Date: _____

Appendix A

Attached to and forming part of the instrument of gift of papers and other historical Materials, executed by _____ (Depositor) on _____ (*date*) and accepted by the _____ (Archives) on _____ (*date*).

Appendix B, C, etc.

The following additional papers and other historical Materials are donated to and accepted by the _____ Archives pursuant to the instrument of gift executed by _____ (Depositor) on _____ (*date*) and accepted by the _____ (Archives) on _____ (*date*).

Figure 3, cont.

Alternative Paragraphs

Paragraph 4. It is the Donor's wish that the Materials be made available for research as soon as possible following their deposit in the _____ Archives. At the same time, the Donor recognizes that the Materials may include some information which, at present, should not be released. Accordingly, the Donee shall have the Materials reviewed and for the present shall restrict access to the following classes of material:

the Donor will choose one or more of the following classes

  a.   Papers and other historical Materials, the disclosure of which would constitute a clearly unwarranted invasion of personal privacy or a libel of a living person.

  b.   Material relating to the personal, family, and confidential business affairs of the Donor or other persons referenced in the Materials.

  c.   Material containing statements made by or to the Donor in confidence.

  d.   Material relating to investigations of individuals and organizations, to proposed appointments to office, or to other personnel matters directly affecting individual privacy.

  e.   Papers and other historical Materials that are specifically authorized under criteria established by statute or executive order to be kept secret in the interest of national defense or foreign policy, and are in fact properly classified pursuant to such statute or executive order.

  f.   Material containing statements or information the divulgence of which might prejudice the conduct of foreign relations of the United States of America or which would adversely affect the security of the United States of America.

Paragraph 7. Materials which have been restricted from access in accordance with Paragraph 4 above shall be restricted until _____ (*specific date*).

or

Paragraph 7. Materials which have been restricted from access in accordance with Paragraph 4 above shall be reviewed by the Donee from time to time and opened to public access when both Donor and Donee agree that conditions no longer require such restrictions. At the death of the Donor, the authority to remove restrictions shall revert to the Archives. (*Alternatively*: The authority to remove restrictions shall revert to the Donor's Designee, _____, and at the death of the Designee the authority shall revert to the Archives.)

Paragraph 8. Subject to the restrictions imposed herein, the Donee may dispose of any of the Materials which the Donee determines to have no permanent value or historical interest, provided that prior to any such disposal and during the lifetime

Figure 3, cont.

of the Donor the Donor shall be notified thereof, and at the Donor's request, the Materials proposed for disposal shall be returned to the Donor.

or

Paragraph 8.   Subject to the restrictions imposed herein, the Donee may dispose of any of the Materials which the Donee determines to have no permanent value or historical interest. If in the opinion of the Archives the Materials should be preserved in a different physical form, such as microform or digital recording, the Archives may perform the necessary processing and the original Materials shall be disposed of as provided herein.

Paragraph 9.   During the Donor's lifetime, the Donor retains all rights of copyright in Donor's works in all papers and other historical Materials donated to the Donee under the terms of this instrument or which may be included in other collections of papers deposited in the _____ Archives. After the Donor's death, all said rights shall pass to the Donee.

or

Paragraph 9.   During the Donor's lifetime, the Donor retains all rights of copyright in Donor's works in all papers and other historical Materials donated to the Donee under the terms of this instrument or which may be included in other collections of papers deposited in the _____ Archives. After the Donor's death, all said rights shall pass to _____, if (he, she) survives the Donor, for (his, her) lifetime or until _____ (*date*), or until the rights expire, whichever event occurs first. Upon that event all such rights shall pass to the Donee.

Figure 3, cont.

Model Deposit Agreement

This deposit agreement has been designed as a model that may be used in whole or in part, as appropriate, for the deposit of historical materials in an archives. Alternative paragraphs that could be substituted for paragraphs in the body of the model deposit agreement are placed together at its conclusion.

Deposit Agreement regarding the Administration
of the Papers and Other Historical Materials

of

_____

Deposited in the

_____ Archives

1.   Subject to the terms, conditions, and restrictions hereinafter set forth, I, _____, (hereinafter referred to as the Undersigned) hereby deposit in the _____ Archives my papers and other historical materials (hereinafter referred to as the Materials and which are described in Appendix A attached hereto).

Figure 4

2.   Title to the Materials shall remain in the possession of the Undersigned with the clear intent that said title will be conveyed to the _____ Archives at the Undersigned's future convenience.

3.   The Materials shall be maintained in the _____ Archives. At any time after delivery and subject to the provisions of paragraph 5, the Undersigned shall be permitted freely to examine any of the Materials during the regular working hours of the _____ Archives where they are preserved.

4.   It is the Undersigned's wish that the Materials be made available for research as soon as possible, and to the fullest extent possible, following their deposit in the _____ Archives. The Director of the _____ Archives or his delegates (hereinafter referred to as the Director) shall have the Materials reviewed and shall restrict access to those Materials, the use of which should be restricted in accordance with the normal application of the General Restriction Policy of the _____ Archives.

5.   Following the completion of the review provided for above, Materials so restricted shall not be available for inspection, reading, or use by anyone, except regular employees of the _____ Archives in the performance of normal archival work on such Materials, and the Undersigned, or persons authorized by him in writing to have access to such Materials.

6.   Materials which have been restricted from access as herein provided shall be reviewed by the Director from time to time and any papers which, because of the passage of time or other circumstances, no longer require such restrictions shall be opened to public access.

7.   Subject to the restriction imposed herein, the Archivist may dispose of any of the Materials which the Director determines to have no permanent value or historical interest, or to be surplus to the needs of the _____ Archives, provided that prior to any such disposal the Undersigned shall be notified thereof, and at the Undersigned's request, the Materials proposed for disposal shall be returned to the Undersigned.

8.   The Undersigned retains to himself all copyrights which the Undersigned has in (a) the Materials and (b) in such of his works as may be among any collections of papers or historical Materials received by the _____ Archives from others. Upon the Undersigned's death, said copyrights shall pass to the _____ Archives.

9.   The Undersigned exonerates the _____ Archives of liability for loss or other damage to the deposited Materials due to deterioration, fire, or other catastrophe.

10.   In the event that the Undersigned may from time to time hereafter deposit in the _____ Archives additional papers and other historical Materials, all of the foregoing provisions of this agreement shall be applicable to such additional papers and other historical Materials. A description of the additional papers and other historical Materials so delivered shall be prepared and attached hereto.

Figure 4, cont.

11. In the event that this agreement remains in effect at the time of the Undersigned's death, the title to the Materials shall pass to the _____ Archives, to be administered under the same conditions on access herein set forth.

Signed: _____
Depositor

Date: _____

The foregoing deposit of papers and other historical Materials is accepted on behalf of the _____ Archives, subject to the terms and conditions heretofore set forth.

Signed: _____
Archives

Date: _____

Appendix A

Attached to and forming part of the instrument of gift of papers and other historical Materials, executed by _____ (Depositor) on _____ (*date*) and accepted by the _____ (Archives) on _____ (*date*).

Appendix B, C, etc.

The following additional papers and other historical Materials are donated to and accepted by the _____ Archives pursuant to the instrument of gift executed by _____ (Depositor) on _____ (*date*) and accepted by the _____ (Archives) on _____ (*date*).

Alternative Paragraphs

Paragraph 4.   It is the Undersigned's wish that the Materials be made available for research as soon as possible following their deposit in the _____ Archives. At the same time, the Undersigned recognizes that the Materials may include some information which, at present, should not be released. Accordingly, the Director of the _____ Archives shall have the Materials reviewed and for the present shall restrict access to the following classes of Materials:

the Undersigned will choose one or more of the following classes

a.   Papers and other historical Materials, the disclosure of which would constitute a clearly unwarranted invasion of personal privacy or a libel of a living person.

b.   Material relating to the personal, family, and confidential business affairs of the Undersigned or other persons referenced in the Materials.

c.   Material containing statements made by or to the Undersigned in confidence.

d.   Material relating to investigations of individuals and organizations, to proposed appointments to office, or to other personnel matters directly affecting individual privacy.

Figure 4, cont.

e.   Papers and other historical Materials that are specifically authorized under criteria established by statute or executive order to be kept secret in the interest of national defense or foreign policy, and are in fact properly classified pursuant to such statute or executive order.

f.   Material concerning statements or information the divulgence of which might prejudice the conduct of foreign relations of the United States of America or which would adversely affect the security of the United States of America.

Paragraph 7.   Materials which have been restricted from access in accordance with Paragraph 4 above shall be restricted until _____ (*specific date*).

or

Paragraph 7.   Materials which have been restricted from access in accordance with Paragraph 4 above shall be reviewed by the Undersigned from time to time and opened to public access when both Undersigned and the _____ Archives agree that conditions no longer require such restrictions. At the death of the Undersigned, the authority to remove restrictions shall revert to the _____ Archives. (*Alternatively:* The authority to remove restrictions shall revert to the Undersigned's Designee, _____, and at the death of the Designee the authority shall revert to the Archives.)

Paragraph 8.   Subject to the restrictions imposed herein, the _____ Archives may dispose of any of the Materials which the _____ Archives determines to have no permanent value or historical interest, provided that prior to any such disposal and during the lifetime of the Undersigned, the Undersigned shall be notified thereof, and at the Undersigned's request, the Materials proposed for disposal shall be returned to the Undersigned.

or

Paragraph 8.   Subject to the restrictions imposed herein, the _____ Archives may dispose of any of the Materials which the _____ Archives determines to have no permanent value or historical interest. If in the opinion of the _____ Archives the Materials should be preserved in a different physical form, such as microform or digital recording, the _____ Archives may perform the necessary processing and the original Materials shall be disposed of as provided herein.

Paragraph 9.   During the Undersigned's lifetime, the Undersigned retains rights of copyright in the Undersigned's work in all papers and other historical Materials deposited in the _____ Archives under the terms of this agreement or which may be included in other collections of papers deposited in the _____ Archives. After the Undersigned's death, all said rights shall pass to _____, if (he, she) survives the Undersigned, for (his, her) lifetime or until _____ (*date*), or until the rights expire, whichever event occurs first. Upon that event all such rights shall pass to the _____ Archives.

Figure 4, cont.

can have them''), acceptance (''we'd be delighted to have them''), and delivery (''here they are''). Presumably the conversation marking this transfer could be reconstructed at a later time if the question of legal title arose, and it would be buttressed by internal archives documents indicating that the material was received from the donor on a certain date, that the material was processed and made available on the assumption that it was the property of the archives, and so forth.

But if the oral statement and delivery occurred in the past, the archives may find itself with items for which there are absolutely no written records regarding receipt. There is no simple solution to these cases. The best thing for the archives to do is to create a file that describes the nature of the item, the present custody of the item by the archives, and any internal evidence from the archives' files pointing to the length of time the archives has had the materials (the item appears on the comprehensive shelf list of 1952, for example). It may, of course, be possible to guess where the item originated and contact the likely donors or their heirs; interviews with former archives staff members may also prove useful.

Some archivists have worried that if they raise questions about undocumented donations the result may be that a claimant will appear and the archives will lose the items. This is, of course, possible, but not very likely. Undocumented gifts have not been involved in most of the well-known cases of return; these have more often been items whose transfer was documented through deposit agreements. While documenting the items many years after accessioning may be a nuisance, raising questions about the original transfer probably does not involve a substantial risk of losing the gift. It simply clarifies the archives' legal title to the material, allowing the archives to take any subsequent actions (publication, rehabilitation, destruction) it chooses.

Tax Implications

Often the reason a donor chooses to deposit rather than donate, especially if a donor is a private individual not an institution, is the tax implication of the gift. The problem arises from the Tax Reform Act of 1969, particularly sections 201(a) and 514. At one time persons could donate the papers they had created to an archives and take a tax deduction for the appraised value of the papers. The reform act changed all that.

The revision of the tax code was stimulated by the tax deductions taken by presidents for the donation of their papers to the National Archives. During the debates on the reform bill, Senator John J. Williams of Delaware, who was instrumental in developing the legislation, expressed concern over "special tax benefits through the

gift of official papers." "To the extent that they [official papers] do have value," he argued, "they were developed by Government officials on Government time with the aid of Government staff personnel, were typed by Government secretaries on Government paper, and were even stored in Government files."[2] In the Congress a consensus emerged that it was improper to take a deduction for such papers and the law should be revised to eliminate this possibility. While the abuses the tax law revision was meant to correct were those of political figures, the new law was written broadly and caught in its sweep all those persons whose personal papers are also their official business (authors, songwriters, poets, and so forth).

Under the current law, the allowance of a deduction for the donation of personal papers depends upon several factors: (1) the nature of the receiving institution, (2) the nature of the property donated, and (3) whether the donor can "establish a basis" in the property to be donated. To be a tax deductible contribution for an individual, the donated property must be a "capital asset" for the donor. Normally, for the creator of the papers, they cannot be a capital asset. To understand why, we must look carefully at the three factors.

First, the tax law defines organizations to whom a contribution can be made and a tax deduction subsequently taken. These institutions generally include all educational institutions, archives, manuscript collections, and the like. There are no real problems here for archives.

The second factor is the nature of the property donated. If the property donated is not money — as it would not be in the case of personal papers — then the amount of the contribution (that is, the money equivalent of the items donated) is defined as the "fair market value of the property at the time of the contribution." Essentially, this means how much the property would sell for on the open market on the day of donation. This is well within the possibilities of donations of papers to archives, too.

The third factor, establishing a "basis," is the one that causes the trouble for archives and their donors. To understand what a basis is, some background is necessary. The tax code distinguishes between property the value of which includes long-term capital gains and property the disposal of which would lead to ordinary income or short-term gains. By definition, only the sale or exchange of a capital asset can create long-term capital gains. The question, then, is whether personal papers are capital assets.

---

[2]Remarks, Senator John J. Williams, 115 *Cong. Rec.* 20461 (1969).

The tax law is very clear about capital assets and personal papers. Specifically excluded from the definition of a capital asset are:

> a copyright, a literary, musical, or artistic composition, a letter or memorandum, or similar property, held by —
> (A) a taxpayer whose personal efforts created such property,
> (B) in the case of a letter, memorandum, or similar property, a taxpayer for whom such property was prepared or produced, or
> (C) a taxpayer in whose hands the basis of such property is determined, for purposes of determining gain from a sale or exchange, in whole or part by reference to the basis of such property in the hands of a taxpayer described in subparagraph (A) or (B).

Consequently, donations from a person described in category A, B, or C cannot be capital assets.

Since personal papers cannot be capital assets for these individuals, they cannot by definition have long-term capital gains. For tax purposes, then, personal papers are property the disposal of which would lead to ordinary income or short-term capital gains.

Having learned that personal papers are property that would give rise to only ordinary income or short-term gains, the basis question can be answered. According to the tax law, for the donation of property that would give rise to ordinary income or short-term capital gains, the allowable deduction is limited to the donor's cost or other basis in such property. Basis here generally means the out-of-pocket costs in the creation of the material. Consequently, these donors can take deductions for the cost of the paper and ink, typewriter ribbons, and floppy disks, but not for the autograph value or the intellectual content of the items.[3]

The clearest test of the new law was a court case involving the donation of former Congressman James H. Morrison's papers to Southeastern Louisiana University.[4] The sole question before the court was whether Morrison was entitled to a deduction for donation of the papers he had accumulated during twenty-four years in the U.S. House of Representatives. The Internal Revenue Service, and the court, said no.

Importantly for archivists, the court in the Morrison case did not distinguish between incoming and outgoing correspondence. (Some archivists had feared that a donor might be able to separate his papers into incoming and outgoing mail, taking a deduction on the value of the incoming, which he did not produce, but not on the outgoing, which he did.) In fact, the court explicitly stated that "third party documents — letters, memoranda, or similar property prepared by third parties (such as constituents, Government employees, or other Members of Congress) and delivered to petitioner — are considered to have been prepared or produced for petitioner."[5] This judicial decision affirms the archival view that the papers of a person are a unitary entity, including both the documents created and the documents received, and are to be treated as an indivisible whole.

Another tax case involved the donation of Hubert Humphrey's papers. In early 1975 Humphrey signed an agreement with the Internal Revenue Service to surrender all income tax deduction claims for the vice-presidential papers he donated to the Minnesota Historical Society. The issue, which was not taken to court, apparently was whether a twenty-five-year restriction on access, and literary rights reserved to Humphrey, made this a gift of "future interest" rather than an outright donation. The result seemed to be that any restrictions on the use of the donated materials would cancel out immediate deductions because the donation would be considered a gift of future interest. (Although the tax dispute arose over deductions in the years 1969-72, the deeds to the material were made between 1966 and 1969. The question of whether the 1969 Tax Reform Act prohibited "carryover" deductions from deeds signed prior to the passage of the act was not answered by the out of court settlement.)[6]

A third well-publicized case involved the appraisal of the papers of former Illinois Governor Otto Kerner, which brought to the fore the methods used by manuscript appraisers. Kerner's appraiser used a simplistic mathematical formula to determine the value of the papers: he estimated the total number of pieces of paper in the collection; he concluded that the average minimum value of each page was ten cents (based on the supposed cost of storing a page of paper, the cost of photocopying a page, and the acceptance of the papers by the Illinois State Historical Society); he multiplied the total number of pages by ten cents a page; he added to this the value of certain letters that had a definitely ascertainable market value. The court rejected this appraisal process. It decided that the relevant factors in determining the fair market value of the Kerner papers were Kerner's accomplishments and general popularity; the significance of the specific papers; the relative place

---

[3]Tax Reform Act of 1969, PL 91-172. The amendments embodied in the act are codified in 83 Stat. 549, 643.

[4]Although the tax case involving Richard Nixon and the donation of his vice-presidential papers to the National Archives is famous and did much to alert the public to the change in the tax law, it was a case that turned on the question of the date of the deed, not on the substantive contents of the papers or the interpretation of tax law.

[5]Morrison v. Commissioner, 71 United States Tax Court Reports 683 (1979).

[6]"HHH Agrees to Repay Huge Tax Deductions," Washington Post, March 14, 1975, A1; M. B. Schnapper, "Public Papers and Private Gain," The Nation 229 (November 24, 1979): 524-526.

and importance of the contributed papers in Kerner's career; the condition and content of the papers; whether the papers were originals or photocopies; whether the papers were handwritten or typed; whether the mental processes of Kerner were revealed by the papers; the composition of the market for such papers; and the intensity of demand among potential buyers.[7]

Each of these cases focused on an individual's donation of his own papers. Archives also receive donations from heirs and from purchasers, and here the tax situation is very different. Heirs can take a tax deduction on the donation of personal papers, and some persons have refused to donate their papers during their lifetimes, leaving the tax deduction to the heirs. To take a tax deduction, however, the heirs must first pass the papers through the estate of the creator, in the process paying inheritance taxes.[8] Purchasers can take deductions for the donation of purchased items.

Because appraisal for tax purposes has often been a key to donation, archivists have debated whether it is ethical for the archival institution itself to appraise papers, either before or after donation. The passage of the Deficit Reduction Act of 1984 has ended that debate.[9] The act included some amendments to the tax laws aimed at stopping the abuse of the appraisal process on property donated to a qualified charitable organization. Besides holding the donor to a higher standard of proof of the value of donated property, the amendments also place some burdens on the donee (the recipient). The new law, which was effective January 1, 1985, requires the donor of property valued in excess of $5,000 (other than publicly traded securities) to obtain a qualified appraisal of the property. The appraisal cannot be made by (1) the taxpayer (the donor), (2) "a party to the transaction in which the taxpayer acquired the property" (such as a manuscript dealer who sold to the donor the materials to be donated), (3) the donee (the archives), (4) "any person employed by any of the foregoing persons or related to any of the foregoing persons under section 267(b) of the Internal Revenue Code of 1954", or (5) "to the extent provided in such regulations, any person whose relationship to the taxpayer would cause a reasonable person to question the independence of such appraiser." Either the donor or the donee (or, for that matter, anyone else) can hire another party to appraise the material. The donor must attach a summary of the appraisal to the tax return in which a deduction is claimed for the donation. The donee must also be presented with the summary appraisal that is attached to the tax return and must acknowledge it. The amendment also requires the donee to report to both the donor and the Internal Revenue Service any disposition of the donated property occurring within two years after its receipt. In summary, for gifts worth more than $5,000 an archives cannot make the appraisal, it must acknowledge the summary appraisal, and it must report any subsequent disposition of the property within two years of its receipt.

An archives can provide prospective donors with the name of an appraisers association. Providing a list of names of individual appraisers is less desirable, because it gives the aura of an endorsement and because if an appraiser's name is omitted from the list he or she may make public charges of favoritism. Working through professional organizations is a safer way to provide information on appraisal services for prospective donors.

Historical Materials Purchased by an Archives

The general reduction of funds available to archives at present means that the purchase of collections occurs less frequently than it did in the past, but some purchases do still occur. The primary concern in a purchase must be that of the legitimacy of the seller. Does he or she have clear title to the property? A seller can only pass along such rights as he has in the property, and if those rights are clouded or are not susceptible to convincing demonstration, the purchaser should be wary. It is possible that an institution purchasing a set of documents where clear title has not been conveyed could be forced to give up the materials if a previous owner who can demonstrate superior title appears and claims the items.[10]

When purchasing items it may also be wise to record more information than the purchase price in the agreement with the seller. While this is not legally required, it may save disagreeable publicity later. In a recent example, a woman who had sold papers to the Sigmund Freud Archives, who in turn transferred the materials to the Library of Congress, wrote an open letter to the *New York Review of Books*. In her letter she complained that the materials she had sold and had assumed would be available for research were now closed under restrictions agreed on by the Freud Archives and the Library. Significantly, she said she sold the materials "believing that these papers would be accessible to

[7] *Kerner* v. *Commission*, 35 T.C.M. 36 (1976).

[8] Donations by the estate itself can become very complicated. See, for example, the problems over the Stravinsky papers as chronicled in "Stravinsky Papers Saga Continues," *SAA Newsletter*, July 1983, p. 8, September 1983, p. 7; *New York Times*, May 15, 1983, I, 1:2, June 4, 1983, I, 15:1, June 24, 1983, III, 26:1.

[9] Deficit Reduction Act of 1984, PL 98-369 §155-6.

[10] This is at the heart of the problems over the Hebrew books and manuscripts sold by Sotheby's in the summer of 1984. See, for example, *New York Times* June 24, 1984, A:23; August 14, 1984, C:13; August 30, 1984, C:17.

serious students and research workers." "No agreement to that effect was made," she continued, "but it seemed a natural and reasonable supposition in dealing with a reputable and responsible institution."[11] A careful statement, in writing, at the time of the purchase would have clarified both access policies and the rights to subsequent disposition of the materials, which became another issue in the incident. While institutions may not want to enter into such agreements in fear of burdening themselves with restrictive conditions, agreements may in the long run avoid difficult relations with past and prospective private sellers.

Conclusion

Donations and purchases are legal transactions where the title to the physical form and the intellectual contents of documents pass from one party to another. These are fundamental changes in the property rights in the items, and archivists should treat the transfers seriously. The documentation of the transfers need not be verbose nor does it require any magic legal words, but it should be clear and unambiguous. Care in this area will repay the archivist many times over, for all further work with the materials will be influenced by the conditions established at the time of donation. Taking time at the beginning saves time later, especially if litigation arises.

If legal problems do occur, remember that the law developed from generations of rational people trying to solve practical problems. At bottom it is a simple system, although it is complex in operation. The better the documentation the archives has of its activities, the clearer the legal issues will be. The clearer and simpler the issues submitted to the law, the clearer and simpler will be the solution. Lawyers frequently say, "Hard cases make bad law." The simpler the case submitted to the legal system, the better the chance that the archives and the public will get a fair and just answer.

3 Access Concepts

The archivist has two parts to play in managing access to records: apply the concepts governing access to the records and administer the procedures for access. Both of these activities, the intellectual and the practical, have greatly perplexed archivists in the past twenty years. Of course there were problems before then; from the beginning of recordkeeping archivists have had to contend with restricting access to certain records, as Ernst Posner's definitive *Archives of the Ancient World* shows.[1] But the passage of the first federal Freedom of Information Act in 1966 did usher in a new era in access practices. State governments also adopted freedom of information or open records acts, and this legislation, when joined by the privacy and sunshine acts of both federal and state governments and the Buckley Amendment on access to student records in institutions of higher education, fundamentally changed the access rules that most archivists had to use. Increasingly, too, this legislated openness influenced the conditions of access to records and personal papers outside the direct purview of the records laws, as archivists accustomed to the new provisions sought easier access to donated material and advocated opening the records of private institutions.

The dramatic change in the way archivists think about access is forcefully demonstrated by rereading Margaret Norton's 1944 presidential address to the Society of American Archivists. In it she discusses the legal aspects of archives, but allots only one paragraph to the problems of administering access to public records. Today access is surely the greatest legal problem faced by archivists, and Norton's conclusion — "the knowledge that information can be obtained only by going through certain formalities also acts as a definite check to sensation mongers" — now seems quaint.[2]

The joint statement issued in 1979 by the American Library Association and the Society of American Archivists on access to original research materials in libraries, archives, and manuscript repositories (reprinted in Appendix 1) reflects the increased importance that archivists place on access. The statement incorporates a general consensus on openness and represents a major professional cooperative milestone. The statement, however, focuses on the administration

---

[11]Diana Riviere to the Editors, *New York Review*, June 2, 1983. See also correspondence on the Sigmund Freud Archives in the issues of February 3 and March 31, 1983.

[1]Ernst Posner, *Archives in the Ancient World* (Cambridge: Harvard University Press, 1972). See, for example, pp. 54, 83, 152, 182.

[2]Margaret Norton, "Some Legal Aspects of Archives," *American Archivist* 8 (January 1945): 1-11.

of access policies rather than on the underlying concepts of access. On access theory the statement merely acknowledges "that every repository has certain obligations to guard against unwarranted invasion of personal privacy and to protect confidentiality in its holdings in accordance with law and that every private donor has the right to impose reasonable restrictions upon his papers to protect privacy or confidentiality for a reasonable period of time." This elevated language glides over a multitude of issues relating to the release of archival holdings for research purposes.

The application of access concepts and the administration of access procedures are the subjects of Chapters 3 and 4. This chapter reviews the most common access concepts that form the basis for access determinations, and the following chapter turns to the problems of putting those determinations into practice.

General Considerations

Access as an archival term means the authority to obtain information from or to perform research in archival materials. While the purpose of an archives is to preserve and make available historical materials, access policy serves as a major brake to full and free availability. Archivists are committed to the principle that everything in their holdings will eventually be available for reference use, but archivists cling equally tenaciously to the idea that a balance must be struck between the public's right to know and the need for confidentiality. The result of this balancing may be to close some research materials to public access for some period of time. It is the tension between these two ideas — to provide access to research materials and to protect confidentiality — that creates the frustration archivists feel when confronted with access problems.

As with questions of appraisal and transfer, provenance is the key to determining access. Again the principal distinctions are between records of the institution of which the archives is a part, with a further distinction between public and private institutions; donated records of another institution; and donated personal papers, artificial collections, and ephemera. The restriction authority for particular materials within each of these types comes either from law, from conditions established by the institution, or from conditions established through instruments of transfer.

It is important to be entirely clear and consistent with the terms used in discussing restricted records. Three terms are often used to describe records to which there is no general public access: restricted, classified, and privileged. "Restricted" is the general, generic term that means closed to public access. It can be used to describe any type of material restricted for any reason.

Restricted items may be entirely closed to public access or may be open only to designated individuals or only under certain conditions. "Classified" has an older meaning of records that were organized in a special classification scheme by the office of origin; that usage has mostly disappeared and now the term normally refers to those federal government materials that contain information concerning national defense and foreign relations that must be protected against unauthorized disclosure *and* that are marked "Confidential," "Secret," or "Top Secret." "Privileged" is another term that was previously often used to designate materials that were not classified national security information but were nevertheless restricted from general public access. Because "privileged" carries a connotation of privileged, or unequal, access, archivists have generally ceased to use the term.

Five restriction categories are common to archives, whether the materials are records or personal papers, donated or held within the creating institution. These are privacy, business information, personnel data, investigative information, and statutory restrictions. The application of these concepts varies by type of material and type of archival institution (for example, personnel data are unlikely to be found in donated personal papers in a historical society; in government archives operating under freedom of information acts, business information may be subject to special prerelease treatment, and so on). The bulk of the chapter will consider access within specific institutional contexts, but a brief review of the five common categories may be useful.

Privacy

Privacy is by far the most pervasive consideration in restricting materials in archives. Exactly what privacy means is a little hard to define, however. The Constitution does not explicitly state that there is a constitutionally protected right to privacy, but many of the provisions of the Bill of Rights do safeguard privacy. Courts in the nineteenth century recognized some of the rights now generally considered to be part of the ambit of personal privacy, but the definition of privacy as a distinct and independent right can be traced to a law review article in 1890. In it the authors, two young lawyers named Samuel Warren and Louis Brandeis, "synthesized at one stroke a whole new category of legal rights and . . . initiated a new field of jurisprudence."[3]

Privacy, in its simplest terms, is the right of an individual to be let alone, to live a life free from unwarranted publicity. The violation or invasion of privacy is

---

[3]62 *Am Jur 2d,* "Privacy," sec. 2; Samuel Warren and Louis Brandeis, "The Right to Privacy," 4 *Harvard Law Review* 193 (1890).

legally a tort, or civil wrong. The basic reference book on torts defines four different forms of invasion of privacy: (1) intrusion upon the individual's seclusion or solitude, or into his private affairs; (2) public disclosure of embarassing private facts about the individual; (3) publicity that places the individual in a false light in the public eye; and (4) appropriation, for another person's advantage, of the individual's name or likeness.[4]

The invasion of privacy is similar to but not the same as libel of an individual. In libel (see page 44) the truth is a defense; that is, if the statement made about the individual is true, it cannot be libelous. In a case of invasion of privacy, however, the statement may be true but the primary damage is the mental distress from having the information exposed to public view. Generally speaking, the motives of the person purveying the information are unimportant in determining whether there is a right of action for invasion of the right of privacy, because the presence of malice is not required in a privacy case.

In any specific instance these broad principles about privacy must be judged in the light of the governing statutes. There is no federal statute of privacy that applies to all records everywhere: the federal Privacy Act applies only to the records of the federal government. Privacy acts have also been passed by a number of state governments (see the list in Appendix 2), although they are by no means as common as state freedom of information acts. In the absence of a specific act, privacy issues will be judged by common law principles and by the holdings of courts in previously litigated cases.

Litigation alleging that some person or institution invaded another's privacy is quite common. Privacy is an issue in lawsuits over contraception and abortion rights; privacy is litigated when citizens believe the government has spied on them unjustly; privacy is an issue in various cases involving use of photographs of persons taken without their permission. Consequently, the issue is usually couched in terms of what is an invasion of privacy, not what is privacy per se.

Privacy tests involving written materials, especially unpublished ones (there are a number of cases in which news media have been sued for invasion of privacy), are a special category of privacy questions. While there is some disagreement over the application of privacy principles to documents, there are a few points on which most archivists and lawyers can agree. First, medical and psychiatric files relating to an individual are usually withheld from public access by privacy considerations. Second, certain materials containing information developed or imparted during a client relationship (such as

with a lawyer or clergyman) are also normally assumed to have a privacy element. Third, the right to privacy is a right of living individuals, and there is normally no privacy right for the dead (see page 53 for a fuller discussion). Finally, once information about an individual is in the public domain, it usually remains open to subsequent users.

Until the federal Freedom of Information Act was passed, actual legal tests of privacy in unpublished written items were few. A review of the privacy principles that have emerged from federal FOIA cases begins on page 53. While the law that has emerged from these cases is undeniably federal in nature, every archivist needs to know and understand it. The federal FOIA interpretations on privacy are the most substantial body of court-tested privacy concepts extant. As such, their precedential value would likely be considered by any court if an archives is charged with violating a citizen's privacy rights.

Business Information

A second major concept used in restricting access to documents is the confidentiality of business information. Two types of material are covered: the information an institution holds about itself and information it holds about the business of others. The heart of the restriction of business information is the need to protect the competitive position of the institution or organization or individual to whom the documents refer. The information may range from the formula for making a product to a list of contributors to a charity to the amount of stock a person holds in a particular company. The information may be financial and technical, but it may also be information about future plans for the organization, exact membership lists for volunteer groups, and the cancelled checks of a person. It is under the general rubric of business information that institutions and organizations usually assert their privacy rights. (While privacy is usually discussed in terms of an individual, a private corporation also has a right to be let alone, so far as the assertion of privacy for the corporation is consistent with the law.)

Governments, as public institutions, cannot use the business information concept to bar citizen access to its records of income, expenditure, and administration. But governments handle enormous amounts of information submitted to them by businesses and organizations, from tax data to bids on government contracts to labor relations reports. The federal Freedom of Information Act recognized this substantial body of information in federal records and provided a specific exemption to cover it. Because the test that is used to withhold business information under the federal statute is, "What could a business reasonably seek to protect from

---

[4]*Prosser on Torts*, quoted in 62 *Am Jur 2d*, "Privacy," sec. 1.

disclosure?'' the decisions in lawsuits brought under the federal Freedom of Information Act provide an excellent review of protectible types of business information. In addition, because businesses and organizations have been active in litigation focusing on this exemption, the emerging judicial interpretation of business information attempts to balance the privacy needs of businesses with public needs for information. A discussion of the FOIA business information exemption begins on page 49.

Personnel Information

A third frequent restriction is on personnel information. While this restriction has elements in common with both privacy and business information, it is often handled separately to provide special notice to users and reassurance to the employees themselves that the data is restricted. Normally some information about employment is available to the public: who works in the institution, what jobs are held by which individuals, the dates of employment of an individual, and so forth. Salary figures are usually protected, except in governmental employment, where salary schedules are public and, in some cases, state law may require publication of personal salaries in excess of a particular dollar figure.

Again, cases litigated under the federal Freedom of Information Act provides some guidance for archivists trying to decide whether or not to open certain types of personnel information. Most likely, however, the federal standards are more liberal (that is, more information would be released) than those of the private sector. The federal FOIA restriction of personnel information is part of the general protection of privacy (see page 54).

Investigative Information

The fourth restriction concept found in most archives is the protection of information generated during investigations. Many institutions have quasi-law enforcement units (for example, campus cops, corporate security forces). In addition many more kinds of investigations exist: the fitness of candidates for ordination into the clergy; investigations of charges of plagiarism in academic publications; various checks and reviews before hiring new employees. All of these may contain information that if disclosed would violate the privacy of the individuals involved; moreover, some of them may reveal procedures (such as the exact way in which campus police rounds are scheduled) that would hamper further effective operation of the institution or organization.

By its very nature, an investigation probes areas where an individual might reasonably assert a right of privacy. For that reason, releasing investigative infor-

mation requires careful review and decision-making. Two kinds of privacy are involved: that of the individual who is the subject of the investigation and that of the persons who provided information to the investigators. In addition to the privacy issues, there is the need to protect the institutional processes and, occasionally, the persons who carried out the investigation on behalf of the institution.

The federal courts have repeatedly struggled with the problem of investigative information. To be sure, there is a great difference between an investigation of a tenure track candidate and an investigation of drug smuggling on the U.S.-Mexican border. But at bottom many of the principles are the same, and any archivist dealing with records of investigations would be well advised to follow the decisions courts make on federal FOIA exemption (b)(7) on investigative information. In particular, archivists need to pay attention to the decisions in cases on the subparts (C) and (D) of exemption (b)(7), for these deal with personal privacy in investigative information. A discussion of the current interpretation of exemption (b)(7) begins on page 55.

Statutory and Other Directed Restrictions

Finally, many archives have restrictions based on statute or on binding institutional decisions. Governmental closure statutes are familiar to most archivists, such as state adoption statutes, the federal statute regulating release of student records in colleges and universities, and so on. In addition, boards of directors, boards of regents, and other governing bodies may formally declare certain records restricted. A corporate board may establish a dual set of minutes, with one open to the public and a fuller set restricted; a charitable organization's board may declare its membership list closed for ten years; and so on. Whatever the origin of the binding restriction, archivists live with it and must restrict records accordingly.

These five general access categories underlie most archival restrictions. Their application depends on the type of archival institution holding the material and the legal authorities that the creator of the materials had. A private individual usually has the most authority over his documents and a donation of these materials to a private archival institution is probably unhindered by any law or regulation. A donation of institutional records may involve some statutory provisions, particularly if the recipient is a public archives. If the creator is a private institution and the records remain in that institution's archives, another set of rules may apply. The most closely regulated access is found in public archives of governments.

The remainder of this chapter considers these restrictions in terms of the creating and receiving institutions.

In all these cases, it is always worth referring to the prevailing federal and state case law on particular access concepts. These are the issues that have been tested in and interpreted by the courts, usually in freedom of information act cases. Even if the archives ultimately decides not to adopt the FOIA application, the archives should know and understand the current legal trends and be able to explain why the particular situation in the archives called for an alternative solution.

Donated Materials

Donated records or personal papers often have restrictions on access. In general, if the archives and the donor can reach an agreement, the material specified by the donor can be restricted. If the receiving institution is a public one, the conditions under which a donation can be accepted may be defined in the authorizing legislation. If the legislation permits gifts but sets no standard (for example, the federal government's phrase "restrictions agreeable to the Archivist"), then the question of conditions on a gift is not one of legal acceptability but of practical and ethical considerations. If the authorizing legislation is silent on the entire question of accepting gifts from private sources, the archives would have to rely either on a legislative enactment defining the general policy of the government about accepting gifts from private sources or on an opinion from the government's legal counsel.

One of the recurrent questions in archival circles is what to do if restrictions are placed on private materials that upon subsequent archival examination are found to reveal criminal activity. The theoretical answer here is easy: an instrument of gift is a contract, and a contract clause cannot be enforced against a crime. In other words, if information in donated materials clearly reveals a crime, the archivist — like any other citizen — has an obligation to report the evidence to the legal authorities, whether or not the donor has specified that those materials be restricted. The catch here is *clear* evidence. In most cases, archives hold documents that seem to imply questionable activities, but the documents rarely give solid evidence. There is no single answer to what is clear evidence, and legal advice may be required. It is not easy to tell a smoking gun from a water pistol.

With that single exception, assuming that the person who is donating the material has clear title to it (see the previous chapter), almost any set of restrictions can be legally upheld. Even material that was previously open and available in private hands can be restricted upon donation to another institution, although the receiving archives will surely point out that if the purpose of the restriction is to protect the confidentiality of the information, the information is already outside the scope of

the protection that can be afforded by restricting the original records.[5]

Donors have proposed an enormous variety of restrictions. Sometimes a particular item is restricted; other times categories are named, often corresponding to privacy and business information. If the donor is a senator or congressman or government executive, a provision to restrict national security information or a provision to protect the advice given by staff members and other confidants may be included in the deed. Sample restriction statements for all these are found in the model deed of gift, Figure 3.[6]

Privacy is by far the most important issue in handling private papers. The widely used language restricting materials that would "embarrass, damage, injure or harass" living individuals is a privacy statement. Because the best current case law on privacy is found in federal FOIA cases and because the potential damage to the individual may lead to an invasion of privacy or libel action against the archives, the model deed phrases the privacy restriction in those terms.

Donors have been known to be cavalier about the release of information in their papers, particularly information relating to persons other than themselves. If the donor does not specifically protect the privacy rights of persons named in the donated materials, the archives should to avoid potential lawsuits. Here a reference in the deed of gift to applying the archives' general restrictions will help solve the problem.

Private Records

Federal Laws and Private Records

As discussed in the introduction to this manual, in general federal access laws apply to federal records, state access laws apply to state and local records, and governmental records laws do not apply to private institutions. There are two major exceptions to these general propositions, for there are two major federal laws governing access to nonfederal records: the law governing records of identifiable students attending schools that receive federal financial aid and the statute

---

[5]See, for example, the Sigmund Freud Archives case described in Chapter 2, where records open in the Freud Archives were closed when they were transferred to the Library of Congress. One other exception is worth mentioning. If the donated papers are those of a journalist and contain names and information from the journalist's sources and informants, these items of information may in some states be protected from disclosure by state "shield laws" designed to protect sources. The Supreme Court has upheld the shield law protections. The application of the shield law is normally permissive, not mandatory, and the archives would have to decide whether to invoke it.

[6]For information on restricting documents that are security classified, see the discussion of exemption (b)(1), page 46.

regulating records of credit-reporting firms pertaining to identifiable customers. Although the latter affects archivists as individuals, few archives hold records of credit-reporting firms, still fewer such firms have archives, and even fewer such archives would have control of active credit records. While it is an example of a federal law pertaining to private records, for archivists it has little practical effect.[7]

That is most decidedly not true of the student records law, the Family Educational Rights and Privacy Act of 1974. Commonly known as the Buckley Amendment for its congressional sponsor, James Buckley, this law has a direct effect on archives of educational institutions. The law applies to "all educational agencies or institutions to which funds are made available under any Federal program for which the Secretary of the U.S. Department of Education has administrative responsibility." The law defines educational records covered by the act as any "records, files, documents, and other materials which (i) contain information directly related to the student; and (ii) are maintained by an educational agency or institution, or by a person acting for such agency or institution." Excluded from the records coverage are institutional personnel records, institutional law enforcement records that fall within a narrow definition, and medical records of students who are either eighteen years of age or older or who are attending postsecondary institutions. The law establishes the rights of parents of students under eighteen to review records on the students and the rights of students eighteen or over to review records on themselves excluding records relating to the financial conditions of their parents or to certain letters of recommendation. The law then enumerates the persons who have access to those records, with the exception that "directory information" (name, address, major field of study, participation in officially recognized activities and sports, and so forth) can be provided if the institution has publicly announced that it will do so and has given parents and students an opportunity to request that such information be withheld in their cases.[8]

For archivists there are two major problems with the language of the Buckley Amendment. First, because educational records are not defined in terms of records systems, all records in which student names appear may be covered (except, of course, the three categories of exclusions). The amendment could be interpreted to cover records reporting, say, spontaneous campus events as well as the classic student records of the registrar's office. Second, the amendment sets no time limit whatso-

ever on the duration of the restrictions. It is conceivable that this section could be interpreted to close down the nineteenth-century student records of an institution that currently receives federal funding.

Several court cases have tested the application of the Buckley Amendment. Although no case answers the two major archival questions of breadth and duration of the restriction, the courts appear to be taking a common-sense approach. In a North Carolina case, the court suggested that disclosure about students that is incidental and not part of an established policy or practice is not a Buckley violation. The cause of the suit was a public law school faculty meeting where student information was discussed, and the principal question was whether the meeting was covered by the state open meetings law. Logic suggests that the minutes of this meeting are also open. This in turn suggests that incidental releases outside identifiable series of student records are not violations of the Buckley statute.[9]

The question of duration is also probably moving toward a less severe interpretation than the face of the statute suggests. Two courts have held that the amendment provides only a procedural remedy — the withholding of funds by the secretary of education — and does not itself provide a right for an individual to sue to receive money damages from the educational institution. In other words, if a person sues under the Buckley Amendment, and if he wins, the school may lose its funds but the individual will not get money. That may reduce the number of individuals willing to bring suit under the amendment.[10]

Finally, an Oklahoma court in 1976 explicitly linked the Buckley provisions to personal privacy. The court carefully said that the amendment established a procedure for advising or identifying a person when educational records pertaining to that person are to be released. As mentioned above, privacy rights are generally considered rights of the living. Consequently, by interpreting the Buckley Amendment as a privacy statute, only living parents and students would have the standing to bring suit for violations of the provisions. With that, any threat that nineteenth-century records would be closed by the amendment evaporates. It is, of course, possible that the Department of Education could bring an action against a school without a suit first initiated by a student or parent. That likelihood is remote, however, in the absence of a living individual whose privacy is invaded by the release of information. Risk

[7]Fair Credit Reporting Act, 15 U.S.C. §1681; Right to Financial Privacy Act of 1978, 12 U.S.C. §3401 et seq.
[8]20 U.S.C. §1232g.

[9]Student Bar Ass'n Bd. of Governors, of School of Law, University of North Carolina at Chapel Hill v. Byrd, 239 S.E.2d 415, 293 N.C. (1977) 594.
[10]Ibid.; Girardier v. Webster College, 563 F.2d 1267 (8th Cird. 1977).

analysis suggests that opening nineteenth-century student records (or, for that matter, records seventy-five years old) is safe.[11]

In the administration of records under the Buckley Amendment, archives will be just one part of the institution-wide procedure. Requirements for inspection, recordkeeping, and notice will affect the whole institution, and archivists should make sure that the institution's lawyers and administrators are aware of the unique archival needs when the institutional procedures are established.

Libel and Private Records

Outside the two federal statutes discussed above, the records of private institutions can be made available or restricted by the institution that created them. As mentioned above, there is no federal privacy statute that operates on all records everywhere; at most, private organizations have as a guideline the law of libel. The legal definition of libel is "a malicious publication, expressed either in printing or writing, or by signs and pictures, tending either to blacken the memory of one who is dead or the reputation of one who is alive, and expose him to public hatred, contempt, or ridicule." Although release of records is not technically a libel, a further provision of the law of libel is that a person who passes on a libelous statement, knowing it to be untrue (known as "publishing a libel"), is also guilty of libel.[12]

Although the definition of libel includes the defamation of both dead and living individuals, it does not follow that a legal action can be brought on behalf of both the quick and the dead. The *Restatement of Torts* specifically reports that "one who publishes defamatory matter concerning a deceased person is not liable either to the estate of the person or to his descendants or relatives." This means that libel, like the general doctrine on privacy mentioned above, can only be used as the basis of a lawsuit by heirs of the person libeled if the libelous material reflects upon and injures them as well.[13]

Archivists in general will not have much cause to worry about the laws of libel. Archivists could, as a part of reference service, theoretically be involved in publishing a libel, but the very definition of publication suggests that a legal action against an archives for publication would not stand up. The condition of absolute previous knowledge of the untruth of the information — the basis for a lawsuit on publication of a libel — is simply not a usual condition for archivists. The best additional protection archivists have against a charge of publishing a libel is to follow well-defined procedures

for reviewing and opening materials in their custody (see Chapter 4).

Other Access Conditions

Private institutions, including businesses, churches, colleges and universities, and voluntary and eleemosynary organizations, will generally restrict for a period of time two categories of records: those whose release might be an invasion of personal privacy and those relating to personnel, especially files relating to disciplinary actions. Beyond these common denominators practices diverge sharply. Businesses are naturally sensitive about records relating to trade secrets, company financial matters, and commercial and financial information of the type protected in the federal Freedom of Information Act by exemption (b)(4). In addition, most businesses will protect records of their legal counsel, such as those covered in FOIA exemption (b)(5), and some businesses are loath to release the records of the board of directors and the executive committee.[14]

Churches are extremely sensitive about records relating to the confidential relationship between clergy and parishioners, a special variation of the general privacy questions and perhaps also similar to the attorney-client privileges covered by federal FOIA exemption (b)(5). Some religious groups do not release records relating to doctrinal disputes within the church, while others hold these debates in the full light of the press. Some churches, like some colleges and voluntary organizations, are cautious about releasing information on contributions made by specific individuals; others publish this information routinely.

Like businesses, colleges and universities may also have records relating to research that was later patented by the university or an affiliated foundation. In these instances, the confidentiality of the information in the publicly filed patent application is gone, but related information may be protected as a trade secret. Voluntary organizations are often extremely secretive about the exact numbers of their memberships, and these records may be withheld for a period of years, and so forth. Because there is no law to guide the archivists of these private institutions, common-sense tests and procedural considerations are key.[15] Restriction statements, as discussed in the following chapter, will serve a useful function here.

[11]*Reeg* v. *Fetzer*, 78 F.R.D. 34 (D.C. OK 1976).
[12]50 *Am Jur 2d*, "Libel and Slander," sec. 3.
[13]*Restatement of Torts 2d*, sec. 560.

[14]See Anne Van Camp, "Access to Corporate Records," *American Archivist* 45 (Summer 1982): 296-298.
[15]Some of these common-sense tests are: there is no privacy right for the dead; if information is published or public in some way it can generally be made available if found in archival documents; a person requesting information about himself will receive more information than will a third party requesting information about him; the necessity for restriction wanes over time.

Public Records and Freedom of Information Acts

Federal and state governments all have freedom of information statutes that cover some portion of the records of governments. Appendix 2 is a summary table of these statutes. The federal act covers only records of the agencies in the executive branch of government, excluding legislative and judicial records and records of the presidents. State acts may or may not cover legislative, judicial, and gubernatorial records, and they may also cover the records of county and local governments.[16]

The federal Freedom of Information Act made explicit what had been implicit in the guarantees of the Bill of Rights: the right of the people to information about the business that the government conducts on their behalf.[17] But if there is continuity in the concept, there was change in its realization in the 1966 act and its amendments in 1974, 1976, and 1978. Two changes are especially important for archivists. First, the act focuses on "information." While it acknowledges that information is normally embodied in a document, it is the information that is to be made available, not the physical record. This is very different from the concept behind previous federal records legislation, which was to retain the physical document in order to retain the information for the public. Second, rather than enacting this legislation as part of the general legislation governing government records, the Congress created this as an independent act lying wholly outside the records statutes. This meant that for the first time since the creation of the National Archives, major records legislation left no specific role for the Archives to play. Each agency must administer the act independently, relying for advice on the Department of Justice. Consequently, the implementation of the act has revolved around the Department of Justice and its interpretation of the act. In practice this has created a major cleavage in authorities over records: access (Justice Department dominant), administration (agencies dominant), and disposition (National Archives dominant).

Two basic assumptions underlie both federal and state freedom of information acts. The first is that all records are open unless specifically closed by law. The second is that the freedom of information acts create the exclusive means by which the public can be denied access to records covered by the acts. In other words, records covered by a freedom of information act may be withheld from public review only if the records fall within an exemption to the disclosure provisions.

But must all records falling within an exemption category be withheld? In the important Supreme Court decision in *Chrysler* v. *Brown* the Court said no, the federal FOIA exemptions are discretionary not mandatory.[18] State freedom of information laws are divided on this issue, with some expressly stating that they are permissive, and some unclear.[19] But if the exemptions are permissive, government archivists, like all other government officials and like archivists everywhere, have to exercise judgment in restricting records.

The federal Freedom of Information Act established nine categories of executive agency records that might be withheld. While each of the fifty states and the District of Columbia has its own freedom of information act, there are many parallels between the statutes. Some twenty-five states have specifically modelled their freedom of information statutes upon the federal act. Because of these similarities, and because the federal Freedom of Information Act has been extensively litigated while the state statutes often have not been, federal precedents can be helpful when dealing with state FOIA exemptions. Indeed, attorneys bringing suits under state information laws look to federal precedents if state case support is lacking. Archivists should do likewise.[20]

The nine federal exemption categories actually reflect five principal ideas or "protectible interests." Three interests relate to confidentiality for the government: national security, law enforcement, and governmental efficiency in operation (confidentiality in decision-making, for example). The other two relate to private

---

[16]Iowa's law, for example, covers "all records and documents of or belonging to this state or any county, city, town, township, school corporation, political subdivision, or tax-supported district in this state, or any branch, department, board, bureau, commission, council, or committee of any of the foregoing." Iowa Code Ann. Sec. 68A.1. State colleges and universities must review the state law carefully to decide whether it applies to their records. For a further discussion of coverage, see Chapter 4.

[17]Previous laws governing access to government information provided no statutory remedies for the citizen if the government refused to disclose records; these statutes were principally the housekeeping statute of 1789 (5 U.S.C. §301) and the Administrative Procedures Act of 1946. See also Harold Relyea, "The Presidency and the People's Right to Know," in Relyea, ed., *The Presidency and Information Policy* (New York: Center for the Study of the Presidency, 1981), pp. 1-33.

[18]*Chrysler Corp.* v. *Brown*, 441 U.S. 281 (1979). For exceptions, see the discussions of exemptions (b)(1) and (b)(3). The best source for the government's position on the exemptions is "Short Guide to the Freedom of Information Act," written by the Office of Information and Privacy of the Department of Justice. There have been a number of editions; the most recent is incorporated in *Freedom of Information Case List: September 1984 Edition* (Washington: Government Printing Office, 1984).

[19]For the single best analysis of state FOI laws, see Burt A. Braverman and Wesley R. Heppler, "A Practical Review of State Open Records Laws," *George Washington Law Review* 49 (May 1981): 723-760. The discussion of state records laws that follows has drawn heavily upon this article.

[20]The federal FOIA is codified as 5 U.S.C. §552. The interrelationship of state and federal FOI laws suggests that an amendment of the federal law will have an impact far beyond the bounds of the federal government alone.

interests in confidentiality: individual privacy, and business and trade confidentiality. In addition, the federal statute has a "pass-through" provision, which cross-references other federal withholding statutes and says that these, too, can be used to restrict records under the Freedom of Information Act. Although the acts in some states (like Wisconsin) specify no exemptions and in other states (like Michigan) as many as twenty are allowed, a recent analysis of state freedom of information laws concluded that they generally include the five categories of protectible interests named above plus the pass-through provision found in the federal law. It is important to note that the state pass-through clauses may exclude from disclosure records whose release is prohibited by either state *or* federal law, making it vital that state archivists be familiar with federal records provisions.[21]

The federal exemptions are found in subsection (b) of the act and are often referred to by subsection and number, such as "(b)(1)," "(b)(6)," and so on. They read as follows:

(b) This section does not apply to matters that are —

(1)(A) specifically authorized under criteria established by an Executive order to be kept secret in the interest of national defense or foreign policy and (B) are in fact properly classified pursuant to such Executive order;

(2) related solely to the internal personnel rules and practices of an agency;

(3) specifically exempted from disclosure by statute (other than section 552b of this title), provided that such statute (A) requires that the matters be withheld from the public in such a manner as to leave no discretion on the issue, or (B) establishes particular criteria for withholding or refers to particular types of matters to be withheld;

(4) trade secrets and commercial or financial information obtained from a person and privileged or confidential;

(5) inter-agency or intra-agency memorandums or letters which would not be available by law to a party other than an agency in litigation with the agency;

(6) personnel and medical files and similar files the disclosure of which would constitute a clearly unwarranted invasion of personal privacy;

(7) investigatory records compiled for law enforcement purposes, but only to the extent that the production of such records would (A) interfere with enforcement proceedings, (B) deprive a person of a right to a fair trial or an impartial adjudication, (C) constitute an unwarranted invasion of personal privacy, (D) disclose the identity of a confidential source and, in the case of a record compiled by a criminal law enforcement authority in the course of a criminal investigation, or by an agency conducting a lawful national security intelligence investigation, confidential information furnished only by the confidential source, (E) disclose investigative

techniques and procedures, or (F) endanger the life or physical safety of law enforcement personnel;

(8) contained in or related to examination, operating, or condition reports prepared by, on behalf of, or for the use of an agency responsible for the regulation or supervision of financial institutions; or

(9) geological and geophysical information and data, including maps, concerning wells.

Although agencies can and frequently do cite more than one exemption for withholding a single document, such as both (b)(6) and (b)(7)(C), each exemption is evaluated on its own merits. The salient features of the current theory and application of each exemption follow.

Exemption (b)(1), National Security

The first exemption, (b)(1), covers national security and foreign policy information that has been properly classified under the standards and procedures of an executive order on classification. These executive orders date from 1940 and have been revised, rewritten, refocused, and reissued periodically since then, including three times in a recent eleven-year period: 1972, 1978, and 1982.[22] Not mere tinkering, each of these revisions has signaled a substantial shift in the direction of governmental security policy.

The relationship between the executive order and the Freedom of Information Act is close but complex. In 1973 the Supreme Court decided that if the agency classification of documents was procedurally proper, judicial review was barred.[23] The Congress reacted to this decision by incorporating into the 1974 FOIA amendments a statement that courts have the right to order the production of agency records for examination in camera (that is, in the judge's chambers, not in open court). This amendment was designed to ensure that classification would be both procedurally *and* substantively correct. Not surprisingly, a large number of FOIA lawsuits since that time have tested the review procedure. While courts often rely on affidavits submitted by an agency assuring the court of the correctness of the classification, some courts have also demanded — and obtained — production of documents.

A fundamental principle of the executive order is that the agency that classified the information, or the successor to that agency (the Department of Energy for the

---

[21]Braverman and Heppler, "A Practical Review."

[22]Executive Order 11652, 37 F.R. 5209, March 8, 1972; Executive Order 12065, 43 F.R. 28962, June 28, 1978; Executive Order 12356, 47 F.R. 14874, April 2, 1982. For a useful comparison of the 1982 order with its predecessors, see Richard C. Ehlke and Harold C. Relyea, "The Reagan Administration Order on Security Classification: A Critical Assessment," *Federal Bar News and Journal* 30 (February 1983): 91-97.

[23]*EPA* v. *Mink*, 410 U.S. 73 (1973). The most important procedure was the affixing of the marks on the documents indicating one of the three levels of classification, i.e., Confidential, Secret, or Top Secret.

records classified by the U.S. Atomic Energy Commission, for example), must declassify it. If the classified information has been accessioned into the National Archives, the archivist of the United States has the authority to declassify it under guidelines issued by the agency of origin. In addition, the archivist can declassify classified information in presidential papers and in certain other materials.[24]

The first question that must be answered in a declassification review is whether the agency will confirm or deny that the records requested are in its possession. The argument is that in some cases admitting that the requested records exist would seriously damage the protectible interests the FOIA exemptions are meant to safeguard. Denials under (b)(1) on the basis of refusing to confirm or deny have been upheld by the courts, and are often called "Glomar denials" because the Central Intelligence Agency successfully used this argument in a case where the requester wanted records relating to the ship *Glomar Explorer*.[25] Glomar denials are also used in other types of requests, especially those involving privacy interests (see page 54).

A second question is whether there has been prior disclosure of the documents. The current executive order on classification, no. 12356, prohibits the automatic declassification of information because of "unofficial publication or inadvertent or unauthorized disclosure." This is contrary to the normal archival position that if information has already been disclosed at sometime in the past, it is open. In practice, the circumstances surrounding the prior disclosure of the currently classified information have often determined whether the information is officially released subsequently. In general, if the first disclosure either was to fulfill a legitimate governmental purpose or was unauthorized, the agency can later withhold the same information. The government can circulate documents among agencies of the executive branch and, if conditions are controlled, to legislative and judicial branches as well, without its being considered prior disclosure to the public. In some cases even nongovernmental institutions have received documents that have later been withheld with court approval. Unauthorized disclosures (usually called "leaks") have been considered by the courts, and the documents leaked have been withheld. Consequently, applying the prior disclosure test requires a "careful analysis of the circumstances surrounding the prior disclosure, including its extent, recipient, justification, and authorization."[26]

A third question to be asked when releasing classified information is whether it passes the "mosaic test." This test comes from the executive order's definition that information is classifiable if "either by itself or in the context of other information" its release "reasonably could be expected to cause damage to the national security." The idea is that pieces of information that individually are harmless may, when assembled, reveal classifiable information. If a piece of information contributes to a revealing pattern, it must be withheld. Courts have acknowledged the "mosaic-like nature of intelligence gathering" and have upheld the concept in restricting information.[27]

Because an executive order has the force of law only within the executive branch of the federal government, in theory classified information that finds its way outside the executive branch or its negotiated controls (such as with a contractor) loses its protection. In certain instances members of Congress have made public classified information, but these instances of disclosure are rare.[28] The executive order generally requires that information disseminated outside the executive branch be given equal protection to that afforded within the branch. This also applies to classified information contained in personal papers donated to a private repository, where the receiving archives is responsible for protecting the classified information until it is declassified.

One of the most substantial changes embodied in the current order is a provision for reclassification of information. Although intended primarily to control information within the government, it was this authority that was used by the National Security Agency to reclassify

---

[24]The 1978 order required agencies reviewing records for possible declassification to "balance the public's interest in access to Government information with the need to protect certain national security information from disclosure." A number of court cases incorporated reviews of the balancing done by the agencies; however, the 1982 order eliminated the balancing test. In the case of *Afshar* v. *Department of State*, 702 F.2d 1125 (DC Cir. 1983), the Court of Appeals said records were properly classified even if they were classified under the old order requiring balancing *and* the agency had *not* applied the balancing test; because the case was tried under the new order, the court declared, the balancing question was "moot."

[25]*Phillippi* v. *Central Intelligence Agency*, 546 F.2d 1009 (DC Cir. 1976); *Gardels* v. *Central Intelligence Agency*, 689 F.2d 1100 (DC Cir. 1982); E.O. 12356, §3.4(f)(1); *Miller* v. *Casey*, 730 F.2d 773 (DC Cir. 1984).

[26]"The Effect of Prior Disclosure: Waiver of Exemptions," *FOIA Update* 4 (Spring 1983): 6; *Schlesinger* v. *Central Intelligence Agency*, Civil No. 82-1749 (D.DC March 5, 1984). This test is also used in other exemptions and is sometimes called the "waiver" issue, because the question is whether the government has waived its right to withhold the document by previously making it available.

[27]E.O. 12356, §1.3(b); *Halperin* v. *CIA*, 629 F.2d 144 (DC Cir. 1980); *Salisbury* v. *United States*, 690 F.2d 966 (DC Cir. 1982). For administration of the "mosaic test," see Chapter 4.

[28]Perhaps one of the most emotional of these congressional releases came on the night of June 29-30, 1971, when Senator Mike Gravel first tried to read portions of the "Pentagon Papers" on the floor of the Senate but, raising no quorum, read them out in a committee room.

certain records at the George C. Marshall Research Library.[29] It is possible that other nonfederal archives holding papers of former government officials could find themselves visited by security officers seeking to review papers in the archives.

To reclassify previously open information, the agency must state in writing both that the information requires protection in the interest of national security *and* that the information "may reasonably be recovered."[30] In an open archives, where dozens of researchers may have seen the material, the latter provision will be particularly hard for the government to sustain. If it *is* sustained, however, and the material in the nonfederal repository is classified following the agency review, then to remove the classification the archives will have to follow the declassification procedure described in the executive order.

With the pass-through provisions of state freedom of information laws, states would be required to protect any classified information that may be found in state records. If such material is found, it should be segregated from other records and stored "under conditions that will provide adequate protection and prevent access by unauthorized persons."[31] Then the state should seek advice for further handling and declassification from either the agency of origin, the Federal Information Security Oversight Office, or the declassification unit of the National Archives. Under the current order there is no automatic declassification, so positive action is needed to remove the classification.[32]

If classified material is in nonfederal custody, a researcher probably cannot request declassification of it under the federal Freedom of Information Act. The act applies to records of agencies of the executive branch of the federal government and has no force in nonfederal institutions. Instead, a researcher seeking access to classified material in nonfederal hands would have to write to the agency that classified the information and request declassification under the mandatory review provisions of the executive order on classification. The order requires an agency, upon request, to review

materials for potential declassification and release, irrespective of where they may be located.[33]

Handling classified records and applying declassification guidelines are highly technical procedures. Only an archivist working in this area on a daily basis can be reasonably certain to be applying current standards, guidelines, and tests. Anyone else who encounters such records should seek help before deciding to make the classified records available.

Exemption (b)(2), Agency Personnel Rules and Practices

Exemption (b)(2) is one of the exemptions that is designed to protect the orderly workings of government by allowing the withholding of information "related solely to the internal personnel rules and practices of an agency." (Although the word order is confusing, the current interpretation is that "personnel" modifies both "rules" and "practices." Routine administrative "practices" not related to personnel are covered also, such as law enforcement practices.) Oddly, this provision does not cover information about individual employees of the government; that is found in (b)(6). Instead it covers rules, regulations, manuals of procedure, and the like.

A recent case suggests that (b)(2) may become particularly significant in computer records. In December 1983 a district court ruled that a Department of Commerce computer program, used to calculate whether a foreign steel producer had violated antidumping laws, can be withheld under (b)(2). Since the issue was the program not the data, it suggests that an accession of software-dependent computer records would have to be examined for the releaseability of both the substantive information and the procedural format, that is, the program.[34]

Exemption (b)(3), Statutory Withholding

The (b)(3) exemption is the cross-reference or pass-through provision requiring the withholding of any information specifically exempted by a statute other than the Freedom of Information Act. It is the most burdensome of the provisions to administer, for it assumes total knowledge of relevant statutes that may be found anywhere in the law codes. A recent survey of federal statutes by a private group found agencies using 135 laws with specific restrictions (for example, the restriction of raw census information for seventy-two years).[35]

[29]See stories on the Marshall Library in the July 1983 *SAA Newsletter*, pp. 1-2. On February 15, 1984, the American Historical Association, the Organization of American Historians, the American Library Association, and others, filed a lawsuit challenging the NSA's authority to order the library to prohibit access to previously available unclassified documents. The suit does not include a challenge on classified documents. "NSA Authority to Prevent Access to Unclassified Material at Private Library Challenged in Court," *Access Reports* 10 (February 29, 1984): 7.

[30]E.O. 12356, §1.6(c).

[31]E.O. 12356, §4.1(b). The executive order is not a law and so might not technically fall under a state's pass-through provision, but states would be unwise to ignore the presence of classified material in their holdings.

[32]E.O. 12356, §1.4.

[33]E.O. 12356, §3.4.

[34]*Windels, Marx, Davies & Ives* v. *Department of Commerce*, C.A. No. 83-0820, D.DC December 9, 1983. For the reinterpretation of Exemption 2, see "The Unique Protection of Exemption 2," *FOIA Update* 5 (Winter 1984): 10.

[35]*The (b)(3) Project: Citations by Federal Agencies (1975-1982)* (Washington: American Society of Access Professionals, 1984).

States have an even greater problem. In addition to worrying about the federal laws that might apply through the state's own pass-through provision, there are state statutes that close off access to adoption records, to state income tax return information, to information submitted in compliance with environmental control laws, to identities of state welfare recipients, and a host of others.[36] There is simply no substitute for a thorough review by archivists of the statutes pertaining to the government of which they are the records custodian.

The major legal issue in exemption (b)(3) cases has been what statutes qualify. The original language of the Freedom of Information Act amendments in 1974 merely said that exemption (b)(3) protected information "specifically exempted by statute." In 1976, in an attempt to narrow the broad interpretation given this phrase by the courts, the Congress amended the exemption (b)(3) language to establish two tests for statutes. To be a (b)(3) statute under the current law, a law must either require "that the matters be withheld from the public in such a manner as to leave no discretion on the issue" or establish "particular criteria for withholding or [refer] to particular types of matters to be withheld." Courts have found few statutes that meet the first test (the census act mentioned above is one). A few statutes meet both tests, but most of the questions have involved the second. The lawsuits over (b)(3) have tended to focus on the clarity and severity of the criteria established in the law that the agency seeks to use as an exemption (b)(3) statute.

Two matters of special controversy are whether the Federal Privacy Act is a (b)(3) statute and whether the rules of federal criminal and civil procedure are statutes and are thereby covered by (b)(3). Congress recently passed a law declaring that the Privacy Act is not a (b)(3) statute. This means that a person can use both the Privacy Act, with its standards for releasing information, to gain information about himself, and also the Freedom of Information Act, with its separate standards, to gain other information. Because the Congress has said the two statutes must be used separately, an individual may be able to obtain information about himself under the Freedom of Information Act that would not be available to him under the disclosure standards of the Privacy Act.[37]

The relationship between privacy and freedom of information acts in the states is murky. Only ten states now have formally designated privacy laws, but many of them have specific laws restricting access to certain categories of privacy information (for example, adoption records). Because a state freedom of information law rarely specifies which state statutes override it (that is, the FOIA passes through to them), each state must examine its statutes to decide what the relationship is between freedom of information and privacy legislation.

Another (b)(3) issue has been whether the Federal Rules of Civil Procedure and the Federal Rules of Criminal Procedure are (b)(3) statutes. Courts have ruled both ways. Generally (b)(3) applies only to statutes, not to exccutive orders or regulations. The Federal Rules, which govern proceedings in federal courts, are not statutes: they are rules, issued by the Supreme Court, but Congress has the power to review, amend, or reject them. After some controversy, it is now settled that Rule 6(e) of the Federal Rules of Criminal Procedure, which prohibits (except in rare instances) the disclosure of "matters occurring before" a grand jury, is a (b)(3) statute. This means that grand jury information is withheld under exemption (b)(3) of the Freedom of Information Act.[38]

Similar rules of civil and criminal procedure are in force in all states for the proceedings in the state court system. In each case a determination must be made as to what extent these rules do indeed serve as a bar to disclosure and whether they are statutes in terms of the state FOIA's pass-through provision. Probably only court tests will resolve the question. Materials containing grand jury and other information barred from release under judicial procedures will be found principally in the records of departments of justice, investigatory agencies, and courts. Archivists should be extremely wary in releasing grand jury information.

Exemption (b)(4), Business Information

Exemption (b)(4) is the business information exemption, covering "trade secrets and commercial or financial information obtained from a person and privileged or confidential." Most states either have a similar provision in the freedom of information act or have separate statutes protecting such information that are covered by the FOIA pass-through provision. This is one of the most controversial areas of access, with a host of litiga-

---

[36]Braverman and Heppler, "A Practical Review."

[37]The congressional statement that the Privacy Act may not serve as an exemption (b)(3) statute under the FOIA is found in the Central Intelligence Agency Act, PL 98-477, 98 Stat. 2209, §2(c), which amends subsection (q) of the Privacy Act of 1974, 5 U.S.C. §552a(q).

[38]*Founding Church of Scientology* v. *Bell*, 603 F.2d 945 (DC Cir. 1979). Not all federal grand jury materials are restricted. Rule 6(e) itself lists three exceptions: grand jury information can be made available to (1) a government attorney in the performance of his duties, (2) upon a demonstration that grounds exist to dismiss an indictment because of irregularities in the grand jury proceedings, and (3) for a matter preliminary to a judicial proceeding. In addition a series of court decisions have established that if the documents in question do not elucidate the inner workings of the grand jury, they may be released. See *Murphy* v. *FBI*, 490 F.Supp. 1138 (D.DC 1980).

tion, a number of congressional hearings, and a sensational release to call attention to the sensitivity of the records.

The release was exactly the sort of event that figures in the nightmares of every archivist who handles materials in which there is potentially sensitive information. In response to an FOIA request, the Environmental Protection Agency inadvertently disclose the secret formula for the Monsanto Company's herbicide named "Roundup," which at the time of the disclosure was the best-selling herbicide in the world. The release created an uproar and escalated the strong urgings by industry that Congress revise the FOIA's business information exemption.[39]

Unlike the (b)(1) exemption, where the material in question must be marked, or the (b)(3) exemption, where the material to be withheld must be so clearly identified as to "leave no discretion on the issue" or must meet particular criteria, the business information exemption does not define just what constitutes a trade secret or commercial or financial information. It is ironic that the notorious EPA disclosure was of a trade secret, for that is the information usually thought to be the best defined and easiest to recognize under (b)(4). A trade secret, under the *Restatement of Torts*, is "any formula, patent, device, or compilation of information which is used in one's business, and which gives him advantage over competitors who do not know it or use it."[40]

Commercial and financial information, on the other hand, is a much vaguer concept. One way to approach the problem is to assume that all technical information from a person or a business firm is commercial or financial information. That covers an enormous spectrum of records, since business information comes to the government through regulatory, procurement, statistical, analytical, and almost any other kind of government activity. The existing court cases that attempt to define this concept have tended to resolve the disputes on a case-by-case basis rather than by establishing general guidelines. The same patchwork appears in state court decisions, with New York, for example, holding that computer programs and mathematical models used by an insurance company in pricing are exempt, Iowa excising production data about individual mines in state mine inspection reports, and so forth.[41] In the absence of a positive ruling that certain business information is not to be considered "commercial or financial," it is probably safest to assume that all of it is.

Making that assumption does not mean that the information must be withheld, of course. Because this exemption has three parts joined by "and," to withhold documents under the exemption they must meet all three tests. That means that the information must be (1) commercial and financial, (2) obtained from a person, and (3) confidential and privileged. Once the determination is made that the information is commercial or financial, the next step is to determine if it was obtained from a person. In the eyes of the law a corporation is a person — a fictive one, but a person nonetheless. Foreign governments have also been held to be persons for purposes of this exemption, but the federal government itself is not. There is some question of whether information that a federal agency obtains by testing a product submitted to it by a private business is commercial information of that business (for example, results from tests of the flammability of children's pajamas conducted by the Consumer Product Safety Commission). A very early case, even predating the (b)(4) exemption, held that agency-produced test information was not "obtained from a person."[42] Whether the ruling would be the same under the current (b)(4) language is questionable.

Most of the exemption (b)(4) litigation has centered on the words "privileged or confidential." The key federal case is *National Parks and Conservation Association* v. *Morton*, and its ruling has been drawn upon by several states as well. In it the court proposed two tests to determine whether business information is confidential. Test 1 was whether the disclosure of the information would "impair the Government's ability to obtain necessary information in the future"; test 2 was whether disclosure would "cause substantial harm to the competitive position of the person from whom the information was obtained." In other words, the exemption protects both a governmental interest (obtaining information) and a private one (maintaining competitive advantage). The court further said that neither a submitter's claims of confidentiality nor an agency's promise that the information would not be released were

[39]"EPA Lets Trade Secret Loose in Slip-up, to Firm's Dismay," *Washington Post*, September 18, 1982, p. A1; "EPA Gets Bad Press on Attitude Toward and Handling of FOIA Requests," *Access Reports* 8 (September 29, 1982): 6-7.

[40]*Restatement of Torts*, §757, comment b (1939). In the case of *Public Citizen Health Research Group* v. *FDA*, 704 F.2d 1280 (DC Cir. 1983), the appeals court narrowed the trade secret definition by requiring a trade secret to have a "direct relationship" to the productive process. Because this varies from all other court decisions, it remains to be seen whether the narrower definition will prevail.

[41]*Belth* v. *Insurance Department*, 95 Misc. 2d 18-20, 406 N.Y. S.2d 649, 650 (Sup. Ct. 1977); *Iowa Op. Atty. Gen.* 7481 (1973). There is some question as to whether information from a nonprofit entity can be considered "commercial or financial information" under (b)(4). See *Washington Research Project, Inc.* v. *HEW*, 504 F.2d 238 (DC Cir. 1974) (cannot); but see also *American Airlines, Inc.* v. *National Mediation Board*, 588 F.2d 863 (2d Cir. 1978) (*Washington Research* held to be too narrow).

[42]*Comstock International* v. *Export-Import Bank*, 464 F. Supp. 804 (D.DC 1979); *Stone* v. *Export-Import Bank*, 552 F.2d 132 (5th Cir. 1977); *Consumers Union* v. *Veterans' Administration*, 301 F. Supp. 796 (S.D.NY 1969).

controlling; these two facts were simply factors to be considered in making a determination but were not themselves determinative.[43]

To withhold information under the first *National Parks* test, the information must have been provided in support of a function of the agency, have been provided voluntarily, and would not have been provided by the submitter if the information was known to be subject to release. On the other hand, if the business has been required to provide the information by statute, regulation, some other mandate, or as a condition for a benefit, it tends to undermine the argument that disclosure would impair the government's ability to obtain such information in the future.

To apply the second *National Parks* test, the government must be able to identify the specific types of competitive harm which would be risked by release and be able to explain why release of the information in question is likely to have those results. Based on various court decisions, several categories of information are likely to be protectible, including technical designs or data of value to the company or to its competitors; internal cost information for current or recent periods; information on financial conditions, the release of which might injure the company; resumes of key company personnel and data on how the personnel are utilized; and information on customers, sources of supply, or business plans that are valuable to the company and not known to competitors. Some courts have applied the "mosaic test" (as discussed relative to (b)(1) above) to business information, but they have generally held that if the information is publicly available from other sources (the prior disclosure test) the government cannot claim "competitive harm" would result from release.[44]

In addition to these two tests, a recent court case has held that the government can use exemption (b)(4) if the release of the information would harm an "identifiable private or governmental interest." This broadens the application of (b)(4) beyond the usual two interests outlined in *National Parks*.[45]

Of all the exemptions, (b)(4) concerns information which ages the most rapidly. The passage of time tends to erode the applicability of the exemption, and this relieves archivists of much of the burden of handling commercial and financial information exclusions. For example, a document containing the future plans of a business firm (such as the introduction of a new product or the acquisition of a new company) may lose its confidential character after the plans become known or have become obsolete. A statement of the holdings of a company in a foreign country that has subsequently nationalized the industry (for example, tobacco company investment in Cuba) may be releaseable. A bid on a government contract that includes technical specifications if subsequent product development has made the product noncompetitive (early computer bids, for example) are probably releaseable, as are other types of bids if the passage of time has been such that a competitor cannot easily extrapolate from the data to determine a current status (the intervention of a major political or social change, a war, or similar watershed event is usually a good clue.)[46] The type of information that does not easily lose a confidential character is information relating to natural resources such as land, coal, timber, oil, gas, and the like.

Exemption (b)(4) is also notable because it has been the focus of "reverse" FOIA cases. These are cases in which a person or corporation that has submitted information to the government seeks to block the government's release of the information under the Freedom of Information Act. The first Supreme Court review of the "reverse" FOIA issue came in the case of *Chrysler Corp. v. Brown*. There the Court decided that the Freedom of Information Act itself did not create a right for a person to sue to prevent release but the Federal Administrative Procedures Act did.[47]

Subsequently numerous "reverse" cases have been decided. More importantly, Congress has repeatedly considered and sometimes passed legislation either to prohibit the release of particular types of business information without the consent of the submitter or to create a government-wide waiting period before business information could be released in order to allow submitters to take legal actions to prevent release. Another proposed solution to the problem of releasing business information is to allow a business to request confidentiality at the time the information is submitted and thereafter to require the government to abide by the company's wishes.

The problem with most of these laws, proposals, and policies is that they have not taken into account the

---

[43]*National Parks and Conservation Ass'n v. Morton*, 498 F.2d 765 (DC Cir. 1974).

[44]*Timkin Co. v. United States Customs Service*, 491 F. Supp. 557 (D.DC 1980), Aff'd, No. 80-1794 (DC Cir. 1980); *Continental Stock Transfer & Trust Co. v. SEC*, 566 F.2d 373 (2d Cir. 1977).

[45]*9 to 5 Organization for Women Office Workers v. Board of Governors for the Federal Reserve System*, 721 F.2d 1 (1st Cir. 1983).

[46]In *Racal-Milgo Government Systems, Inc. v. Small Business Administration*, Civil Action No. 81-1840 (D.DC December 28, 1981), federal government contracts were ruled to be public. However, in *Sperry Univac Division v. Baldrige*, Civil No. 82-0045-A (E.D. VA June 16, 1982), contract information was ruled to meet the competitive harm test. This emphasizes the case-by-case nature of the (b)(4) decisions. Some 35 states with FOI laws also state in law that contracts are public. Even in these cases, bids for contracts may not be.

[47]*Chrysler v. Brown.*

rapidity with which business information goes out of date; in general, there has been no termination date on notification requirements. Some of these laws and regulations require notification of the business before any release of information about it, even if the records have been open for decades: it is conceivable that nineteenth-century information could fall under these provisions. The administrative burden of such procedures in an archives would be enormous.[48]

Although most states protect business information from disclosure in some way, there has not been much "reverse" litigation in the states. Notably, however, New York in 1981 amended its freedom of information law to require notification to submitters before release of information on which the submitter has requested protection.[49] Federal practices in this area, as in so many of the FOIA issues, will have a significant influence on state policies.

Exemption (b)(5), Governmental Deliberative Privileges

Exemption (b)(5) is the major exemption designed to protect governmental deliberative privileges. Although a broad reading of its language ("inter-agency or intra-agency memorandums or letters which would not be available by law to a party other than an agency in litigation with the agency") would suggest that almost any records could be closed under this exemption, in practice it has been used more narrowly. One major use has been to protect information that is specified in the rules of civil or criminal procedure as not discoverable in the course of litigation. This includes information releating to attorney-client privilege (that is, the working relationship between an agency and its lawyers) and attorney work-product (that is, the documents a lawyer prepares during or in reasonable anticipation of litigation). A second major use has been to defend "deliberative process privilege," which in a major 1979 case the Supreme Court held existed "to insure that a decision maker will receive the unimpeded advice of his associates." An emerging third use is to protect government research, development, or commercial information if the release of such information would put the government at a competitive disadvantage (such as release of information during the process of awarding a contract).[50]

A series of cases has examined specific documents claimed as exempt under (b)(5), and a number of general principles have evolved. First, time of preparation of the document is critical: it must be a predecisional document to be protected by (b)(5). If, however, the predecisional document is either adopted as a final decision or is incorporated into a final decision, it loses its protection unless protected by one of the other exemptions. Second, matters of fact are excluded; the exemption is to protect advice, comments, suggestions, and so forth. Finally, (b)(5) also does not protect documents that report, explain, or justify a final decision.[51]

Because (b)(5), like (b)(1), falls within the category of a protectible interest relating to confidentiality for the government itself, the question of prior disclosure is again an issue. Generally the courts have followed the same guidelines for (b)(5) as in (b)(1) (see discussion above).

Perhaps the best thing to say about exemption (b)(5) from an archivist's point of view is that it probably will not often be used for accessioned records. The very nature of the exemption suggests that it is most important to agencies still actively using the records, and by the time the documents are transferred to the archives much of the necessity for protecting the decisional process is past.[52] It is true, however, that one case involving holdings of the National Archives and the (b)(5) exemption was extremely difficult to resolve, although the agency with an interest in the document finally agreed to the release.[53] The Archives has also used the exemption to withhold administrative records of the National Archives itself.

Both Texas and the District of Columbia have adopted the same language as the federal statute, and a dozen other states have language that is close to that of (b)(5). State cases are few and tend to mirror the federal ones. Again, federal case law is influential.

---

[48]To pick only three examples, the Export Trading Company Act of 1982 (PL 97-290, 15 U.S.C. §§4016, 4019) prohibits the disclosure of commercial or financial information submitted to the Commerce Department by individuals or companies seeking immunity from criminal prosecution under antitrust laws; in 1983 the Postal Rate Commission established procedures for providing submitters of confidential business data an opportunity to object to disclosure under FOIA, both by asserting confidentiality when the data is delivered and getting a second chance before it is released; a 1982 law (15 U.S.C. §2055; 16 CFR 1101) requires the Consumer Product Safety Commission to ensure the accuracy of complaints about consumer products before the information is released.

[49]2 *McKinney's 1981 Session Laws of N.Y.*, ch. 890.

[50]*Federal Open Market Committee* v. *Merrill*, 443 U.S. 340 (1979).

[51]*Coastal States Gas Corp.* v. *Department of Energy*, 617 F.2d 851 (DC Cir. 1980); *NLRB* v. *Sears, Roebuck & Co.*, 421 U.S. 132 (1975). Drafts are a category likely to be exempt under the deliberative process provision; for full discussion see "Short Guide."

[52]The Supreme Court has ruled that the termination of the litigation does not likewise terminate the protection of attorney work-product information. *FTC* v. *Grolier, Inc.*, 103 S. Ct. 2209 (1983). Remember, however, that this is a permissive, not mandatory, exemption.

[53]In this case, a requester had asked for a memorandum written by the deputy solicitor general to the solicitor general. The letter agreeing to the release of the memorandum contains a legal analysis of the applicability of (b)(5). Frank H. Easterbrook to Milton O. Gustafson, October 17, 1978, copy in possession of the authors.

Exemption (b)(6), Personal Privacy

Privacy is the subject of (b)(6), exempting "personnel and medical files and similar files the disclosure of which would constitute a clearly unwarranted invasion of personal privacy." The first question is who is a person for purposes of this exemption. The courts have been quite clear on this, saying that this exemption is to protect individual human beings, not corporations or associations. The one exception to this is information about a small business, which can be considered a question of privacy "when the individual and corporation are identical."[54]

A second question is whether the exemption covers dead individuals. Again, the evolving case law is that there is no privacy right for the dead. It is possible, however, that the disclosure of information about a dead person would violate the privacy rights of surviving heirs or other close associates; in those cases the withholding would be based on the privacy rights of the living individuals even though the information was about a deceased person. An example might make this clearer. Suppose, for instance, the dead person once received medical care at a military hospital because he was a veteran. The hospital records reveal that he had a serious, inheritable disease that the children of the deceased have a good chance of contracting. Releasing the information about the deceased may tend to invade the privacy of the living children and the withholding of the information could be justified on (b)(6) grounds. For (b)(6) purposes, it is safest to assume that persons named in the documents are alive unless there is proof of death or the passage of time is such that it is reasonable to assume death.[55]

Having decided who is a person for exemption (b)(6) purposes, "personnel and medical files and similar files" must be defined next. There are no major problems in deciding what are personnel and medical files, but the "similar files" phrase has raised questions. In the first place, do these have to be entire files on an individual, or does the exemption also cover information about an individual that is scattered in several files? In the second, what is a "similar" file? Both the Justice Department and the courts have interpreted this phrase broadly. In the words of the attorney general's "Blue

Book" interpreting the 1974 FOIA amendments, personal information is the issue, not files. The Justice Department includes in that phrase any "information about an individual which he could reasonably assert an option to withhold from the public at large because of its intimacy or its possible adverse effects upon himself or his family."[56]

In 1982 the Supreme Court affirmed this position. A lower court, in the case of *Department of State* v. *Washington Post Co.*, had ruled that "similar files" meant only files containing the type of data found in personnel or medical files, information of a "highly personal or intimate" nature. The Supreme Court disagreed. It declared that "similar files" was to have a broad scope and that the government may withhold information that "applies to a particular individual" to protect that person from "the injury and embarrassment that can result from the unnecessary disclosure of personal information." This ruling appears to settle the question.[57]

Several other points are also quite well settled for exemption (b)(6). For one, protecting the identity of the individual includes not just withholding his name but also any other information that might serve to identify him. For example, if the archivist is releasing a file on a person who is probably still alive and in the records he is referred to as "the secretary of the union local at J. F. Cook Railways Corporation," to protect the person's identity both his name and descriptor would have to be deleted. The exemption protects information identifying a person, not just the name or Social Security number of the individual.

A second area where there is common-sense agreement is that a person requesting information about himself will receive more information than a third party would; in fact, there is some doubt that exemption (b)(6) can be used to deny an individual any information about himself at all.[58]

A third matter usually agreed upon is that public information that names an individual (a newspaper article, a press release, a book) does not need protecting. This is a logical approach that has been questioned on occasion, such as whether the privacy of a person who was involved in a publicized case of embezzlement is invaded if documents reporting the same facts are released thirty years later (in general the answer is no). But the basic idea is that once information is in the public do-

---

[54]*Sims* v. *CIA*, 642 F.2d 562, 572n.47 (DC Cir. 1980); *National Parks* v. *Morton*; *Providence Journal Co.* v. *FBI*, 460 F. Supp. 778 (D.RI 1978), rev'd other grounds 602 F.2d 1010 (1st Cir. 1979).

[55]*Williams* v. *Department of Justice*, 556 F. Supp. 63 (D.DC 1982) (agency's good-faith processing sufficient); but see *Diamond* v. *FBI*, 532 F. Supp. 216 (S.D.NY 1981) (research required on whether subject of the files was deceased); *Lesar* v. *Department of Justice*, 636 F.2d 472 (DC Cir. 1980).

[56]*Attorney General's Memorandum on the 1974 Amendments to the Freedom of Information Act* (Washington: Government Printing Office, 1975), pp. 9-10.

[57]"Short Guide;" *Department of State* v. *Washington Post Co.*, 456 U.S. 595 (1982).

[58]*Nix* v. *United States*, 572 F.2d 998 (4th Cir. 1978).

main, it is not possible to return it to a privacy sphere.[59]

These, however, are nearly all the easy answers on personal privacy. The problems surrounding exemption (b)(6) are many. They involve the "Glomar test," the balancing of competing interests, the rights of public figures, and the perennial problem of lists of names, particularly mailing lists.

The Glomar test, again, is the decision as to whether or not the agency will confirm or deny the existence of information. If the archives decides that either confirming or denying would itself invade the privacy of the person who is the subject of the inquiry (for example, "Do you have a case file on John Q. in the records of the state mental hospital?") the Glomar test may be invoked. Although this test may occasionally be used by an archives, it is much more commonly used by agencies when current records are requested. In general, historical interest overrides the "confirm or deny" issue in archival records.[60]

Having confirmed the existence of the records, the next decision is which portions of the file can be released. This stage is known as the "balancing test" or the "balancing of competing interests." Many court decisions have recognized the need to balance the public interest in disclosure with the public interest in nondisclosure, that is, balancing the invasion of privacy (the foreseeable harm) against the benefit that will accrue to the general public from the release of the information. This means that archivists must judge the seriousness of the invasion of personal privacy that will result from the release, such as the likelihood of injury, damage, harassment, or embarrassment.

To balance privacy against public interest, both concepts must be understood. The language of the Freedom of Information Act assumes that privacy is a generally recognized term and provides no specific definition. From a series of court decisions, however, it appears that the working definition is roughly the individual's ability to control dissemination of personal, intimate details of his life and the lives of members of his family.

The types of information regularly protected are marital status, birth legitimacy, medical condition, welfare status, family rights and reputation, and religious affiliation. The balancing test described above serves as a brake on absolute privacy (as, of course, does the mere fact that information about the individual is in the hands of the government.)

The public interest in disclosure is perhaps even harder to define. Courts have held that to be considered a "public interest" the release must benefit the general public or substantial numbers of the public, not just benefit an individual or a commercial interest. For example, researchers have sometimes found courts holding that the release of information for research is in the public interest, and nonprofit organizations serving groups whose needs will be benefited by release of the information have also prevailed. Courts have, however, also found that a number of claimed "public interests" do not overweigh privacy claims. Courts have ruled that "general public curiosity" is insufficient, as are general claims of public service, such as a vague statement about serving as a public watchdog.[61]

If the requester is found to be speaking for a public interest, the next step is to determine what is the public interest in disclosure. Courts have found several areas in which public interest can be assumed to be high. One, and the most widely acknowledged, is if the requested information would inform the public about proven violations of the public trust (that is, government wrongdoing). Second, in a line of cases unique to the D.C. Circuit, the professional and business conduct of an individual's business dealings with the federal government, such as the names of suspected violators of the EPA "Superfund" law, are considered to be of public interest. A third is a vague set of issues in which the public is believed to have special interests and rights, such as the operations of courts and the conduct of union elections.[62] Finally, the public is assumed to have a right to basic information about public employees, both military and civilian, such as their names, present and past position titles, grades, salaries, and duty stations.[63]

---

[59]Note the contrast between this argument and the positions on "waiver" in exemptions (b)(1) and (b)(3). In the case of (b)(1) and (b)(3), both examples of a protectible interest in confidentiality for the government, information that reaches the public domain through leaks or through necessary agency selective disclosure can later be withheld under FOIA. In the protectible interest relating to private interests in confidentiality (business and personal), a prior disclosure is considered to destroy irretrievably the private nature of the information.

[60]It is essential that the Glomar test be applied consistently. In the example of the mental hospital's files, if the Glomar denial is used when there is a file but a simple "we have no file" is issued when there isn't, the Glomar is tantamount to admission that a file exists. An archives must make a decision on whether to use the "refuse to confirm or deny" for a series of records and then do so irrespective of whether the files do or do not exist.

[61]*Getman* v. *NLRB*, 450 F.2d 670 (DC Cir. 1971); *Disabled Officers Ass'n* v. *Rumsfeld*, 428 F. Supp. 454 (D.DC 1977); *Fund for Constitutional Government* v. *National Archives and Records Service*, 656 F.2d 856 (DC Cir. 1981); *Aviation Data Service* v. *FAA*, 687 F.2d 1319 (10th Cir. 1982); *Harbolt* v. *Department of State*, 616 F.2d 772 (5th Cir. 1980); *Miller* v. *Bell*, 661 F.2d 623 (7th Cir. 1981).

[62]*Columbia Packing Co., Inc.*, v. *Department of Agriculture*, 563 F.2d 495 (1st Cir. 1977); *Tax Reform Research Group* v. *IRS*, 419 F.Supp. 415 (D.DC 1976); *Cohen* v. *EPA*, 3 GDS 83,223 (D.DC 1983); *Ferri* v. *Bell*, 645 F.2d 1213 (3d Cir. 1981); *Getman* v. *NLRB*.

[63]Courts generally protect personal details of an individual's federal service, such as home addresses, performance studies and award recommendations, complaints made against supervisors, medical and related details in employee claims, marital status, college grades, etc. For discussion, see "Short Guide."

Balancing the competing interests has been particularly difficult in two areas: information about public figures and lists of names. The privacy rights of individuals are eroded to the extent that they are "public figures." A number of lawsuits, including two against the National Archives for disclosure of information from the records of the Watergate Special Prosecution Force, have established some rather conflicting case law on the rights of public figures. It appears settled that public figures have a narrower orbit within which they can assert privacy rights than the average citizen. If the public figure is a governmental official, information about him that reflects his part in the operations of government generally cannot be protected by the privacy exemption, although it might be protected by another exemption category. But it is equally true that public figures do not forfeit all rights to privacy. One court, in fact, suggested that the "degree of intrusion is indeed potentially augmented by the fact that the individual is a well known figure."[64] Perhaps the most common-sense approach is to realize that if dealing with records relating to a public figure, much of the information may have already been disclosed, either by the person or by press reports about the individual. If the archivist can ascertain the degree of public knowledge about the person about whom information is requested, that will simplify the task by reducing the number of items of information on which a decision must be made. Those items of information that are not known to the public must be afforded the balancing test.

When asked about the "hard areas" in applying a privacy test to agency records, the Defense Department's FOIA coordinator named several problems and then concluded, "And lists, don't forget the lists."[65] Government records are replete with lists of names. These can range from lists of people who received methadone to lists of borrowers of books from public libraries. The issue of making lists of names and addresses available, particularly if they are to be used for commercial mailing lists, has been so controversial that some proposed revisions of the federal Freedom of Information Act have included express language protecting lists that could be used for solicitation purposes. Absent such a provision, however, FOIA administrators and the courts have come to a number of barely compatible positions on the disclosure of lists.

An early FOIA case held that an address list could be withheld if the information was sought solely for commercial purposes. Several other cases have concluded that in the absence of commercial exploitation and in the presence of a demonstrated public interest in disclosure, the balancing test may be applied and an agency may choose to disclose the list. At present, this use of the balancing test is a key exception to the general proposition that the purpose for which a requester seeks the information under the Freedom of Information Act is irrelevant to the determination to release or withhold.[66]

State laws have similar difficulties with privacy provisions, and state courts have generally required a balancing test. A few state laws also provide specific guidance on information that is nondisclosable, such as adoption records. Because many of the state laws closely parallel the federal statute, federal case law is again pertinent. On the issue of lists, particularly for circulation records in libraries, states have been very active. Maryland, Virginia, Iowa, and California, for example, have a statutory exemption for circulation records, while New York, Nevada, and Texas have opinions by the state attorneys general that circulation records may not be released.[67] Archivists in those states may find that the language of the statutes is such that is also covers the user records maintained by the archives.

As is apparent from this brief discussion, there are no absolutes in the categories of information that must be considered private. Context is all-important; a person's name in the public telephone directory is one thing, the same name in a list of drug-treatment patients is quite another. Prior disclosure can make the most intimate information — birth legitimacy, for example — public information.

Perhaps the single most important quality of information relating to an individual is that the claim of privacy is very slowly eroded by time. Unlike business information, which often ages quickly, information about an individual has a privacy aura throughout his or her lifetime. Similarly, the damage that can be done by the release of such information cannot normally be compensated in dollars. Monsanto can develop a new herbicide, but it is not possible to build a new reputation so easily. Archivists must always be cautious when handling personal information about living individuals.

Exemption (b)(7), Investigatory Information

The federal Freedom of Information Act and a majority of state FOIAs have an exemption for "investigatory records" that are compiled for "law enforcement purposes." The federal statute then goes on

---

[64]*Fund for Constitutional Government* v. *NARS*.

[65]"Privacy Protection Practices Examined," *FOIA Update* 3 (September 1982): 1.

[66]*Wine Hobby USA, Inc.* v. *IRS*, 502 F.2d 133 (3d Cir. 1974); *Getman* v. *NLRB*; *Disabled Officers* v. *Rumsfeld*; *Minnis* v. *USDA*, Nos. 83-4089, 83-4209 (9th Cir. May 22, 1984).

[67]"Basic Confidentiality/Access to Information Conflict Continues to Plague the Nation's Libraries," *Access Reports* (November 3, 1980): 7.

to list six types of harm that may be caused by release, denominated A through F, and records that would cause any one of these types of harm may be withheld under (b)(7).

Before turning to the six tests, records must be defined as investigatory in nature and compiled for "law enforcement purposes." "Investigatory records" are records "which reflect or result from specifically focused inquiries by an agency." These do not include records relating to routine administration or oversight of federal programs. The "law" covered by this exemption includes federal civil and criminal statutes, statutes authorizing regulatory proceedings, and state and foreign laws as well. "Law enforcement purposes," a series of federal courts have concluded, can include either civil or criminal investigations, and civil investigations can encompass administrative, regulatory, personnel background security, and similar investigations. On the other hand, general agency audits and reviews of itself are held not to be within the meaning of this exemption.[68]

The first harm test, (A), is if the release of the records would "interfere with enforcement proceedings." This is very significant to the investigative agencies — and, consequently, has been extensively litigated — because it can be used to protect pretrial and on-going investigations, identities of cooperative prosecution witnesses, and strategy information, such as plans in prison crisis situations. It can also be used in certain circumstances to protect records of closed or dormant investigations if information in those files may be used in related future enforcement cases. Although it is technically possible that such records could be found in an archives (long-term plans for protecting the chief executive are a possibility, for example) it is unlikely that there will be many and this exemption is used rarely in an archives.[69]

Similarly, the second harm cited, (B), covers records that will also be found infrequently in archival holdings. These are records that if released would "deprive a person of a right to a fair trial or an impartial adjudication." The Department of Justice believes this exemption is directed toward protecting prejudicial publicity, which makes its use in an archives even more remote. No significant cases have tested the application of (b)(7)(B).

Exemption (b)(7)(C) allows the withholding of records the disclosure of which could "constitute an unwarranted invasion of personal privacy." This again is a privacy test, and many of the decisions on exemption (b)(6) can serve as precedents here. In particular, the Glomar and balancing tests are applicable, as are the general principles that historical interest in the material may outweigh privacy interests in some cases (a particular kind of balance) and that public information about the investigation or the notoriety of the individual involved tend to weaken the exemption claim. Finally, too, here as in (b)(6), time erodes the privacy claim very slowly.

The distinction between the language of (b)(6) "clearly unwarranted invasion of personal privacy" and (b)(7)(C) "unwarranted invasion of personal privacy" has received a lot of attention. Briefly, the difference is assumed to be deliberate on the part of the Congress and to reflect the general opprobrium that surrounds the finding of a person's name in an investigative file. This stigma in itself is held to be such that the burden of proof needed to justify withholding is lower — hence the omission of the word "clearly." The scales, in other words, are weighted more heavily toward the privacy interest in (b)(7)(C) than in (b)(6).[70]

The privacy test in investigative case files has been used to withhold the identities of several different categories of persons. One use is to protect the identities of persons who are not the subjects of the investigation nor are confidential sources but are merely mentioned in the case file. This is an example of the theory that the mere presence of an individual's name in a law enforcement case file carries a stigma. The courts have generally upheld such withholding, although in the case of *Lamont* v. *Department of Justice* the court ordered disclosure of the identities both (1) of acquaintances of the subject of the investigation who were mentioned neither as FBI sources nor in a derogatory context and (2) of persons who participated prominently in events that are part of the public records.[71]

A second major use of (b)(7)(C), often linked to the use of (b)(7)(D), is to protect the identities of persons who give information to law enforcement agencies in civil investigations not related to national security (criminal investigations and national security civil investigations are covered by the (b)(7)(D) exemption). In these cases, if the individual named in the record is providing information that relates strictly to a formal relationship with the subject of the investigation (for example, landlord, employer, college registrar), the information can generally be made available, but if the individual goes on to express opinions, or if the relationship between the individuals is informal, such informa-

---

[68]*Williams* v. *IRS*, 479 F.2d 317 (3d Cir. 1973); *Rural Housing Alliance* v. *Department of Agriculture*, 498 F.2d 73 (DC Cir. 1974); "Short Guide."

[69]"Short Guide"; "The 'Generic' Aspect of Exemption 7(A)" and "Can Exemption 7(A) be used to protect the records of closed or dormant investigations?" *FOIA Update* 5 (Spring 1984): 3-4, 6.

[70]*Deering Millikin* v. *Irving*, 548 F.2d 1131 (4th Cir. 1977); *Miller* v. *Bell*; *Department of Air Force* v. *Rose*, 425 U.S. 352 (S.D.NY 1976).

[71]*Miller* v. *Bell*; *Lesar* v. *Department of Justice*; *Lamont* v. *Department of Justice*, 475 F.Supp. 761 (S.D.NY 1979).

tion and identities are normally deleted. Notice here that two types of privacy are being protected: (1) if the individual making the statement is known but may be making unsubstantiated allegations about the subject of the investigation, the allegations are deleted to protect the privacy of the individual who is the *subject of the file*; (2) if the information is known or not derogatory to the subject individual but the source of the information is not known to the subject individual, the name of and any other information tending to identify the *source* is deleted.[72]

A third use of the (b)(7)(C) exemption is to protect the identities of persons investigated but not prosecuted; here very careful balancing is required.[73] Finally, provision (b)(7)(C) is also used to protect the identities of law enforcement and other governmental personnel involved in investigations.[74]

Provision (D) of exemption (b)(7) protects the identity of a confidential source and, in certain cases, all confidential information furnished only by the confidential source. The first clause allows the withholding of all information that would "disclose the identity of a confidential source." At least two courts have held that balancing is not required.[75] In other words, the courts suggest that if the information would disclose the person's identity, public interest in the disclosure does not override withholding.

The trend in cases that turn on the (b)(7)(D) exemption is to adopt what is called a "functional approach," in which confidentiality is assumed to exist if the agency's "investigatory function depends for its existence upon information supplied by individuals who in many cases would suffer severe detriment if their identities were known." This suggests that the test of confidentiality is not whether there was an express promise of confidentiality either given to the individual or specifically recorded in the document in question but instead whether the agency depends on and the source could have reasonably inferred an assurance of confidentiality.[76] In practice, this means that names and all other data that would tend to disclose the identity of a

source are deleted. This provision does not apply to other federal agencies as sources, although it may apply to individual federal employees.

There has been controversy over whether (b)(7)(D) applies to official agencies of state, local, and foreign governments and to institutions and organizations. The emerging position is that it does in order to avoid revealing an on-going confidential relationship that must be protected if federal law enforcement agencies are to continue to obtain information from these sources. Here the claim of confidentiality erodes particularly slowly because it is based on protecting an enduring relationship.[77]

The second clause in exemption (b)(7)(D) focuses on information, not identity. It carefully describes the records it protects as "compiled by a criminal law enforcement authority in the course of a criminal investigation, or by an agency conducting a lawful national security intelligence investigation" and containing "confidential information furnished only by the confidential source." The provision is used to protect information itself and may be used to withhold information that is sensitive to the supplier but not to the recipient (that is, to the government) on the ground that its disclosure would damage further cooperation.

Very little significant litigation focused on this clause until the 1980s. Then, with a number of important cases, courts interpreted the language of (b)(7)(D) very broadly. The current interpretation is that even if the information does not identify the source it can be protected, and it may even be used to protect information provided by a source whose identity is known. It has been held to protect information provided by deceased sources (in at least one case it was used to protect information that had been provided by a deceased individual who had testified in open court) and to protect the identities of local law enforcement agencies even when their participation is known. This elastic interpretation suggests that in the future (b)(7)(D) will form the backbone of the government's cases involving criminal law authorities and national security intelligence investigators.[78]

In its guide to the Freedom of Information Act, the Justice Department bluntly warns that "the protections afforded by Exemption 7(D) are not lost through the mere passage of time." The two cases that have led the department to that position involved, in one case, docu-

---

[72]*Lesar* v. *Department of Justice; Maroscia* v. *Levi*, 569 F.2d 1000 (7th Cir. 1977); *Shaver* v. *Bell*, 433 F. Supp. 438 (N.D. GA 1977).

[73]*Kuhnert* v. *Webster*, 620 F.2d 662 (8th Cir. 1980) *Common Cause* v. *National Archives and Records Service*, 628 F.2d 179 (DC Cir. 1980). In the *Fund for Constitutional Government* case, the court said the identities of those investigated but not charged must be withheld unless "exceptional circumstances militate in favor of disclosure."

[74]*Lesar* v. *Department of Justice; Maroscia* v. *Levi; Baez* v. *Department of Justice*, 647 F.2d 1328 (DC Cir. 1980); *Kelly* v. *FBI*, 2 GDS 82,059 (D.DC 1981).

[75]*Lane* v. *Department of Justice*, 654 F.2d 917 (3d Cir. 1981); *Sands* v. *Murphy*, 633 F.2d 968 (1st Cir. 1980).

[76]*Lamont* v. *Department of Justice; Radowich* v. *United States Attorney*, 658 F.2d 957 (4th Cir. 1981); *Pope* v. *United States*, 599 F.2d 1383 (5th Cir. 1979).

[77]*Baez* v. *Department of Justice; Kelly* v. *FBI*.

[78]*Radowich* v. *U.S. Attorney; Duffin* v. *Carlson*, 636 F.2d 709 (DC Cir. 1980); *Cohen* v. *Smith*, No. 81-5365, mem. op. at 3 (9th Cir. March 25, 1983) (unpublished memorandum); *Kiraly* v. *FBI*, 3 GDS 82,466 at 83,138 (N.D. OH 1982); *Stassi* v. *Department of Justice*, Civil No. 78-0536, slip op. at 9-10 (D.DC April 12, 1979); *Lesar* v. *Department of Justice*.

ments from the Joseph McCarthy era and, in the other, documents that were twenty-seven years old.[79] In archival terms, these time spans are the blink of an archivist's eye. Still, because of the longstanding relationships apparently protected by the clause, it is quite conceivable that (b)(7)(D) information can be found in archival holdings. Archivists should proceed warily in making judgments to release documents that contain information that appears to fall within the (b)(7)(D) provision.

Test (E) in (b)(7) protects information that would "disclose investigative techniques and procedures." The sensitive investigatory techniques included in this definition are those not generally known outside the government and do not include such routine procedures as fingerprinting, standard ballistics tests, and so forth. In some cases, it can be used to protect the very fact that a particular technique was used in a particular instance. In a number of rulings, however, the courts have ordered the agency to describe the general nature of the technique while withholding the details.[80] Fortunately for archivists, by the time files arrive at an archives these techniques will probably be sufficiently out of date that this consideration can be waived.

The final test in (b)(7) is whether the release of the records would "(F) endanger the life or physical safety of law enforcement personnel." The most obvious cases here are those where undercover agents are identified, but other persons can be considered for protection under the exemption, including foreign, state, and local police, prosecutors, judges, parole and probation officers, and prison guards, among others. The Justice Department believes that, as in (b)(7)(D), no balancing test is required here. Again, the passage of time may lessen the burden of applying this restriction, but with the seriousness of the potential consequences, archivists cannot be secure about releasing this information until natural, and not unnatural, mortality has taken its toll.[81]

Most states have an exemption for law enforcement records, and the language of these exemptions may be broader than that of the federal statute. State law enforcement exemptions have often been litigated, and state case law may be available to guide the state or local archivist. The state attorney general's office could certainly provide up-to-the-minute information on the application of these provisions.

Exemptions (b)(8) and (b)(9), Financial Institutions and Geological Information

The last two federal FOIA exemptions are little known and little used and neither has been reviewed by the Supreme Court. The first of these, (b)(8), protects information "contained in or related to examination, operating, or condition reports prepared by, on behalf of, or for the use of an agency responsible for the regulation or supervision of financial institutions." The few courts that have interpreted this have viewed it as a broad exemption affording virtually absolute protection for data that falls within it. One circuit court of appeals concluded that (b)(8) had two purposes, to "protect the security of financial institutions by withholding from the public reports that contain frank evaluations of a bank's liability" and "to promote cooperation and communication between employees and examiners." Another court found that the exemption also was designed to safeguard the relationship between the banks and their supervising agencies. Within these sweeping interpretations, a broad band of records can be withheld. One court even ruled that records could be withheld in toto without sanitization (see Chapter 4), and another ruled that records relating to defunct banks could be withheld. Although the significance of this provision may become more apparent as the records relating to bank failures accumulate, the case law is hardly sufficient at present to point the way for application in the daily work of an archives, except to suggest that the courts find the protection afforded by (b)(8) to be very broad.[82]

Exemption (b)(9) protects "geological and geophysical information and data, including maps, concerning wells." The provision has never been tested in court. Two cases relating to (b)(9) exist, but both were "reverse" FOIA cases contesting the propriety of discretionary disclosure not the applicability of the exemption itself.[83]

Other Considerations

Although only nine exemptions are found in the federal statute, state freedom of information acts contain many other specialized exemptions. Perhaps the most common of the provisions found in state laws but not in the federal act are those covering tax return data (it is a (b)(3) pass-through statute in the federal FOIA) and land value information. A number of states also prohibit disclosure of licensing, employment, or academic examinations, and a few protect information on government procurement and bidding processes. The

[79]*Diamond* v. *FBI*, 707 F.2d 75 (2d Cir. 1983); *Abrams* v. *FBI*, 511 F. Supp. 758 (N.D. IL 1981).

[80]*Hayden* v. *CIA*, No. 76-285 (D.DC 1980); *Stassi* v. *Department of the Treasury*, No. 78-533 (D.DC 1979); *Malizia* v. *Department of Justice*, 519 F. Supp. 338 (S.D.NY 1981).

[81]"Short Guide."

[82]*Atkinson* v. *FDIC*, 1 GDS 80,034 (D.DC 1980); *Consumers Union of U.S., Inc.* v. *Heimann*, 589 F.2d 531 (DC Cir. 1978); *Gregory* v. *FDIC*, 631 F.2d 896 (DC Cir. 1980).

[83]"Short Guide."

remaining specialized state provisions are either unique to a state or shared with only one other state, thus limiting the possibility of gaining insight into the meaning of a provision by looking at applications and decisions in other jurisdictions.[84]

One event that may increase the uniformity of state freedom of information and privacy laws is the July 1980 adoption of the Uniform Information Practices Code by the National Conference of Commissioners on Uniform State Laws. This code provides a model state law governing access to public records, and it contains twelve exemptions from mandatory disclosure of records. The government's protectible interests are found in exemptions for materials relating to law enforcement, deliberative proceedings, prelitigation activities, licensing examinations, government procurement, acquisition of property, and the security of record-keeping. Protectible personal interests are covered by exemptions for proprietary information, business and trade secrets, and records that identify an individual. In addition, there is a pass-through provision referring to federal and state laws and to rules of evidence. Perhaps the most unusual exemption permits the withholding of "library, archival, or museum material contributed by private persons to the extent of any lawful limitation imposed on the material"; the explanatory text says that this exemption is incorporated "to overcome the reluctance of many private individuals to donate personal papers or other materials to the state for preservation."

The model law has generated considerable opposition from groups that feel its real impact will be to reduce access to government records. A major problem is that the model law defines a "personal record" very broadly as "any item or collection of information in a government record which refers, in fact, to a particular individual, whether or not the information is maintained in individually identifiable form." If information meets this vague test, the agency cannot disclose the information to any person other than the individual to whom it refers unless disclosure is not a clearly unwarranted invasion of personal privacy. Even more seriously, whereas the federal Freedom of Information Act contains a presumption that government records are open, the model law turns that on its head for "personal records" and requires a person requesting a record that contains the name of an individual to show why disclosure would be in the public interest.[85] Archivists will want to watch carefully if states begin considering the adoption of this model law.

Knowing the general lines of application of the FOIA

provisions, the question remains as to the act's relationship to exemptions and disclosure requirements in governmental privacy and sunshine acts. Again the specific answers will depend upon the particular provisions of the federal, state, and local statutes. Some general observations can be made, however.

At the federal level, the relationship between the freedom of information, privacy, and sunshine acts is complex. These three statutes were drafted at different times without specific reconciliation of the various provisions, a situation that is generally true in states as well. This disharmony has resulted in some contradictory court decisions, such as a recent Federal Privacy Act case in which a judge ruled that the release of the name of an individual who is the subject of an investigation is not in itself an unwarranted invasion of privacy, a ruling in direct contradiction to the majority of holdings on FOIA exemption (b)(7)(C).[86] Fortunately, the Congress has now clarified the relationship between the Federal Privacy Act and FOIA privacy exemption, as mentioned above. Also fortunately for the National Archives, it has an exemption from the most onerous burdens of the Privacy Act, obtained in part by persuading the Congress that through its regular access policy the privacy of individuals named in the records is protected. The National Archives must, however, publish an annual notice of the systems of records in its holdings that contain privacy information and have formal rules for managing those records.

One of the provisions of the Federal Privacy Act allows an individual to request any agency to "make any correction of any portion" of a record pertaining to him that he "believes is not accurate, relevant, timely, or complete." Corrections can range from adding information to the file to expunging information from it. The National Archives has vigorously resisted expunging records in its custody, but at times it has allowed individuals to submit a written statement about the contents of an archival record maintained in the National Archives, with the understanding that the submission would be retained by the Archives and made available to any requester using the files to which it pertains.[87] More serious, however, are the expungements and other corrections carried out in agencies, some of which the Ar-

[84]Braverman and Heppler, "A Practical Review."

[85]Uniform Information Practices Code, 1980 Handbook of the National Conference of Commissioners on Uniform State Laws 149.

[86]*Gough, Kenney and Lebert* v. *FBI*, F83-008 CIV (D.C. AK December 1983).

[87]5 U.S.C. §552a. There are two possible ways to handle such submissions: one is to identify them clearly as submissions after the records were retired to the National Archives (such as marking the submissions with a stamp or maintaining them within a specially-marked envelope) and to insert them into the file; more preferable, but more cumbersome, is to maintain a parallel file with these submissions and insert into the original file only a cross-reference, clearly marked as generated by the Archives and not by the agency of origin, leading the researcher to the parallel file.

chives has also protested. These expungements are undertaken at the request of an individual, which means that they are spotty and unsystematic. In practice they also tend to occur disproportionately often in the files of more prominent individuals, as these are the persons most likely to request "corrections" in files that have been determined to be of permanent value. Consequently, archivists must be concerned about the impact of the act upon the comprehensiveness of files and their integrity as historical sources.

The federal sunshine act has only an indirect influence upon federal archival holdings and practices. The sunshine act specifically provides that it does not expand or limit any person's rights under the Freedom of Information Act, but because the meetings covered by the act are open, it does serve to ensure that the records of those meetings are open. It may also tend to open records the contents of which were discussed at open meetings.[88]

State and local archives' problems with privacy acts are more severe than the federal ones. Unless the state archives has managed to obtain a waiver similar to the federal one, the state privacy act must be assumed to apply to archival holdings, either directly or indirectly (if the state privacy act is held to be a pass-through statute under the state's freedom of information act). Each state and local archives will have to determine the applicability of the privacy act to archival holdings, most likely in consultation with the state attorney general. State schools may also be covered by the provisions of the privacy act, with direct effects on the archives of those schools. As with the federal sunshine act, the state sunshine acts will have only indirect impacts on the administration of access in archival records.

Conclusion

Every archivist wishes there was a nice little checklist that could be followed to determine whether a particular record or set of records must be restricted. The plain fact is that there isn't. Restricting records is making judgments. It is a matter of knowing the applicable law and its interpretation, looking carefully at the records, and deciding if the records meet the test. It means doing research to find out how much is already in the public domain about the subject of the records, understanding the context of the documents, and deciding. It means understanding when the access problem involves a law and when it involves an ethical or practical issue. And ultimately the archivist just has to decide.

---

[88] 5 U.S.C. §552b. The best discussion of the relationship between the federal FOIA and the sunshine act is Stephen S. Ostrach, "Relationship Between the Sunshine and Freedom of Information Acts," *Federal Bar Journal* 38 (Fall 1979): 182.

4 Administration of Access

The intellectual problems of access discussed in the last chapter are complex and challenging. People like to argue about concepts of privacy and national security, where personal philosophical predilections can come into play. Administering restricted records seems dull by comparison: the decision has been made that some of the information in this body of material needs to be restricted; now it is a matter of handling the details of withdrawal and notification. Yet it is precisely here that many institutions run into trouble. Administering access is a time-consuming, detail-oriented business with two keys: established procedures and consistent application.

Administration of access proceeds in stages. First, the institution establishes a coherent access policy and prepares a written statement of that policy that can be made available to staff, researchers, and prospective donors. Second, the archivists make determinations about the nature of the materials and the level of screening that must be done before reference service can be provided. Third, screening, withdrawal, and cross-referencing are completed. Finally, periodic or systematic re-reviews of restricted materials are made to ensure that all materials for which the reason for the restriction has expired are released to the research public. This chapter discusses each of these stages, then closes with a brief review of the specialized administration of records under the freedom of information acts.

Statements of Access Policy

As we have seen in previous chapters, records can be restricted by law, by conditions established by the institution of which the archives is a part, and by conditions documented in instruments of transfer. Personal papers are restricted by negotiated restrictions, but they may also be restricted by conditions established by the archival institution. In administering access to materials archivists have two basic responsibilities to the public: providing notice of the existence of restrictions and providing notice that specific materials are restricted pursuant to those restrictions.

Clearly stated access policies are the bedrock of access administration. The purpose of an access policy statement is to alert researchers, staff, prospective donors, and other parts of the institution of the existence of restrictions, the authority of the restrictions, the authority for removal of the restrictions, and, when possible, the method of implementing the restrictions. In addition, the restriction policy establishes a prima facie case of professional integrity and responsibility if, at some future time, the implementation of a particular restriction is called into question.

Statements of general access policies may be couched either positively or negatively, that is, "all records are open unless" or "such records may be disclosed only." Although on balance it is sounder to state restrictions positively, sometimes the only feasible way to write them is to use a negative format. The important thing is to be clear and responsible.

Most institutions will have a general policy statement about protecting personal privacy; many will also protect business and financial information. In addition, most repositories will want to point out that specific bodies of records may have additional restrictions and that there are donor restrictions on certain materials.

Access statements are best understood if they are placed in a context of general archival policies. In an introduction to the statement, the archives might refer to the Society of American Archivists-American Library Association policy on access, reaffirm the institution's commitment to making materials available on terms of equal access[1], and mention the institution's attempts to balance the needs to know with the needs for confidentiality. Following the general introduction specific sections would discuss each general type of document that is restricted. (See Figure 5.)

Because all persons using an archives, whether as staff, researchers, or donors, will need to have information on access policy, it is useful to provide as many copies of the access statement and as many references to it in as many places as possible. A single printed sheet is one possibility, but other places that such statements might be reprinted are guides, inventories, registers, researcher application forms, solicitation packets, and, for governmental archives, agency rules.

General restriction statements that state access guidelines for all the holdings are supplemented by specific restriction statements that explain restrictions on a particular type of records for one agency. In the National Archives, specific restrictions are tied to particular FOIA exemptions if the records to which they pertain are FOIA-controlled. State and local archives have similar practices for handling specific restrictions.

It is clear that an institution can establish restrictions on its own records. But can an archival institution impose restrictions upon a collection irrespective of the donor's wishes? The answer to that question depends upon the view one takes of the nature of donor agreements.

There are two ways to look at an agreement between a donor and an archives: one view is that records other than those specified in restrictions *must be opened*; the other view is that the records specified in the restrictions

must be closed and the archivist can make the determinations about which other materials to open. In the discussion on restrictions, we pointed out that a contract cannot be enforced if enforcing it would be a crime. Under that logic, if the application of a donor restriction would restrict records that appear to provide evidence of crime, the archives is freed of that restriction and, in fact, is bound to call the evidence to the attention of law enforcement officials. But is the reverse true? That is, if a donor's restrictions fail to cover a body of materials that would libel some living individual or cause a person a clear and definable harm, does the archives have the responsibility to close the records to protect the individuals named in the records? In general, the answer is yes, because just as citizens have a responsibility to report evidence of a crime, so also persons have a legal responsibility to avoid a civil wrong — for example, an invasion of personal privacy. Institutions here have a right and a responsibility to close such materials whether or not the items were specified by the donor for restriction.

Perhaps an example will make this clearer. An archives has been negotiating with a congressman for the donation of his papers. He has been defeated in the election and is quite bitter. He refuses to allow the archives to take a look at the papers, saying, "You either want them or you don't: make up your mind." The man is also very proud of his public service and signs a deed in which portions of the papers, such as constituent mail, are restricted for ten years. The archives takes the papers, and as it begins processing the donor dies. In the constituent mail are heartbreaking pleas for assistance in solving welfare problems, providing aid for battered wives, obtaining help in finding missing children, desperate accounts of old age medical problems, and so on. Just protecting them for ten years is certainly not enough; many if not most of the people are still alive. At the end of ten years can the archives extend the restriction or is it absolutely bound by the contract to open the files? The answer is that the archives can extend the closure to protect the individuals who are living.

Presented in the way that the previous paragraph does, the problem does not seem difficult to resolve. Part of the trick of administering access to records is stating the problem clearly and accurately. Sometimes a "balance sheet" approach, laying out in columns what will happen if one course is selected and then what will happen if another path is chosen, will help clarify what is really the key problem. Is it donor relations or privacy? Sanctity of contract or institutional authority? And so on. Clearly stated access policies, especially if incorporated by reference in the deed of gift, will help clarify the legal authority of the archives for restricting materials not specifically named as restricted in the deed itself.

---

[1]See discussion of the concept of equal access on page 72.

Model General Restriction Statement

This general restriction statement has been formulated as a model that may be used in whole or in part by an archives. Alternative paragraphs that could be substituted under varying circumstances for paragraphs in the body of the statement are placed together at its conclusion.

General Restriction Statement

of the

_____ Archives

The _____ Archives is committed to making research materials available to users on equal terms of access. This is in accordance with the standard professional policy on access adopted jointly by the Society of American Archivists and the American Library Association. Equal access does not mean that all materials are open to research use. It is the responsibility of the _____ Archives to balance the researcher's need for access with the needs for confidentiality of persons and institutions whose activities are reflected in the material. Consequently, the use of some materials in the _____ Archives, especially those of recent date, is subject to restrictions.

Two types of restrictions exist. Restrictions on access that apply to more than one group of materials are termed "general restrictions." They are applicable to particular kinds of information or designated classes of materials, wherever they may be found among the holdings. The other kind of restrictions are known as "specific restrictions." These are restrictions specified by the transferring agency or donor and apply to a specific body of material, sometimes for a specific length of time. Information about specific restrictions will be found in the accessioning dossier that covers the body of materials to which the specific restriction applies.

The following is a list of the general restrictions that are applied to the materials held by the _____ Archives. These general restrictions are established pursuant to _____ (*authority, such as an action of the Board of Directors or a statute. If a single authority does not exist, a separate authority line may be added to each of the restrictions as part (c).*) of _____ (*date*).

1.   Materials containing information, the disclosure of which would constitute a clearly unwarranted invasion of personal privacy or a libel of a living person.
       a.   *Definition.* Materials containing information about a living person which reveal details of a highly personal or libelous nature which, if released, would constitute a clearly unwarranted invasion of privacy or a libel, including but not limited to information about the physical or mental health or the medical or psychiatric care or treatment of the individual, and which personal information is not known to have been previously made public.
       b.   *Restrictions.* Such records may be disclosed only:
             i.   to regular employees of the _____ Archives in the performance of normal archival work on such materials.
             ii.   to the named individual or his authorized representative, provided that access will not be granted if the records are restricted pursuant to any other general or specific restrictions.

Figure 5

2. Materials containing confidential business and financial information.

a. *Definition.* Materials which contain trade secrets and commercial or financial information which was obtained with an expressed or implied understanding of confidentiality.

b. *Restrictions.* Such information may be disclosed only:

i. if the information consists of statistical totals or summaries and does not disclose the source of the information or identify individual parties, or

ii. if the party with whom the confidential relationship has been established agrees to its release, or

iii. if, in the judgment of the archivist, the passage of time is such that release of the information would not result in substantial competitive harm to the parties identified in the materials.

3. Materials containing confidential employment or personnel information.

a. *Definition.* Materials containing information on appointment, employment, performance evaluation, disciplinary action, and similar personnel matters.

b. *Restrictions.* Such information may be disclosed only:

i. if the information is a summary statement of service, or

ii. if the information does not identify particular individuals, or

iii. if the individual or his legal representative agrees to its release, or

iv. if the individual is deceased or the passage of time is such that the individual may be presumed to be deceased.

4. Materials relating to investigations.

a. *Definition.* Materials containing information related to or compiled during an investigation of individuals or organizations.

b. *Restrictions.* Such information may be disclosed only:

i. if the release of the information does not interfere with ongoing litigation or similar proceedings, and

ii. if confidential sources and information are not revealed, and

iii. if confidential investigative techniques are not described, and

iv. if the release of the information would not endanger the safety of law enforcement personnel, or

v. if the passage of time is such that:

(a) the safety of persons is not endangered, and

(b) the public interest in disclosure outweighs the continued need for confidentiality.

5. Materials restricted by statute, regulation, executive order, or court order.

a. *Definition.* Materials containing information, the access to which is restricted by statute, regulation, executive order, or court order.

b. *Restrictions.* Such information may be disclosed only:

i. in accordance with the provisions of such statute, regulation, executive order, or court order.

Figure 5, cont.

Alternative Paragraphs

The following elements or paragraphs may be substituted or added to the model general restriction statement, as appropriate, to meet the needs of the archives.

General Restrictions 1-4.

    iii. to those officers and employees of the agency of origin or its successor in function who have a need for the record in the performance of their official duties.

    iv. to the Donor of the materials or to the Donor's Designee, pursuant to the provisions of the Donor's deed of gift.

General Restriction 1.

    v. to researchers for the purpose of statistical or quantitative medical or psychiatric research when such researchers have provided the archives with written assurance that the information will be used solely for statistical research or reporting and that no individually identifiable information will be disclosed.

General Restriction 6. Materials containing information regarding confidential decision-making.

    a. *Definition.* Materials which contain information that was given in confidence in the period before a determination was made, including but not limited to advice given by attorneys, public accountants, and staff advisors.

    b. *Restrictions.* Such information may be disclosed only:

        i. if the decision has been made public and the nature of the determinations leading to the final decision is known, or

        ii. if the passage of time is such that release of the information would not impede current decision-making, or

        iii. if, in the judgment of the archivist, the public interest in disclosure outweighs the continued need for confidentiality.

Figure 5, cont.

All this may seem like a very complicated process to handle the few documents that are restricted. But there are mutual suspicions between archivists and users of archives, and a clear statement of what the archives does when it restricts records will help deflect some of the natural cynicism about archival motives. Then, too, archivists must understand that we live in a litigious age. The archival institution's best protection in the case of litigation is a clear understanding and written statement of its access policies.

Procedures for Review

Just as important as a general policy statement is an established procedure for handling the review of materials. Unless the archives is very small, it is impossible to review every page of every set of records or personal papers for items that possibly should be restricted. Instead, each archives must decide on some general ground rules that give guidance on when to screen on a page-by-page basis, when to screen at a file level and when to screen at the series level. For example, if the records came from the institution's press office, the series of press releases would be spot checked to make sure there was no intermingling of backup materials but would not be screened further before opening. Similarly, a series of case files from a mental hospital and dating from the 1950s would probably also be spot checked but then restricted. And so on. Archivists familiar with the general type of material coming into an archives can generally make quick and quite accurate determinations of those series that can be handled as a whole.

If the records must be reviewed at the file or document level, the archives can choose to review the materials during the processing stage or can wait until there is a request for the records. There are arguments in favor of both approaches. Handling the records at the processing stage ensures that all records open for research are reviewed and can be served quickly. On the other hand, because some records may not be used for years, it is possible to spend a significant amount of time withdrawing and then refiling materials with no intervening use.

Private institutions can and often do adopt a policy that records will not be made available to research until archival processing is completed; archives working under governmental freedom of information acts usually cannot enforce such a policy but instead must be willing to review for release any records in their possession. If an archives does have a policy that records will be closed pending processing, this should be clearly stated in material sent to prospective users. Almost all archival institutions have a backlog of unprocessed items, and a "closed pending processing" policy can mean delays in access for all users.

If the archives waits for a specific request before reviewing the materials for restrictions, this, too, can occasion serious delays that will affect the researcher. Once a request is in hand, the archivist must determine what materials pertain to the request, and for those documents selected, what restrictions cover them. Are these records covered by a freedom of information act? By a law establishing special access conditions? By a donor's instrument? By a specific restriction negotiated at the time of transfer? Do any of the archives' own restriction policies cover the materials? If item level review is necessary, the researcher may wait for weeks while the processing is completed.

Screening and Withdrawal

Whether working during processing or following a reference inquiry, the archivist, having refreshed his memory about the precise criteria governing access, now turns to actual review. Any physical form of material may contain restricted information: sound recordings from law enforcement agencies (to say nothing of the Nixon tapes); photographs taken by military or law enforcement agencies or photographs included in medical and welfare files; maps and architectural drawings prepared by security agencies, and so on. But these are quite special cases, most likely well-known to the archivist handling the materials and specifically restricted in the provisions of the transfer document. At present most of the records the archivist must review for release are in paper format; ever more frequently, however, they will be on electronic media — computer tape, disk, diskette, or some as yet unknown form.

Some archival institutions will not review below the file level; that is, if something within the file must be withheld the whole file is restricted. Increasingly, however, the pressure of the freedom of information acts and the general openness stance of archival institutions has moved archivists toward a position of releasing as many individual documents as possible. At the other extreme from withholding at the file level is withholding at the word level. The federal Freedom of Information Act, and some state acts as well, require the release of any "reasonably segregable" portion of a document. This means that individual paragraphs or even words are excised in order to provide the researcher with a "disclosure free" copy (see page 69). If the policy of the archives is to withhold on an item level (that is, to remove the entire document if something in it must be restricted but not to make deletions within the document), the task is simpler than withholding portions within the document.

Whether withholding involves a file, a document, or a portion of a document, the archivist's key responsibility is to alert the user to the existence of the restricted material, that is, to tell the user that something has been removed from the records. With paper documents restricted at the item or file level, the normal practice is to insert a sheet into the file in place of the restricted document; this inserted page is usually called a "withdrawal sheet" (see Figure 6). On it the item or file withdrawn is described in as much detail as possible without giving away the restricted information. It is often possible, for instance, to identify the correspondents, the date of the item, and the general subject. The withdrawal sheet also should specify the reasons for the withdrawal (for example, "donor's deed of gift, §4.2," "FOIA provision 7, records of land appraisal"), the date of withdrawal, and the name of the staff member withdrawing the document. Some archives complete only one withdrawal sheet per file, listing on it all withdrawn items and filing it in the front of the file folder. A few archives even file individual sheets for each item *and* a summary sheet in the front.

Once the item is removed from the file, it must be sequestered but must also maintain its provenance and identity. Many archives choose a system known as "parallel files." In this method, a document that is removed is placed with a copy of the withdrawal sheet in a file folder with the same title as the one from which it was withdrawn but marked (by color, by stamp, or a similar fashion) as restricted. These file folders are then placed in a separate box, similarly marked as restricted, and stored in a separate area of the archives. This method is a relatively good guarantee that the restricted items will not be served to a researcher by accident. If, however, a large amount of material must be withdrawn, leaving the original storage containers half empty, the amount of storage space needed to accommodate the same amount of material (that is, the original boxes plus the parallel files) is greatly increased.

In view of this storage problem, which is especially serious in large records series, some archives have adopted a practice of putting the withdrawn material in a specially marked envelope and filing it at the back of the original storage container. While this solves the

---

Withdrawal Notice

In the review of this file the item(s) identified below has been withdrawn because access to it is restricted. Restrictions on records in the _____ Archives are stated in general and specific restriction statements which are available for examination. Restrictions on donated materials are stated in instruments of gift which are also available for examination.

File Title:

Form: (*letter, report, memorandum, etc.*)

Date:

To:

From:

Subject:

Authority for the restriction: (*General Restriction Statement No.* _____; *Specific Restriction Statement* _____; *Donor's Deed of Gift, paragraph* _____, *provision* _____; *etc.*)

By: (*signature of archivist withdrawing item*) Date:

Figure 6

space problem, it means that before a container of records can be served it must be checked for restricted items and the special envelopes removed. This greatly increases the risk of accidentally serving restricted records to a researcher; in fact, it has happened in at least one archives using this method. If restricted records are accidentally served to a researcher and if that results in a legal action against the archives, the central question would be whether the archives had taken all reasonable and prudent steps to prevent disclosure. Either policy can, of course, be defended, but parallel files would provide a better demonstration of responsible stewardship.

If the records to be restricted are on microfilm or microfiche, the administrative problem is much greater than for paper records. Obviously a whole roll or card can be withheld, but what if only one document in the entirety needs restriction? It is possible to splice a copy of the film to eliminate the offending frames, but if many documents are involved this is an extremely costly and entirely impractical solution. Similarly, an electrostatic copy can be produced and the restrictions worked out on that physical format while the original film is withheld; again this is expensive and depends upon getting a good quality paper copy from the film. One ar-

chivist even suggested standing behind a researcher using film containing restricted frames and pulling the plug on the reader at the appropriate moments! None of these are good solutions, and archivists should be wary of agreeing to accept microform as a record copy if the records are likely to contain substantial amounts of restricted information.

If the records to be restricted are in electronic form and if the records are numerical and statistical ones or ones with defined data elements, the review process may begin by reading the computer documentation package that explains the layout of the file. If, however, the records are general correspondence on electronic storage devices, review will probably consist of turning the electronic pages, just as in reviewing paper records the paper pages are turned. In the latter case it is possible to print out those documents that the user requests and follow the normal paper excising process, although with large volumes of records for review this is not very practical. With statistical information this is not very practical, either, both because of the enormous volume of records to be printed and because the user will probably want to manipulate the records in machine-readable formats. All this means that after the archivist decides on those items that will have to be excised, the archivist will have to work closely with computer programmers to ensure that the machine-readable copy provided to users has all the restricted information removed.

One other variation is possible with machine-readable records, and that is a requirement by the agency of origin that information in a database identifying a single individual or organization cannot be released but that aggregated totals can. In this case, to make the records available a programmer will have to write instructions to the computer to compile and aggregate certain types of information.[2] Just as paper records are marked to indicate removals, the computer records provided to researchers with deletions or aggregations should be accompanied by a clear written explanation of the changes made in the record.

A useful practice that some archives have adopted is establishing administrative "precedent files." This is a set of files, one each on the general types of restrictions found in the holdings (e.g., privacy, business information, confidential decision-making). If, during review, the archivist confronts and resolves a difficult problem that might create a precedent for future restriction decisions, a copy of the item is made, annotated with the decision, and placed in the file. It is essential that both decisions to open and decisions to withhold are included in the precedent files; consequently, the files themselves must be sequestered where they will not be accidentally read.

Precedent files serve several purposes. First, they keep an archives from making divergent decisions, both over time and among different staff members: it is essential to be consistent in applying restrictions. Second, they are an ideal training tool for new staff members who must be introduced to the access policy of the institution. Third, they become an accumulating body of knowledge about the nature and meaning of the restrictions on the holdings. Finally, in case of challenge to the validity of the application of restrictions, they serve as yet more evidence that the archives has been a responsible custodian, trying to apply the restrictions aptly.[3]

Periodic Review

Archives that must manage substantial bodies of restricted material will find it necessary to institute controls over the materials to facilitate re-review and eventual reintegration of the temporarily restricted items. In small archives, this can be managed by making a third copy of the withdrawal sheet (the first is in the original file from which the item was withdrawn, the second is with the withdrawn item as a record of where it should be refiled) and filing it in a control file. Increasingly, however, institutions are turning to computers and word processors to handle the information. Control files can then be reviewed periodically to determine which of the restrictions need no longer be applied (a computer can do much of the searching automatically, especially for restrictions keyed to a particular date). Those items that from the control file appear to lack a continuing need for restriction can be re-reviewed and, if appropriate, reintegrated into the files.

At the time of reintegration of the formerly restricted items, the withdrawal sheets are removed or, if there is only one sheet for the entire file, the entry for the particular item returned is lined through or marked in some way to indicate that it is no longer restricted. If a third copy of the withdrawal sheet has served as a control, it can also be withdrawn and reunited with the other two. It is, however, important that a record be maintained showing what items were once restricted and have since been returned. One way to do this is to place one of the cancelled withdrawal sheets in the control file or processing file or accession file for the entire group of records; another is to maintain a separate file on removed restrictions. The latter is particularly easy to do if the restriction information has been maintained on a computer, for the information can be deleted automatically from a "currently restricted" file and transferred to the "formerly restricted" one.

Researchers should have access to the information about the return of records to the holdings. One scholar complained to an archives about the policy of returning records without maintaining a list of returned items; the practice, he said, resulted in his having to go through the body of material in question every year or so as he worked on his book just to see what else had been released. Either maintaining a printout of "recently released records" or placing a set of the cancelled withdrawal sheets in a reference area accessible to users or maintaining an "openings book" listing releases will solve the problem.

For specific sets of records with high public interest it may be easiest to maintain a separate log of all releases so interested persons can write to the archives and learn exactly what has been released since the last visit. In

---

[2]For a full discussion of anonymization in machine-readable records and, in particular, techniques of aggregation, see Harold Naugler's forthcoming *The Archival Appraisal of Machine-Readable Records: A RAMP Study with Guidelines* (Paris: UNESCO General Information Program and UNISIST, 1984).

[3]In the case of donor restrictions, a user would normally have no ground on which to challenge the agreements to restrict that are incorporated in the instrument of transfer. What a researcher *may* be able to challenge is whether the archives properly interpreted the donor's instructions. We know of no case law on this question.

some cases, where the records have exceptionally high interest, an annual list may even be prepared. Again, electronic recordkeeping makes the maintenance of such lists a relatively simple matter.

Administration Under the Federal Freedom of Information Act

Unlike the intellectual side of access, where the interpretations of the federal Freedom of Information Act now set the standard for interpreting such common archival concepts as privacy and business confidentiality, the administration of access under the act is peculiar unto itself. The special problems include determining which records are covered by the act, reviewing to excise items of information within the document, preparing lists of records denied and identifying for each record the reason for the exemption, understanding appeal and litigation rights, and recording the process of handling requests. All of these are specialized problems, requiring substantially more detailed handling of requests for records than archivists employ if records not covered by the act are requested. Likewise, although some state freedom of information acts are as stringent as the federal act, most are not, and archivists in each state must determine what requirements exist for the procedural handling of FOIA requests.

Coverage

As discussed in previous chapters, courts have broadly construed the coverage of the federal Freedom of Information Act. The act applies to records of agencies of the executive branch of government, with some special peculiarities for presidential records. Records of the legislative and judicial branches lie entirely outside the reach of the act. In that sense the coverage is very narrow. It is broad, however, in its inclusivity for information in executive branch records. In particular, courts have held that documents that originated outside an agency but are in the possession of an agency generally can be reached by the Freedom of Information Act. (This is an application of the "received" part of the "made and received" definition of records that archivists normally use.)

On the troublesome question of records made with agency funds but not in the possession of an agency, the Supreme Court has ruled on records of grantees but not on the records of contractors. In the case of *Forsham* v. *Harris*, the Court decided that grantee records that had not been obtained by an agency were not agency records: "an agency must first either create or obtain a record as a prerequisite to it becoming an 'agency record' within the meaning of the FOIA." Commenting on the *Forsham* decision, the Justice Department concluded:

The Court's decision reflects concepts from the law of personal property, in which possession indicates ownership and control unless another person has a better claim to the property. Thus, a strong presumption exists that when a record is in an agency's possession, it is an "agency record" for FOIA purposes. This presumption is not affected by the fact that an entity which is not an agency may also have a copy of the record but . . . it may be rebutted by other factors.[4]

A growing body of FOIA law tries to define these "other factors" that tend to rebut the presumption of record status. If the records in question were obtained by an agency from the federal judiciary or the Congress, especially if there is clear evidence of intent not to relinquish control of the records at the time they were transferred to the agency, they are generally nonrecord for FOIA purposes. A related issue that finds courts deeply divided is the record status of a document "jointly possessed" by an FOIA-exempt and an FOIA-covered agency. Presentence reports jointly used by courts and parole commissions have been particular problems, and decisions have gone both ways.[5] In addition, materials which are physically located within the agency but which are determined to be personal property are not records for FOIA purposes.[6]

It must be understood that just because a document falls outside the reach of the Freedom of Information Act it is not necessarily a nonrecord; judicial and congressional documents, for example, are clearly records. It merely means that the provisions of the act cannot be used to gain access to that document.

---

[4]*Forsham* v. *Harris*, 445 U.S. 169 (1980); "A Short Guide to the Freedom of Information Act," *Freedom of Information Case List: September 1984 Edition* (Washington: Government Printing Office, 1984) p. 40; *McGehee* v. *Central Intelligence Agency*, 697 F.2d 1008 (DC Cir. 1980) (records in the possession of the CIA but originated by the Department of State are "agency records" and the CIA must review for release).

[5]*Goland* v. *CIA*, 607 F.2d 339 (DC Cir. 1978) (congressional records are not agency records); *Carson* v. *Department of Justice*, 631 F.2d 1008 (DC Cir. 1980) (presentence reports by the probation service of the courts and transferred to the Parole Commission are reachable under FOIA as agency records); *Crooker* v. *United States Parole Commission*, 730 F.2d 1 (1st Cir. 1984) (jointly possessed presentence reports are not agency records subject to FOIA).

[6]*Porter County Chap., Etc.* v. *United States Atomic Energy Commission*, 380 F. Supp. 630 (N.D. IN 1974); *Wolfe* v. *Department of Health and Human Services*, 539 F. Supp. 276 (D.DC 1982), aff'd, 711 F.2d 1077 (DC Cir. 1983) (Reagan transition team report of the Department of Health and Human Services, obtained by and in the personal possession of a senatorial staff member who subsequently became an HHS employee, not part of the departmental files, and not used by the department is not an agency record); *The Bureau of National Affairs, Inc.* v. *Department of Justice*, Civil Action No. 82-1211, U.S. Dist. Ct., D.C., November 29, 1982 (appointment calendar existing only for the convenience of the author, not created at the request of the agency and not part of the official recordkeeping program, is not an agency record).

If the records are covered by the Freedom of Information Act, the act may still not cover the request. First of all, the request must "reasonably describe" the records; for example, a request for "all records relating to the Second World War" does not meet that test. Second, the request may ask that records be compiled. Courts have agreed that records must be furnished under the act but do not need to be *created*; if a compilation does not exist, the archives does not have to create one.[7]

An FOIA request can be made by "any person." This includes both U.S. and foreign individuals, partnerships, corporations, associations, and foreign, state, or local governments. The requester does not have to state a reason for seeking access.

Approximately half of the state FOIA laws follow the federal model in matters of coverage. In New York, for example, the law defines agency and specifically excludes the judiciary and the state legislature, although it implicitly covers the records of the office of the governor. A recent New York court decision held that state possession of the minutes of meetings of private companies was sufficient to find that the minutes were records covered by the act. Several other states tie FOIA coverage to public funding, which greatly increases the scope of the application; the Arkansas Freedom of Information Act, for example, covers any "agency wholly or partially supported by public funds or expending public funds." As mentioned above, some states also expressly cover local governmental entities within the scope of their freedom of information acts. In those governments where the FOIA scope is partial, as it is in the federal setting, alternative restriction and access plans may exist for the records excluded from the FOIA ambit[8] (see Appendix 2 for a table of state FOIA citations).

Review Procedures

Having determined that the records are covered and are reasonably described and are extant, the next step is to locate them. Although there is no legal definition of what constitutes a reasonable amount of effort expended on a search for requested records, courts have sent agencies, notably the FBI, back to search records again if the court is not satisfied that the original search was adequate. If the archives has general policy guidance on the amount of time to spend on researcher requests and the archives has met that test, that probably constitutes a reasonable effort.

After the record is located, it must be reviewed, applying the tests of the exemptions. The federal Freedom of Information Act requires that an initial determination be made within ten days of the receipt of the request, and only three grounds are given in the law for a justifiable extension: collecting records from physically disparate offices, processing "voluminous" records included in the request, and consulting with another agency or another part of the same agency that has a "substantial subject-matter interest" in the records. A requester who does not receive an answer within ten days can go directly to court and sue for release of the records. In such situations the court will ask the government to explain the delay and, according to the law, "if the Government can show exceptional circumstances exist and that the agency is exercising due diligence in responding to the request, the court may retain jurisdiction and allow the agency additional time to complete its review of the records." The court may require periodic reports of the progress that is being made in filling the request, and as long as it is satisfied that the review is going forward the court is unlikely to intervene further. A ten-day extension can only be used once per request by the agency, either at the initial request or appeal stage or divided between the two; consequently, appeals offices usually want to be notified before an extension is taken by the office handling the initial request because if the ten days are used on the initial request the appeals office has no time flexibility at all if an appeal is made.

Following the completion of the review, "any reasonably segregable portion of a record" must be released. If the entire document can be released, it is simply a matter of notifying the researcher of the times and places of availability and the price of copying. (If the document to be released is a classified document, the classification stamp must be voided and the document marked for release in accordance with the procedures specified in the current executive order on classification.) If none of the information can be released, the archivist turns to the procedures for denials. But if some information is releaseable and some is not, then the archivist must answer the question of whether there is a "segregable portion" of this document.

The question of what is a segregable portion has been raised repeatedly. Two rules of thumb have evolved, one called the "mosaic test" (based on a court decision), the other called the "swiss cheese test" (based on common sense). The mosaic test, also known as the "jigsaw puzzle" and discussed on page 47, says that if the disclosure of a fact, although innocent of itself,

[7]*NLRB* v. *Sears, Roebuck & Co.*, 421 U.S. 132, 161 (1975); *Krohn* v. *Department of Justice*, 628 F.2d 195 (DC Cir. 1980); *Sears* v. *Gottschalk*, 502 F.2d 122 (4th Cir. 1974), cert. den. 422 U.S. 1056 (1975).

[8]Burt A. Braverman and Wesley R. Heppler, "A Practical Review of State Open Records Laws," *George Washington Law Review* 49 (May 1981): 723-760; *In the Matter of The Washington Post Company* v. *New York State Insurance Department et al.*, No. 73, State of New York, Court of Appeals, March 29, 1984.

could serve as a "missing link" that would allow a person to patch together a mosaic of the whole, the fact should be restricted.[9] This approach requires a good deal of knowledge about the topic under review; in general archivists cannot be expected to apply more than normal knowledge to the implications that might be drawn from the records. The swiss cheese test is the other half of the question. Here the archivist must decide whether, if all the restricted items are deleted, there is anything left that makes sense. Is it more holes than cheese? Worse, is what is left misleading? Archivists cannot protect researchers against drawing erroneous conclusions, but can only ensure that "sanitized" documents (the FOIA jargon for those documents that have had portions excised prior to release) are adequately marked to indicate deletions. Yet if all that would be left after sanitizing is a scattered "he stated" or a "holding that," it is questionable whether the release is worth making. Pages have been released to users with only the page number remaining at the top of the page; paying minimum copying fees for a "2" seems unreasonable.

The actual process of excision can be handled in a variety of ways. With paper documents, working from a copy, items that must be removed can be cut out with an exacto knife, can be covered with an opaque white tape, or can be marked over with a special type of marking pen that will obscure the writing when recopied. Then the excised copy can be recopied onto paper, the excised portions marked with a stamp or by hand to indicate to the user where something was excised, and the recopied, marked document is ready for release.[10] Records in machine-readable format can be excised by electronic means, as described above, and microform is a problem in any system of limited access.

Denials

If some or all of the records requested by a researcher are to be denied to him (and this includes those released with deletions) a denial letter must be written. The law and the courts have made it clear that the burden of proof is on the agency to justify the withholding. This means that denial letters are critically important to the FOIA process, and they must be crafted with care.

Each FOIA response has four basic parts: (1) statement of records requested, date of the requester's letter, and date the letter was received (because the ten days allowed for response are ten working days counted from the date of receipt of the request); (2) decision, with statement of exemptions used (if any); (3) statement of hours of service, availability of copies, and cost of reproductions; (4) notification of appeal rights (if records have been denied).[11]

Included either within the denial letter or as a separate enclosure should be a statement of the deletions and the exemptions used as justification. Courts may require a detailed exemption list, called a "Vaughn list" because the D.C. Court of Appeals first held that such a list was required in the case of *Vaughn* v. *Rosen*.[12] If an FOIA case goes to court, the judge can order the agency to produce the documents for inspection and comparison with the exemptions cited in the Vaughn list, or the court can appoint a special master to do the review. Two or more exemptions can be cited for a single deletion (for example, both (b)(6) and (b)(7)(C) for certain privacy matters), and if the (b)(3) "pass-through" exemption is cited, the particular statute to which it refers must also be cited.

The federal Freedom of Information Act provides that fees charged for document search and reproduction can be waived or reduced by the agency if the agency determines that this is "in the public interest because furnishing the information can be considered as primarily benefiting the general public."[13] Requesters often ask for this "fee waiver," as it is known. The National Archives has chosen not to charge any fees for search costs, believing that, as an institution dedicated to providing those services to the public, search fees are inappropriate. Consequently, only normal copying fees are charged and fee waivers are routinely denied, with an explanation that all search fees have already been waived.

The act may also provide an exception to the general archival principle that if the records are released to one third party requester they are released to all. The Justice Department suggests that "the basic limitation on differences of treatment in releasing an exempt record to one person but not another is that the difference must

---

[9]*Halperin* v. *CIA*, 629 F.2d 144 (DC Cir. 1980) (mosaic test applied to intelligence information).

[10]If the documents to be excised are in a standard format (such as a fill-in-the-blank form) and the restricted information appears in a standard position on the form, it is possible to make a paper template and place it on the copying equipment and then lay the documents to be excised on the template.

[11]Technically the act is a freedom of *information* act, not a freedom of *records* one, but because in most instances the information sought is embedded in documents, physical service of the records or copies of the records is assumed. Each agency must publish in the *Federal Register* the FOIA procedures it has established and the officials who are entitled to make decisions for it on FOIA requests. Although it certainly is true that releases can be as potentially dangerous as denials, it is denials that are usually most carefully controlled, with only a limited number of officials empowered to deny records.

[12]*Vaughn* v. *Rosen*, 484 F.2d 820 (DC Cir. 1973), cert. denied, 415 U.S. 977 (1974).

[13]5 U.S.C. §552 (a)(4)(A).

be reasonable and not unfair.''[14] (The mailing list issue discussed in the previous chapter is an example.) In general, archivists should be wary of advancing these arguments for differential treatment of requesters without first seeking advice of legal counsel.

Appeals

If records are denied to a requester, that person can file an appeal at any time. The appeal is made to a higher level official in the same agency as the official issuing the initial denial. The federal Freedom of Information Act provides no time limit on the right to appeal, although it sets a twenty-day time limit for an agency response to the appeal. If, upon appeal, the denial is continued, the requester has the right to bring suit in federal district court, either the D.C. court, the court for the district in which the records are located, the district in which the requester lives, or the district in which the requester has his principal place of business. In making its decision the court can review the records in question in camera. If the court rules in favor of the requester (the FOIA language is that the requester must ''substantially prevail''), the court can award both attorney fees and costs to be paid by the government for the requester.

Administrative Controls

Because the federal Freedom of Information Act requires an agency to make an annual report to the Congress on its administration of the act, careful controls are maintained over the disposition of the requests in hand. These controls, usually in the form of logs, are keyed to the information Congress requires, which includes such things as the amount of time spent on the request, the number of extensions taken, the number of times an exemption was used, and so forth. FOIA cover sheets in distinctive colors are attached to incoming requests as further insurance that they will not be buried in piles of routine requests.

The National Archives has chosen to treat as FOIA requests only those letters that actually specify that the request is being made under the aegis of the act. The alternative is to treat every routine reference request as a FOIA request, which would totally skew the statistics that Congress is trying to collect to monitor the implementation of the act. Because a requester can invoke the act at any time and because the application of the restrictions is the same whether or not the request is filed under the act, the actual impact of this policy is slight.

Administrative Records of the Archives

Governmental archives, both federal and state, must also remember that the administrative records of the archives as an agency also fall within the provisions of the Freedom of Information acts. Unless the archives is an independent agency, its administration of the act in terms of administrative (as opposed to accessioned) records will be guided by the policies of the parent agency. This may result in the archives administering the act in two rather different ways, depending on whether the request is for administrative or accessioned records.

Conclusion

Administering access policy is based on two principles: the public should know of the existence of restrictions, and the public should know of the existence of records that are restricted. Most archivists do not like to withhold records; for the most part, the days of the secretive archivist who hoarded his trove a la Silas Marner are over. Instead archivists want users, want records open, want records cited in publications. Archivists do not want to bother with the picky procedures of review and restriction. And yet in most repositories some restrictions are necessary.

If an archives finds its restrictions of records challenged, its best protection is to have been following a well-defined, written policy on the administration of access. The archives must be able to demonstrate that its handling of the materials was not arbitrary and capricious, that it has been a responsible custodian of the materials entrusted to it. Clarity and consistency remain the archivist's best friends.

---

5   Reference Service

Archival reference service encompasses five activities: providing information about the institution and its records, providing information from the records, furnishing the records, furnishing copies of the records, and loaning the records. Each of these activities may generate legal problems, although the most serious and frequent arise in the course of providing the actual documents.

Information about the Institution and Its Records

Providing information about the institution is usually quite simple: where it is, what it holds, what services it provides, who can use it, and so forth. But if the general public is not admitted, problems can arise in defining who are researchers eligible to use the holdings.

14"Short Guide."

The archival ethic, expressed in the SAA-ALA joint statement on access (see Appendix 1) is that archives will give equal access to records to all researchers. (The meaning here is equal access for all third party researchers — obviously, the creator of the item and the recipient of the item, parties one and two, have already seen it and there is normally no point in barring their access to it.) The thrust of the statement is that once an item is opened to one user it is open to them all. This does not mean, however, that an institution cannot set some criteria for use. What the statement does suggest is that an institution should clearly define its users and then treat them equally.

Often institutions will refuse to allow minors to use original documents or will allow minors to use them only if accompanied by an adult. Explained in terms of preservation, this policy is reasonable and may even be used in institutions whose policies are governed by the Freedom of Information Act if it is made clear that a minor will be allowed to work from duplicate copies such as microfilm, microfiche, or electrostatic reproductions.[1]

A more difficult situation may arise when the institution limits access to "serious researchers," "scholars," or "qualified researchers." Here the problem is one of defining who is a "serious" scholar. A genealogist who can find the information only in the holdings of that institution? A college student writing a term paper? A congressional aide seeking information for a speech? Although in a private institution it is the right of the institution to limit access in any way it chooses, ad hoc capricious determinations can lead to charges of favoritism and unfair treatment.[2] Whether a lawsuit over exclusion by these terms (e.g., a determination that the applicant is not a "qualified researcher") could actually be sustained is untested, but an institution seeking to apply such an access limitation should have a clear definition of the persons who fall within and without the strictures and should make that definition publicly available. The institution must also make every effort to ensure that the staff members who screen research applicants apply the policy consistently.

Some college and university archives have been pressured to limit access to new accessions, particularly of donated materials, to faculty members for a short period of time. If the archives is in an academic institu-

tion covered by a freedom of information act, this restriction is probably impossible to maintain unless donated materials are exempted from the act. If the archives is in a privately funded school, the legal case is less clear. (The restriction would be a breach of the archivist's ethic of equal access, however.) Assuming that the donor did not stipulate any general access policy, the material is the university's property and access to it can be limited. If the time period is sufficiently brief, it is unlikely that a legal action to compel opening would be heard by the courts in time to make any difference. A more serious issue might arise if a scholar outside the university was completing a manuscript for delivery to a publisher within the year and the donated materials were directly pertinent to his topic. In such a case "right to work" might become an issue, but in that instance, too, the archives would be better served by using a strategy of conflict resolution rather than forcing the researcher to resort to legal measures. Whatever the final policy decision is on restricted access for other than faculty members, the policy must be clearly spelled out in informational handouts provided to all researchers.

Another widespread problem is that of the authorized biographer. Almost every institution that accepts donations of personal papers will at sometime or other acquire a body of material which is restricted in whole or in part, only to find that the donor has given a biographer permission to use it all, even after it is in the custody of the archives. If in the deed the donor reserved the right to authorize access, the archives has no legal choice but to allow the biographer use of the materials (if the items are in "courtesy storage" pending donation the donor retains complete control). If, however, the deed is silent, the control of access can be assumed to be a right transferred to the archives at the time ownership passes. Once again, though, a direct confrontation is probably unwise. The archives might, for example, work with the donor or his heirs to open additional materials to all researchers, with the biographer given first reading after opening.

A similar problem arises when researchers from agencies come to the archives to use records that are restricted from general distribution. This is particularly important when the records are classified for national security reasons, but it also happens with other categories of restricted records. In addition, former officials sometimes are granted access to the records of agencies in which they worked.[3] All of these situations can create

---

[1]Freedom of information acts normally require that the public be given access to *information* but do not require that the public be given the original document. Copies are generally provided to fulfill FOIA requests.

[2]A private institution technically *could* discriminate against categories of researchers based on race, gender, religion, and so forth; however, the institution would probably lose its tax-exempt status, federal and state grants, contracts, and accounts.

---

[3]Access for former presidents and vice-presidents is legislated and codified as 44 U.S.C. §2205(3) and 2207; access to classified records for historical researchers and former presidential appointees is found in E.O. 12356, §4.3; access for agency historians is supplemented by an interagency agreement.

misunderstandings among other researchers. The information the repository provides to all users should clearly state that access to certain records is limited to those persons with pertinent clearances or other permissions.

Occasionally questions have arisen about hours of service. A private repository can normally set whatever hours it chooses or even open only by appointment. Public archives may have hours of service established in legislation, but more likely the archives is allowed to set its own schedule. Could a public body be sued to maintain longer hours if it is only open, say, alternate Tuesdays? Or to have some evening and Saturday hours to accommodate users who work a normal workweek? Or to open all parts of the archives for Saturday hours if one part has them? It is possible that such a suit could be brought, but the success of the litigation would likely turn on why the hours were established as they were. If the archives has not been capricious but instead is opening its doors as frequently as its resources will permit, the suit would probably be dismissed.

Providing information about the records, whether in writing, on the telephone, or in person, is complex. This is the point at which the researcher must be alerted to the existence of restrictions, if there are any, and to the practices the institution employs in withdrawing material. Generally the questions here are a matter of ethics, not law, and the normal procedure is that the archivist will provide the prospective researcher with all pertinent, relevant information.

Some archivists have worried about their liability if a researcher is not led to all materials that are relevant to his topic. Could they be sued if an important set of documents is not shown? This is a hard question to answer in the abstract. Probably a court would evaluate whether the researcher had access to finding aids that were adequate to point him to the materials in question; if he saw the finding aids but did not ask for the materials, it is not the legal responsibility of the archives to bring the latter to him. The problem then turns to the adequacy of the finding aids. If the archives knows that the finding aids are incomplete or otherwise inadequate, it has a responsibility to assist the researcher in attempting to locate relevant materials. A good faith effort by the archivist, an effort that fulfills all standard internal procedures for reference service, is required. If the archives can show that such procedures were followed, it probably has no legal liability if the search fails to uncover references to every relevant document.

Providing information about the records also includes informing the researcher of any institutional publication projects under way on the materials in question, especially if the publication involves the closure to

research of some parts of the holdings.[4] The most famous controversy over an institutional publication project occurred in 1969-70, oddly enough in a case where records were not closed during publication. In this cause célèbre, a researcher named Francis Loewenheim charged that he had not been given full access to records at the Franklin D. Roosevelt Library because the library was using these materials for a publication on Franklin D. Roosevelt and foreign affairs. The complaint, which was aired in the *New York Times*, was investigated by a special joint committee of the American Historical Association and the Organization of American Historians. The committee concluded that "there was no deliberate and systematic withholding of documents from Loewenheim." Although the library was preparing a publication, the committee found that researchers continued to have access to the documents that were being readied for publication. The committee did decide, however, that the library should have been more diligent in informing researchers of the scope, nature, and practices of the library's publication project.[5]

In addition to the policy of closing materials while in final preparation for publication, some institutions not covered by a freedom of information act also have a policy of closing materials until arrangement and description is completed, "closed pending processing." Given the nature of processing backlogs in most archival institutions, these backlogs can persist over many years. The researcher must be informed that records are closed under this policy, for it may directly affect his research strategy. The question is whether a lawsuit to gain access to materials closed for institutional administrative purposes could succeed. The answer probably lies in a question of time. If there is a reasonable expectation that the materials will be available for research use on a fixed date, a court will be more favorably inclined to the justice of the archives' position than if the closure appears to be protracted without a likely date for opening the materials. Furthermore, the nature of the archival institution itself — whether public or private — and the nature of the materials would also be factors that the court could consider. While it is conceivable that a public archives could be required to open

---

[4]Such publication projects include, of course, microfilm publications where after final arrangement for the camera the records are closed until the filming is completed.

[5]*Final Report of the Joint AHA-OAH Ad Hoc Committee to Investigate the Charges against the Franklin D. Roosevelt Library and Related Matters* (Washington: American Historical Association, 1970). One result of the investigation was the establishment of the permanent joint committee of the American Historical Association, the Organization of American Historians, and the Society of American Archivists.

its records (almost certainly if they are covered by a freedom of information statute), it seems much less likely that the court would require, for instance, a business archives to open its records to outside researchers.

Information from the Records

A second major type of reference service is providing information from the records. The fundamental problem here is the utter reliance of the user upon the archivist's selection, extraction, and synthesis of information. One part of the problem is the breadth and depth of the search; the second is the accuracy of the interpretation. What is the archivist's and the archival institution's liability ·if the information provided proves to be in error?

Look at an easy example. If, on the one hand, the information is genealogical and is destined for inclusion in a family memory book, the impact of the error, while regretable, is not great. If, on the other hand, the genealogical information is being collected to establish the eligibility of the individual for certain rights and benefits (for example, inheritance, federal monies), an error can have a substantial and demonstrable impact. While it could be argued that any person entrusting the research to an archives is willingly accepting the risk of a nonexhaustive or inaccurate search, the archives is still open to a possible lawsuit for damages.

The best defense an archives could have if it did fail to provide accurate information would be that it had followed established search procedures and that it had alerted the requester to the nature and extent of the search. As in most areas of archival work, standard written procedures and guidelines and an established pattern of adherence to them is a secure foundation. Such procedural statements are particularly useful if the claim is made that the archives failed to look in all likely places for the information. If the issue is the misinterpretation by the archives of information located, such as misreading handwriting or mistranscribing information, the archives is unlikely to be held liable for the error unless it was malicious or intentional. Even courts acknowledge human failings.

Providing the Records

The majority of the legal issues in the administration of reference service center around the third main area of reference service, that of providing the records themselves. These issues in turn fall into three general areas: establishment of researcher identity, credentials, and liability; delivery, custody, and return; surveillance and enforcement of regulations.

Establishment of Researcher Identity, Credentials, Liability

Most institutions have a well-defined procedure for handling researchers during initial visits. Some archives use a single form that includes both the researcher's registration and a statement of the research room rules, while other institutions separate these two parts. For subsequent enforcement of institutional regulations, it is important that the researcher receive, read, and acknowledge in writing the receipt of a copy of the rules. That means that if a single form is used, the researcher needs to receive a copy of it; if two parts are used, the registration form should include a statement that the researcher signs acknowledging the receipt of a copy of the research room rules.

The information collected on registration forms varies by archival institution.[6] Much of the information is for internal use in the institution (information on the anticipated final product of research, for example), but five items have special significance for potential legal matters: researcher identification and credentials; description of proposed research; subsequent use of information about the researcher; publication controls asserted by the institution; and indemnification of the archives from claims arising out of the use of the documents.

Identity. Fortunately archives have not reached the stage at which all researchers' names must be checked against the FBI's computer list of criminals. It is, however, prudent for the institution to maintain a list of known manuscript thieves and of persons who have previously been excluded from the institution for cause (destruction of property, threatening harm to persons, and so on). In the normal course of archival activity, all the institution will want to do is ensure that it has a good set of facts about the new user. These pieces of information include name, home and local address, institutional affiliation or occupation, and some form of identification number such as a number from a driver's license or other type of identification that includes a photograph that the person interviewing the potential researcher can check. It is unfortunately true that in recent instances of manuscript theft, the identification provided to the archives by the thief was false; however, even false information may on occasion help investigators establish a pattern. Some institutions require references, either in the form of a letter of introduction or a list of names provided by the researcher; these are purely an exercise unless the archives has a policy of checking the references.

[6]See, for example, the registration forms and regulations reprinted in the *Archival Forms Manual* (Chicago: Society of American Archivists, 1982).

Research Focus. While establishing identity, archives normally ask the researcher to provide a brief written description of proposed research. This is usually very sketchy, but it may be valuable if the archives subsequently faces charges that it did not provide all the information the researcher requested. The written statement the researcher provided at the entrance interview would be one bit of evidence of the nature of the request that was actually made.[7]

Subsequent Use of Researcher Information. Archivists have often disagreed about the ethics of telling one researcher of another researcher's work on the same research topic. For public archives, the advent of national and state privacy acts effectively barred the release of researchers' names and unique personal identifiers (such as a social security number) unless certain conditions were met, one of which was often the permission of the named individual. As a result, many archives have adopted the practice of including a statement on the researcher registration form that gives the archives the specific permission of the researcher to inform other researchers of his or her research topic. Absent such permission, public archives would be able to release researcher information only in accordance with the provisions of the state or federal privacy acts. Private archives remain in the position of having the choice of whether or not to disclose topics, but increasingly these archives also are adopting the procedure of a signed statement on the researcher registration.

Legally the issue is whether there is something inherently private in the research topic chosen by an individual and, if so, whether the archivist stands in a confidential relationship to the researcher with regard to that protectible information. Because research goes on for long periods of time and is often conducted in various institutions, it seems unlikely that an argument of "confidential relationship" merely on the basis of the topic alone could be sustained. If, however, the question is whether to reveal to another researcher the exact documents, files, photographs, or data used by the first researcher, the issue becomes more serious. Here the issue is business information, for the exact files used by a researcher may give the subsequent researcher either a clue to the direction of the work or, at the very least, to make the second person's research easier by pointing to a well-trod path. Of course, the second researcher has little way to know what the intellectual

position of the first researcher will be, but access to the exact files served provides the opportunity to do a bit of "reverse engineering." For those researchers whose livelihood is dependent on publication, whether for commercial revenue or for academic tenure, the stakes can be substantial.

But what are the legal remedies for a researcher if an archives provides information about the research to another person? Monetary damages are usually impossible to prove; most research makes no money whatsoever. Even in cases of commercial publication, the time lag between archival research and publication is often considerable and the waiting time for access to archival material is only one of the time factors involved in which of the two researchers would publish first. Perhaps if the first researcher was being harassed by the second, he might be able to get a court order to prevent the harassment and also to bar the archives from any further release of information about him.

In the usual case, this adds up to a lack of serious legal consequences for the archives that makes information on one researcher's materials available to another. This does not mean that archives should be encouraged to begin releasing all researcher information, however. Instead it simply means that ethical issues are paramount, not legal ones.

Publication Controls. Research registration forms often include a statement about permission to publish. In public archives with public records covered by freedom of information acts, governments do not assert control over subsequent use of the materials provided, but registration statements usually inform researchers that if a copyright persists in materials provided to them that it is the responsibility of the researcher to secure the appropriate permissions if publication of the copyrighted material is contemplated. For donated materials in either public or private archives, the publication restrictions must follow the provisions specified in the donor's deed of gift, and the researcher must be notified that the donated materials have publication restrictions that are exercised either by the archival institution or by some other person or institution acting on behalf of the donor. Private archives and archives holding donated or purchased materials where the donor has not specified publication control may themselves choose to control publication of materials. In those cases, the nature and scope of that control should be understood by the researcher at the inception of research.

The publication policy should be defined in writing and a copy should be signed by the researcher indicating acknowledgement (often it is part of the registration form). Whether a public institution such as a state college or university can require researchers to obtain its

---

[7] In its review of the Loewenheim case, the committee members found that part of the problem arose because Loewenheim changed the focus of his research a number of times, until it finally differed markedly from his initial written statement of research. The committee advised future researchers to "supplement their original application with a written statement describing any major project they may initiate while there." *Final Report*, p. 55.

permission before further reproducing its records is a question that should be considered with the university's counsel and the state attorney general. Private institutions can, of course, write anything they choose into an agreement to be signed by the researcher, although the institution's ability to police a complex set of publication restrictions may be limited.

The signing of such an agreement by the researcher constitutes a contract, and if the researcher published in violation of the contract the archives would have all the rights of a breach of contract, including the basis for a lawsuit. It seems unlikely, however, that a court would award damages to an archives that had not, for example, received a copy of a publication that relied heavily on its holdings, even if this did violate the researcher's agreement to provide such a copy. In fact, the most effective threat may not be legal at all but may be the option of barring the researcher from further use of the archives if he violates the agreement.[8]

Indemnification from Claims. Similar to the publication permissions, but pointing in exactly the opposite direction, are the "hold harmless" provisions sometimes written into researcher registration forms. Unlike the publication statements, which attempt to tie the researcher firmly to the archival institution, these hold-harmless statements generally seek to erect a wall between the actions of the researcher and the responsibilities of the archives. The statements usually are a variation of language such as "I agree to indemnify and hold harmless the _____ Archives, its officers, employees and agent, from and against all claims and actions arising out of my use of the documents." While there is no harm in requiring a researcher to sign such a statement, it is scant protection for the archives if problems do arise.

Consider the following example. Penniless graduate student Q comes to the archives to research the papers of famous author A. He has the archives make a copy of an unpublished short story to which the copyright has been retained by the family of A. He subsequently publishes part of the story in an article analyzing the image of the lawyer in author A's work. The family decides to sue. Logically they will sue the graduate student, but they will almost surely sue the archives as well.

Who would be the defendant with the greater ability to pay damages: the graduate student or the archives? In this case the archives would have to defend itself on the grounds of making copies based on fair use and would argue that the hold-harmless statement requires indemnification from Q for any damages awarded. The indemnification will be of no value since Q has no money and the archives will have to pay the judgment against it.

Consider another example. Researcher R, equally as impoverished as Q, being a free-lance writer, comes to the archives to use the donated records of the Schellenberg Steel Company. While the deed of gift clearly stipulates that the records must be screened to remove personal and medical information about living individuals, the archives decides to make all the materials available without screening and to rely on the hold-harmless clause to protect itself if the writer uses materials that should be restricted. The writer publishes an unflattering psychological profile of one of the company's former top managers. Enraged, the subject sues the writer and the archives. Here the hold-harmless clause will do no good whatsoever because the archives had not completed its legal responsibilities to restrict information before providing the records to the writer.

The hold-harmless clause is not a way to avoid responsibilities by shifting the burden to someone else's shoulders, in this case, to the researcher's. And even if the archives has completed its work, if the suit is brought against both the researcher and the archives (perhaps alleging that the archives violated the deed of gift when deciding to open the records to research without screening them first), the plaintiff's attorneys will certainly be looking for the defendant with "deep pockets," that is, with the ability to pay compensation.

The hold-harmless clause may in some cases help mitigate the damages assessed against an archives, but in no way will it prevent the archives from being made a party to a lawsuit. Such a clause might allow the archives in turn to sue the researcher if the archives has had to pay damages, but given the financial state of most researchers that is scant comfort, especially since to enforce the provision would mean again assuming the burden of litigation costs.

Delivery, Custody, and Return

Following the initial interview with the researcher, reference service proceeds to the delivery of the requested records. If questions later arise about loss or defacement of materials believed delivered to a researcher, the archives will need to be able to establish clearly what the researcher received to use and what the researcher returned to the custody of the archivist providing the service. Accurate recordkeeping is essential.

---

[8]In 1980-81 a case involving permission to publish received a good deal of publicity. A researcher named John Halberstadt had used the Thomas Wolfe papers at Harvard University's Houghton Library, having signed an agreement to obtain permission from both the executors and the library prior to publishing any books or articles based on the collection. When he did seek such permission, the library agreed but the estate twice refused. Halberstadt published anyway. The library barred him for one year and the estate took independent action against him. "Wolfe Papers Controversy," *SAA Newsletter* (July 1981): 14. For a case upholding contractual prepublication review, see *Snepp* v. *United States*, 444 U.S. 507 (1980).

In serious cases, if a theft is discovered in one body of materials provided to a researcher, the archives will want to use reference service records to check all other materials delivered to that individual to see if other items appear to be missing. This argues for retaining reference service records for a number of years after the researcher's final visit, for thefts are often not detected for months or even years.

Many archival institutions limit the number of items that a researcher can use at any one time. This makes it easier to establish whether the materials are all returned, but in large bodies of loose materials an item check is virtually impossible. Few institutions can afford to number and identify each document, as an English archives has done with the papers of former Prime Minister Winston Churchill.[9] Instead archives must rely on an attendance and receipting procedure. Researchers should sign a register each time they enter and leave the research area, thereby establishing dates, times, and patterns of behavior. Then, as each increment of material is delivered to the researcher, it should be clearly described in as much detail as possible on a dated reference service slip which the researcher must sign to acknowledge receipt of the documents. Upon occasion a researcher will resist signing such a sheet; the archives should have a firm policy that signing a reference service slip is a precondition for receipt of records and that a researcher refusing to sign will be denied materials. Then, when the researcher is finished with the items, the archivist returning them to storage from the research area should verify that the items delivered are there and should countersign and date the reference service slip. At least this provides evidence that the researcher had access to the items.

Archivists have debated the aesthetics and efficacy of stamping original documents to mark them as property of the archives. From a legal point of view, a document bearing the stamp of the institution in permanent ink is a much better candidate for a replevin action (especially if buttressed by reference records that suggest that the document in question was at one time in the possession of the archives) than is a document without a stamp. Stamps will not deter the thief who simply wants to keep the document for personal pleasure (most often documents with a connection to the individual's family), but they may deter the commercial thief.

Surveillance and Enforcement

Archives can take all reasonable steps to ensure that researchers comply with established institutional reference service regulations. "All reasonable steps" is, of course, vague, but clearly research institutions can have uniformed guards, can require that no bags, briefcases, or papers be brought into the research area, can use closed circuit cameras, and can search bags before the researcher is allowed to leave the building. Researchers should never be left unattended with original materials, whether in the search room itself or in storage areas. Ultimately, if an institution's surveillance practices come into question, a court would decide whether the precautions had been reasonable.[10]

Most enforcement problems are routine. Generally they involve drippy ink pens, eating, drinking, and smoking in the research areas, or the use of prohibited equipment (some institutions prohibit personal copiers, photographic lights, or tape recorders). These can be policed effectively only if the regulations that the researcher signed during the initial interview are clear and prohibit these activities. A posted copy of the regulations in the research area, preferably printed in large type, can help. A researcher who refuses to abide by the regulations must be asked to leave, quietly if possible, but if not, removal is more important than decorum.

If a researcher becomes verbally abusive, threatening, or violent, guards or police should be called at once. In archives researchers have threatened to shoot other researchers, to assault the staff, and to harm people not present. In such situations there is no time for heroics or amateur psychology: get the professionals as fast as possible.

If a staff member of the archives suspects that a researcher is defacing or attempting to steal documents, two things should be done immediately: the researcher should be prevented from continuing with his or her actions and a second staff member should be involved. Normally the easiest way to interrupt the individual's work is to engage him in conversation. This also has the advantage of stalling until a second staff member can arrive, if one is not already present in the area. If possible, the researcher should accompany the staff member to an area of the building away from the research room to avoid creating a major disturbance if other researchers are present. Guards should be alerted to prevent the researcher from leaving the building, and if the situation seems to involve a clear theft, police should be alerted. In general, the approach should be quiet but firm, and the archivist should remember to interrupt the action, keep talking, prevent the researcher from leaving until the issue is resolved, and make sure that there is a credible witness to the discussion (to avoid a case of my-word-against-your-word).

---

[9] Edwin Welch, "Security in an English Archives," *Archivaria* 1 (Summer 1976): 49.

[10] For example, a researcher might raise the issue of the right of an archives to search a bag, or a donor whose papers were stolen might question the adequacy of the preventive measures in effect at the time of the theft.

Every reference room should have a list of emergency telephone numbers, including that of the guard force and the police, and all staff should be instructed in the tactics of handling problem researchers. If the room has only one staff member in it at a time, it should be equipped with a buzzer that can be used to signal for help. A good discussion of the question of what to do if a staff member witnesses a theft can be found in the SAA basic manual on archival security.[11]

If a theft occurs and donated materials are stolen, might the donor bring a legal action against the repository? The answer depends on whether the donor retained specific rights, such as copyright, at the time of donation. If the donor did, then the question would be whether the archives was negligent in its surveillance and security practices. Once again, a court would decide, and a written security and surveillance procedure would be the archives' first line of defense. Recovery would probably be limited to the actual monetary damage sustained by the donor (which in most cases is probably small), unless the archives was flagrantly negligent in providing security. In the latter case, punitive penalties for larger amounts might be assessed. If the materials stolen were on deposit, and if the deposit agreement specified that the archives was liable for any physical damage to the materials, the archives is certainly open to a suit. Here the stakes are much higher, especially if the donor would have been able to take a tax deduction on the materials at the time of the final gift.

A special related issue in the service of records is the problem of identification and authentication of documents. Often reference archivists are asked whether the handwriting is Thomas Jefferson's, if the photograph was taken by Lewis Hine, does the map of the gold mine date from the 1880s. Some institutions have a policy against providing identification and authentication services, preferring instead to provide the researcher with similar documents and to let the researcher come to his own conclusion.[12] This conservative policy protects the institution, but it does not provide much assistance for the researcher. On the other hand, if the institution does provide authentication service and if a document on which an archivist has provided an identification is later involved in a legal proceeding, the archivist may be called to explain how he came to that identification and the archivist's credentials may be examined. Assuming no fraud or negligence and that the archivist was qualified (that is, the archivist was knowledgeable about the records and could render an informed opinion about their authenticity), responsibility for relying on the archivist's judgment would then lie with the person who had sought that opinion. So long as the archivist is qualified, no legal liability should arise.

Service of Restricted Records

A special problem in serving the records arises when researchers arrive to do research in restricted records. Normally an archives insists on written permission from the agency or donor that controls access, and cautious archives will insist that the permission be given directly to the archives by the access authority (not from the authority to the researcher). Not only will direct contact between authority and archives ensure that there truly is permission, but it also will ensure that the archives and the authority mutually understand the scope of the permission granted. (For example, an agency historian may have permission to use classified records generated by the State Department but not those created by the Central Intelligence Agency; a law firm might have negotiated an agreement with an agency to see case files on fare increases in bus rates but not cases files on train rates; a staff member of a legislative committee may be able to see certain restricted agency files but not the classified documents within them.) This sort of reference service is extremely tricky to handle, especially if the researcher is not fully familiar with the nature of archival research. It is vital that the archives and the authorizing agency understand each other completely, including whether the permission to read the documents includes the permission to take notes or to obtain copies (for instance, if a person is authorized to see the papers relating to his adoption, can he also make copies of those papers?).

While the archives must be in touch with the access authority in these cases, the archives normally will not go to the agency or donor on the researcher's behalf. The risk here is one of endorsement; that is, that the archives does not want to put itself in the position of guaranteeing to the authority the bona fides of the researcher. Instead, the archives normally provides the pertinent names and addresses to the researcher seeking access and advises the potential user to communicate directly with the authority and to ask the authority to

[11]Timothy Walch, *Archival Security* (Chicago: Society of American Archivists, 1978), pp. 18-21. See also the model law relating to library theft, pp. 26-27.

[12]"Authentication" in this paragraph is used in its common meaning of verifying that something is authentic or real. Authentication is also a legal term in the law of evidence, where it means the act or mode of giving authority or legal authenticity to a statute, record, or other written instrument, or a certified copy thereof, so as to render it legally admissible in evidence. A discussion of the legal meaning is found in Chapter 7, "Special Problems," in the "Custody and Authentication" section.

contact the archives with a decision.[13] In this way the authority can make its own judgment about the requester and inform the archives and the user of its decision. Normally these negotiations are carried out in writing, and often the archives informs the authority in advance that a request will likely be forthcoming.

After the access permission is granted, the materials must be reviewed for release. This can become extremely complicated, and great care must be taken to identify correctly those documents that can be released. For example, if classified documents are found in a file of personal papers and if the classifying agency has given permission for the researcher to see those classified documents, the documents must still be reviewed before release to see if the documents must be withheld on other grounds, such as a restriction in the donor's deed of gift that documents violating privacy rights of living individuals must be withheld. If the permission involves agency records, the archives will have to review the materials to ensure that, for example, these are bus fare files without train fare files intermixed. And so on.

The actual service of the records is also complicated. Researchers using restricted records cannot be seated in an area where researchers without such authorization can accidentally view the records. This normally means seating the researcher in a separate room and providing surveillance separate from the central surveillance arrangements. Needless to say, the researcher should sign the same logs and reference service forms that are required in the regular search room.

Providing Copies

The fourth basic form of reference service is providing copies of documents. The problems of copyright will be considered in the following chapter, but leaving that aside, the issues surrounding the furnishing of copies are what can be copied, who can copy it, what physical forms of copies will be provided, what charges will be levied, and whether certification services for copies will be provided.

All materials covered by a freedom of information act can be copied in accordance with the provisions of that law. Other materials and materials in private archives can be copied only with the permission of the archival institution. Rationally, if the archives permits note-taking but prohibits electrostatic copying of textual documents, all the archives is achieving is preventing an exact copy of the format and slowing the speed of research. This is not true of photographic materials, however, and some archives have placed strict limits on these reproductions or have effectuated such a limit by placing premium prices on reproductions. Whether or not these are socially desirable policies, they are certainly within the legal rights of the institution if the records are not covered by a freedom of information act.

Archivists faced with a request to copy slanderous statements or libelous writings or, in other days, pornographic items, have wondered whether these items can be copied and what the liability of an archives is in such cases.[14] Technically, passing along a libel or slander to another person is "publication" and may make the "passer" subject to a lawsuit for damages. In truth, however, in an archives this is an access problem not a copying problem. If the archives has permitted a researcher to see or hear the document, the damage has been done and the copying of the item does not compound the infraction.

Who can copy public records may be stated in a freedom of information act, but if the law is silent the general principle is that the legal owner of a document can control the right to copy. This is true for public records, private records, and donated materials (in accord with donor agreements). A quite different issue in copying records is whether researchers will be allowed to bring their own copying equipment into the institution to copy records. If the archives is willing to provide copying service for the researcher, it probably can deny the researcher's personal equipment. If, however, the archives does not provide copying for, say, color photographs and the researcher wants to bring in a camera, it could be argued that by denying the researcher the copy the institution is, in effect, preventing him from working with the materials. Based on a theory of impeding work, a legal argument might be made. Similarly, for documents covered by the federal Freedom of Information Act, copies must be available whether or not the institution owns the equipment; for example, computerized data must be made available even if the archives does not have a computer.

What physical forms of copies will be provided and what charges will be levied, including surcharges for such special services as copies provided within twenty-four hours, are the right of the institution to determine (an exception is public records if the forms and charges are specified in legislation). Some institutions have

---

[13]In rare instances the approving authority for a donor does not want his name and address revealed, usually in fear of harassment. When this happens, the archives must forward the researcher's written request to the authority and provide a sanitized copy of the transmittal to the researcher as proof that the request has been sent out. When the response comes back it must also be sanitized and provided to the researcher.

[14]Slander is spoken and libel is written. Normally these are civil infractions, but can become criminal if done with the purpose of inciting a breach of the peace. An archives could have slanderous materials in oral recordings, video tapes, and so on, but the majority of the problems are with libel in written documents.

adopted the practice of loans in the guise of sales, where a researcher can buy a microfilm copy of documents and can keep it as long as necessary, but periodically (say every six months) the researcher must check back with the archives and when he has finished using the film it must be returned to the institution. If the records provided under such a loan provision are covered by a freedom of information act, it would probably meet the letter of but not the spirit of the act. For other records, such an agreement is certainly legal, and if the researcher agrees to it, it is enforceable. Enforcement is, however, the problem. If the researcher does not return the film, what are the damages to the institution? What price can be placed on research visits? Would the institution be willing to pay court costs to bring a breach of contract suit? Would an institution bar the researcher from further use of records? What if the researcher lives in another state or even in another country?

Public archives often certify copies of documents in their holdings, either for legal purposes or for the personal use of the researcher. This is very different from authenticating the *original* document, for certifying a copy merely assures subsequent viewers that it is an authentic *copy* of a document in the possession of Archives X. These certifications make no claim about the original, only about the copy. Assuming that the staff members preparing the copies are entirely trustworthy, there is little risk in providing such certifications. Courts have repeatedly accepted certifications, thereby allowing the copies to go into evidence instead of the original documents. At worst, the archivist performing the certification may be required to testify that this is a copy of a document in the possession of the archives.

Loans

The final type of reference service is furnishing original documents on loan. Loans are most commonly requested either within the government or institution for research purposes or outside the institution for exhibition. (Occasionally archives are asked to loan original documents outside the institution for research purposes, such as through the interlibrary loan program, but except for copies of oral history transcripts, such requests are usually denied because of the risks of loss in transit.) Requests for loans within the institution, normally back to the office of origin or its successor, are difficult to deny, given the internal nature of the transaction. Archives, whether private or public, have no legal standing to deny such requests, and the ability of the archives to prevent wholesale loans is dependent primarily upon the status and authority of the archives within the institution. Most archives try to persuade intrainstitutional requesters to use the material in the archives facilities or to

use copies. If that fails, or if the amount of material requested is too large to make copying feasible, the archives should at minimum carefully document what items are loaned and obtain a signed receipt from the borrower. The receipt should include the acceptance by the borrower of the conditions of the loan, including maintenance of the original order, prohibition of annotations or insertions into the files, specified storage conditions, the right of the archives to check up on the documents at any time during the loan, the procedure for handling researchers who come to the archives for access to the loaned materials, and the fixed date for return. Again, the ability of the archives to enforce these conditions is entirely a matter of internal persuasiveness. Legally the documents remain within the institution that is the legal owner, and as long as the loan is documented the future legal interests in the documents are preserved.

Loans to outside institutions for exhibit purposes are very different. Here the archives has the legal right and responsibility to protect the institution's property, and almost any conditions can be established, if the lender and borrower can agree. These loan agreements should be as complete as possible, for they form the basis of the lawsuit if something should happen to the item while in transit or on exhibit. The documentation should be sufficient to show the chain of custody of the item, i.e., who is legally responsible for it at each stage of its existence. The borrower should be required to obtain an insurance policy for the value of the document, and it goes without saying that a document should not be loaned without retaining an excellent copy in the archives. A sample loan agreement from the National Archives is found in Appendix 3; others are found in the forms manual published by SAA.

A variation on the loan problem is the transfer of original archival materials to another organization for conservation or duplication. Once again the exchange of physical property should be documented thoroughly, with the recipient agreeing in writing to abide by the terms and conditions established by the archives. Because the transfer may be for purposes of transforming the physical character of the item, the transfer document should either refer to the contract under which the work is being done or recapitulate the specific terms of the contract.

Conclusion

The basis of reference service is the transfer of information in either original, copy, written or oral format from the archives to the researcher. Transfer, especially if physical property is involved, always involves risks, and the purpose of the law is to provide a framework within which such risks can be undertaken. The real question for an archives is not whether legal responsibility for use of the records can be placed on the user, but rather whether the costs of recovery are worth bringing legal action.

The foundation for the recovery of damages from a user is documentation showing that he or she was informed of and agreed to the rules of the institution, whether with respect to handling original materials, making and distributing copies, or exhibiting archival items. Providing reference service, like the records themselves, is fundamentally about documenting the actions at every step of the process. With good documentation, potential legal problems can be minimized or resolved without resort to lawyers and courts. That avoidance should be the goal of the archives.

6 Copyright and the Archives

Rewarding creativity by recognizing and protecting the property rights of the creator in the item created has long been public policy. In Article I, Section 8, of the United States Constitution, Congress is given the power "to promote the Progress of Science and useful Arts, by securing for limited Times to Authors and Inventors the exclusive Right to their respective Writings and Discoveries." It did not take long for Congress to exercise this power. As early as May 31, 1790, Congress passed the first copyright act "for the encouragement of learning, by securing the copies of maps, charts, and books to the authors and proprietors of such copies, during the times therein mentioned."[1] The nearly two hundred years since the first copyright act have seen numerous amendments and revisions to the copyright law; the latest, on October 19, 1976, was a total revision of the act.[2]

The revised act, which became effective on January 1, 1978, provides copyright protection to literary, musical, and dramatic works; pictorial, graphic, and sculptural works; pantomines and choreographic works; and sound recordings, motion pictures, and other audiovisual works.[3] A further revision in 1980 extended copyright to cover computer programs.[4] It is safe to assume that all the holdings of an archives are subject to the copyright protection afforded by the new act.[5]

This chapter will highlight the significant parts of the act, discuss fair use and copying, outline the potential financial losses an archives can suffer for violation of copyright, and offer some solutions to fair use and copying problems in the form of an "archivist's loophole." Finally some specific copyright problems will be identified and addressed.

The Act

The Copyright Act of 1976 changed the time copyright protection begins (or "attaches"), changed the duration of copyright, made registration optional, gave the owner of the copyright certain exclusive rights, and provided for limitation on the exclusive rights. Examination of the new copyright practices requires an understanding of previous copyright methods. Prior to 1978 unpublished materials were protected by common law copyright under the laws of the individual states. At common law an author had a property right in his manuscript and the exclusive right to copy the manuscript until he permitted general publication (this was also known as literary property right). This right was perpetual and passed by inheritance to heirs so long as the work remained unpublished. Upon publication the manuscript was protected only if it contained a notice of copyright and was registered with the U.S. Copyright Office. All of this has changed. As of January 1, 1978, any work created is automatically copyrighted when created and all rights under common law or state statutory law are preempted by the new act. Now publication is no longer the key to copyright protection and the copyright act provides the exclusive copyright protection.

The duration of copyright protection has also changed, from twenty-eight years plus one renewal of twenty-eight years to the life of the author plus fifty years. The act established various key dates and terms of years for copyright protection, depending on whether the work was created, published, or copyrighted before January 1, 1978.[6] Of primary importance to archivists is the provision that works created before January 1, 1978, and not previously copyrighted nor in the public

---

[1]1 Stat. 124, §15. Copyright by definition is a limited monopoly granted by the sovereign to the creator of a work.

[2]*United States Code*, Title 17.

[3]17 U.S.C. §102(a).

[4]17 U.S.C. §101; 17 U.S.C. §117; *Apple Computer* v. *Franklin Computer Corp.*, 714 F.2d 1240 (3d Cir. 1982); *Tandy Corp.* v. *Personal Micro Computers, Inc.*, 524 F.Supp. 171 (D.C. CA 1981).

[5]The major exception here is that any work of the United States government cannot be copyrighted. The U.S. can, however, own copyrights transferred to it. 17 U.S.C. §105. This prohibition does not apply to other public bodies. The prohibition also does not mean that the records of the United States do not contain copyrighted material; if the government obtains, say, a copyrighted article from a private source and incorporates that into the government's files, the copyright protection remains on the article and with the creator. Similarly, private letters to the government and found in the government's files retain private copyright.

[6]17 U.S.C. §301 *et. seq.*

domain are now protected by the life plus fifty years rule, but in no event does the protection expire before December 31, 2002. That means, for example, that an unpublished letter by W. C. Fields is protected by copyright until the end of 2002, even though the life plus fifty years rule would have made it available in 1996 (he died in 1946).

Under the new act, when a work is published a notice of copyright must be placed on all copies but registration with the Copyright Office is not required. There are provisions regarding corrections for the omission of the notice and copyright is not automatically lost if corrective action is taken. However, before a suit of infringement can be brought and before statutory damages or attorney's fees can be recovered, the work, whether published or unpublished, must be registered.[7] (The significance of this requirement will be discussed in the third section of this chapter.)

Finally, the act, subject to certain exceptions, gives a number of exclusive rights to the owner of the copyright.[8] These include the right to copy, publish, transfer ownership, or prepare derivative works and, in the case of some works, display the work publicly. To exercise his right to transfer the copyright, the owner must document the transfer in writing and sign the transfer document. The transfer of ownership may be recorded in the Copyright Office and is, therefore, often referred to as "recordation." No infringement action can be brought by the new owner until the transfer instrument is recorded.[9]

Since all works are now automatically copyrighted upon creation (often described as "from the moment you lift your pencil"), the archivist must presume that, unless the copyright has been donated or sold to the archives, every item in the holdings that comes from a nonfederal source is copyrighted and reproduction could be an infringement of the copyright. Ownership of the copyright is not the same as ownership of the physical object. Transfer of the physical object of the work does not transfer ownership of the copyright because a specific transfer of the copyright by the owner of the copyright is required. In other words, merely donating a letter to an archives does not transfer copyright. A specific provision must be included in the transfer instrument if copyright is to pass from donor to archives.[10]

The presumption cannot be made that the person donating the letter (for example) to the archives owns the copyright to that letter. Only if the donor is the person who created the item or a person to whom the copyright has been formally transferred does the donor own the copyright. Archivists also cannot assume that a phrase in the donor's deed giving the archives "all copyright in such of the materials as are unpublished" covers all the materials in the donation. A donor can only transfer such copyright as he holds, and he clearly does not hold, for example, the copyright in a letter he received, except in the unlikely event of specific copyright transfer from the letter-writer.[11]

The reverse is also true, that transfer of the copyright does not transfer the ownership of the physical object. For example, an archives may own a letter in its collection but not hold the copyright to it, and the copyright in the letter may be passed, say, from one family member to another by recordation but without any notice to or withdrawal of the letter from the archives.

Finally, copyright does not protect ideas; that is the role reserved for the patent laws. Copyright merely protects exact, unique expression of an idea. Nor does copyright restrict access. Copyright restricts copying and certain types of use, such as performance of a play, but not simple viewing or hearing.

Fair Use and Archival Reproduction

The copyright rules are strict and permit no copying unless the archives owns the copyright. Congress, however, enacted two important exceptions to these exclusive rights of the copyright owner. To archivists, the most important of these exceptions are fair use, covered by Section 107 of the copyright act, and reproduction by libraries and archives, covered by Section 108.[12] The archival implications of fair use and reproduction by libraries and archives can be understood thoroughly only by first examining the concepts separately and then seeing how they relate to each other.

§107 Fair Use

The common law doctrine of fair use was developed by the courts to shield some forms of copying from the literal implications of the former copyright act. Over time the doctrine of fair use had been tailored to balance the public's right of access to knowledge of general importance with the author's right to protect his intellectual creation. When writing the new copyright act, Congress decided to codify the existing judicial doctrine of fair use. Section 107 provides that fair use of a copyrighted work "for purposes such as criticism, comment, news reporting, teaching (including multiple copies for classroom use), scholarship, or research, is not an infringement of copyright." To determine whether a use

---

[7]17 U.S.C §411-412; *Burns v. Rockwood Distributing Co.*, 481 F.Supp. 841 (D.C. IL 1979).

[8]17 U.S.C. §106.

[9]17 U.S.C. §205(d).

[10]17 U.S.C. §202.

[11]17 U.S.C. §201(d).

[12]Other limitations on exclusive rights are found in §109-118.

is a fair use, the section specifies four factors to be considered: (1) the purpose and character of the use, including whether such use is of a commercial nature or is for nonprofit educational purposes; (2) the nature of the copyrighted work; (3) the amount and substantiality of the portion used in relation to the copyrighted work as a whole; and (4) the effect of the use upon the potential market for or value of the copyrighted work. Although these factors are clear and simple to state, they provide no easy formula to determine what is fair use. Each use of copyrighted materials must be tested against all four factors.

Faced with a copyright question a court will balance the use against the factors to determine whether the use is fair use; there is no set formula. There is a requirement that the new use be a productive one such as criticism, comment, news reporting, teaching, scholarship, or research. As stated by Justice Harry Blackmun in his dissenting opinion in *Sony Corporation of America* v. *Universal City Studios*:

> The fair use doctrine must strike a balance between the dual risks created by the copyright system: on the one hand, that depriving authors of their monopoly will reduce their incentive to create, and on the other, that granting authors a complete monopoly will reduce the creative ability of others. The inquiry is necessarily a flexible one, and the endless variety of situations that may arise precludes the formulation of exact rules. But when a user reproduces an entire work and uses it for its original purpose, with no added benefit to the public, the doctrine of fair use usually does not apply. There is then no need whatsoever to provide the ordinary user with a fair use subsidy at the author's expense.[13]

Thus, making a copy of a document for a researcher is almost always Section 107 fair use because it is a productive use as defined in the law, and the reproduction is not for its original purpose but for further work of added benefit to the public.

§108 Archives and Library Copying

In order to assist libraries, archives, and scholars, Congress enacted Section 108, "Limitations on exclusive rights: reproduction by libraries and archives." Where Section 107, fair use, applies to everyone copying a work, Section 108 applies only to a library or an archives copying a work. Section 108 provides many standards to govern copying and is a confusing attempt to specify when copying by a library and archives is permissible. (Sections 106, 107, and 108 are reproduced in Appendix 4.)

Even though Section 108 is difficult to interpret, archivists need to understand basically how it permits copying. For an institution to copy a work without infringement, the institution (1) must be open to the public or open to researchers in a specialized field, (2) must not be copying for a commercial purpose, and (3) must include a notice of copyright in the copies produced.[14] Furthermore, the institution's copying activities cannot be part of a concerted or systematic copying of works; however, isolated and unrelated copying of the same material on separate occasions is permitted. This means, for example, that the archives cannot reproduce five hundred copies of a copyrighted letter with the intent of selling them by mail. It does not prohibit normal systematic microfilming for preservation and reference purposes.

Having met tests 1, 2, and 3, an institution can copy certain works (as noted below) at any time if the purpose is preservation, security, or replacement of the work. An unpublished work can be copied for preservation or security purposes within the institution or for the deposit for research use in another institution that is either open to the public or open to researchers in a specialized field.[15] Published works can be copied for the institution itself or for another research institution to replace a damaged, deteriorating, lost, or stolen work if an unused replacement cannot be found at a fair price.[16] Copying of musical works,[17] pictorial, graphic, or sculptural works or motion pictures is permitted *only* under these provisions for preservation, security, or replacement of the work.

Different provisions apply for copying a work for a user (an institution at times can be a user, too). If a user requests an institution to copy a work and provide the copies to him, before proceeding to copy the institution should have a reasonable belief that the copy will be used for private study, scholarship, or research. The notice shown below must be posted at the place where the institution accepts copy orders; it must as well be placed on any order form for copies.

NOTICE
WARNING CONCERNING COPYRIGHT
RESTRICTIONS

The copyright law of the United States (Title 17, United States Code) governs the making of photocopies or other reproductions of copyrighted material.

---

[13]*Sony Corporation of America* v. *Universal City Studios*, 52 LW 4090, 4106 (1984).

[14]17 U.S.C. §108(a). By "commercial purpose" the act intends that copying is not being done to make profits that should belong to the owner of the copyright. The institution can charge for the costs of copying. The notice of copyright is the same as that required by Section 401 and must include the copyright symbol, the date, and the name of the owner of the copyright. If the archives is not sure that the material is copyrighted it should put in a notice with as much information as it has and a warning that the material may be copyrighted.

[15]17 U.S.C. §108(b).

[16]17 U.S.C. §108(c).

[17]17 U.S.C. §108(h). A "musical work" is the sheet music, not the sound recording.

Under certain conditions specified in the law, libraries and archives are authorized to furnish a photocopy or other reproduction. One of these specified conditions is that the photocopy or reproduction is not to be "used for any purpose other than private study, scholarship or research." If a user makes a request for, or later uses, a photocopy or reproduction for purposes in excess of "fair use," that user may be liable for copyright infringement.

The institution reserves the right to refuse to accept a copying order if, in its judgment, fulfillment of the order would involve violation of copyright law.[18]

These requirements apply whether the archives is copying an unpublished or published work for a user. The only copying distinction the statute makes is between (1) a copy made for a user of a small portion of a work or one article or contribution to a collection or periodical and (2) a copy made for a user of all or substantially all of a work. In the latter case, the institution must first satisfy itself that a copy of the work cannot be found at a fair price before agreeing to make a copy.[19] If an institution has an unsupervised copying machine that is made available for users, the institution may escape liability for copies made on it if the equipment displays a notice that copying may be subject to the copyright law.[20] None of these exceptions to the exclusive rights of the copyright holder excuse the user from liability for infringement unless his subsequent use of the copied material is protected by Section 107 on fair use.[21]

Relationship of §107 and §108

As this brief review of the statutory provisions demonstrates, there are no easy formulas to determine when copying is permitted. Basically, under section 108, the archives can copy if it is for (1) preservation, security, or replacement or (2) for a user for research purposes and is not of a musical work, pictorial, graphic, or sculptural work, or motion picture. The flow charts in Figures 7, 8, and 9 explain sections 107 and 108 and demonstrate their relationship to each other. The three charts show the copying permitted when an archives makes a copy for itself or another research institution and when a user requests a copy of the same.

---

[18]17 U.S.C. §108(d) and (e). For regulations concerning the print size and location of the notice see 37 CFR §201.14.

[19]17 U.S.C. §108(e).

[20]17 U.S.C. §108(f)(1).

[21]The Register of Copyrights has taken the position that §108(d) and (e) apply only to published materials. See Carolyn A. Wallace, "Archivists and the New Copyright Law," *Georgia Archive* 6 (Fall 1978): 1. The register's position is not supported by the language of the two subsections or by legislative history and is wholly the opinion of the register.

Infringement and Liability

Every time a copy is made, a possibility exists that the person making the copy is infringing upon the exclusive rights of the owner of the copyright. Despite this risk, copying goes on without many suits for infringement. The reasons for this are varied, but chief among them is that the damages caused by the copying are minimal or hard to prove. Just as walking across someone else's yard is committing a trespass without causing substantial damage, so, too, copying can occur without substantial damage.

Anyone who violates the exclusive rights of the owner of the copyright is deemed an infringer of the copyright. The owner of the copyright has a number of remedies against an infringer. These remedies are: (1) injunction (prohibition) against further infringement, (2) recovery of actual damages, (3) recovery of the profits made by the infringer, (4) recovery of statutory damages, and (5) recovery of costs and attorney's fees. It is easier to obtain an injunction in a copyright infringement case than in an ordinary civil case; however, if copying is done by an archives an injunction against further infringement is not a likely remedy because the copying in most instances is a single occurrence, not continuous copying, and the owner of the copyright has adequate protection through the recovery of money damages. (A more likely candidate for injunctive relief would be, for example, a play being produced every night in violation of the copyright.)

A more probable consequence of a suit against an archives for infringement would be recovery of damages and profits. The infringer of a copyright is liable either for the copyright owner's actual damages and any additional profits of the infringer or for statutory damages.[22] Actual damages may be difficult to prove and there may be no profits; consequently, prior to final judgment in the suit the copyright owner must decide whether to take statutory damages or actual damages plus profits — recovery of both is not permitted. If the court decides the infringement did occur, an award of statutory damages cannot be less than $250 nor more than $10,000 (the $10,000 ceiling can be increased to $50,000 if it is proven that the infringement was willful). The possibility of an award of the maximum amount of statutory damages increases if the infringement was committed willfully and, conversely, the possibility of an award of the minimum amount of statutory damages increases if the infringement was innocent. In addition

---

[22]17 U.S.C. §504. Actual damages here means the real money lost to the copyright owner because of the unauthorized copying: in other words, what could the copyright owner receive for the sale of his exclusive rights. Statutory damages are those specified by statute — in this case, particular sums of money.

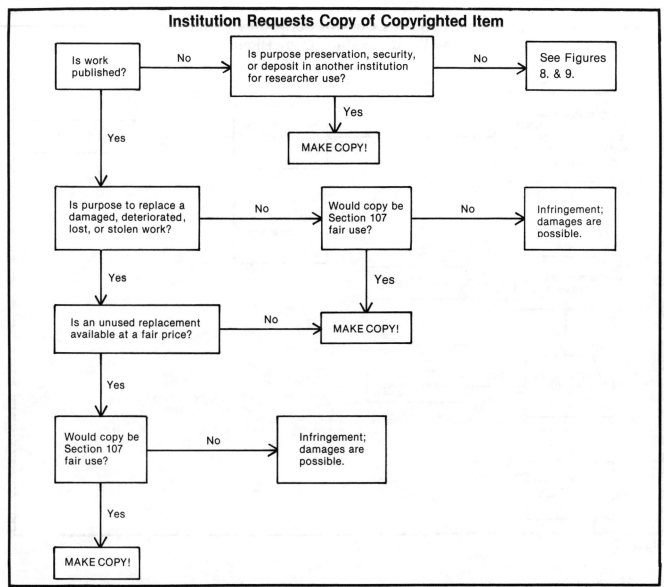

Figure 7

to either the actual damages and profits or the statutory damages, the court may also award the recovery of the costs of bringing the lawsuit, including reasonable attorney's fees, to the prevailing party.

There are, however, limitations on the recovery allowed. No suit for infringement can be instituted until the work is registered.[23] Furthermore, upon registration, no statutory damages or attorney fees can be recovered for any infringement of an unpublished work occuring before registration: only actual damages plus profits of the infringer can be recovered. This scheme of damage recovery leads us to the "archivist's loophole."

If the archives contains mostly unpublished materials that have never been registered with the Register of

Copyrights, and if the archives infringes on the copyright, the owner of the copyright can only recover his actual damages plus the profits of the archives. No statutory damages or attorney's fees would be allowed because the copyrighted item was not registered at the time of the infringement. In most cases, the archives would have received no profit for making a copy and actual damages (what the copy would have been sold for) would be nearly impossible to prove. Thus, if an archives follows the procedures outlined above in the discussion of Section 108, it is doubtful that it will be sued when the owner of the copyright can recover very little if anything.

This conclusion brings back the advice from Chapter 2 on deeds of gift for donated materials: always obtain the copyright. Then the archives can make copies and,

---

[23]17 U.S.C. §411(a).

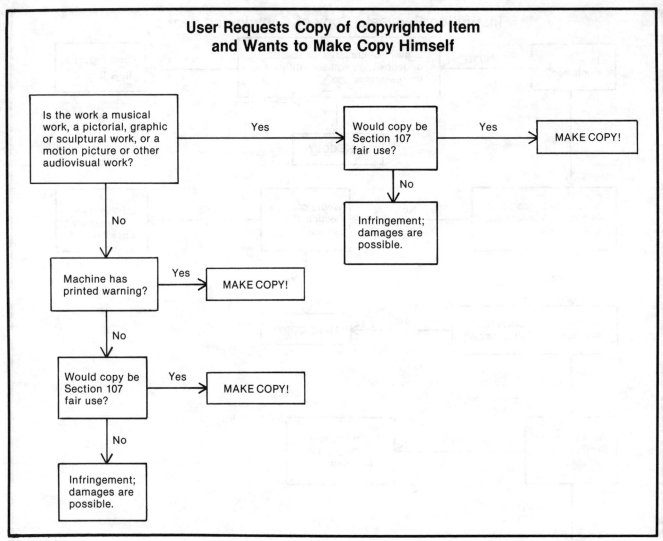

**User Requests Copy of Copyrighted Item
and Wants to Make Copy Himself**

Figure 8

by putting the notice of copyright on the copies, restrict the number of copies made by the recipient. If the archives owns the copyright, it can never be successfully sued for infringement. For those items that were donated but for which the donor does not hold the copyright (all his incoming correspondence, for example) the archives must follow the rules for copying.

If an archives is located within the institution whose records it holds, the institutional records are copyrighted by the institution and can be copied by the archives in accordance with institutional policy. (Naturally, the instituion does not hold the copyright on incoming correspondence from private sources and the archives must follow the copyright law's general rules for copying those documents.) In addition, if an institution holds records of the United States or copies of such records, these can also be copied at will because the law specifies that they cannot be copyrighted.

In sum, archivists must recognize the difference between access and copyright. If there are no access restrictions, a researcher can always have access to copyrighted material. It is only when the researcher wants a copy that the rules on copying arise. If the copy request is a Section 108 copying, a copy can be made; if not, then the copying must be a Section 107 fair use copying. Section 107 is the best support to allow copying for research purposes. All of this requires a responsible archivist who knows that is being copied, for whom, and for what purpose.

Special Problems in Copyright

Many questions on copyright can arise daily within an archives. These questions usually revolve around what copyright the archives can hold by virtue of its creative activity and what copyright researchers can hold in the documents in the custody of the archives.

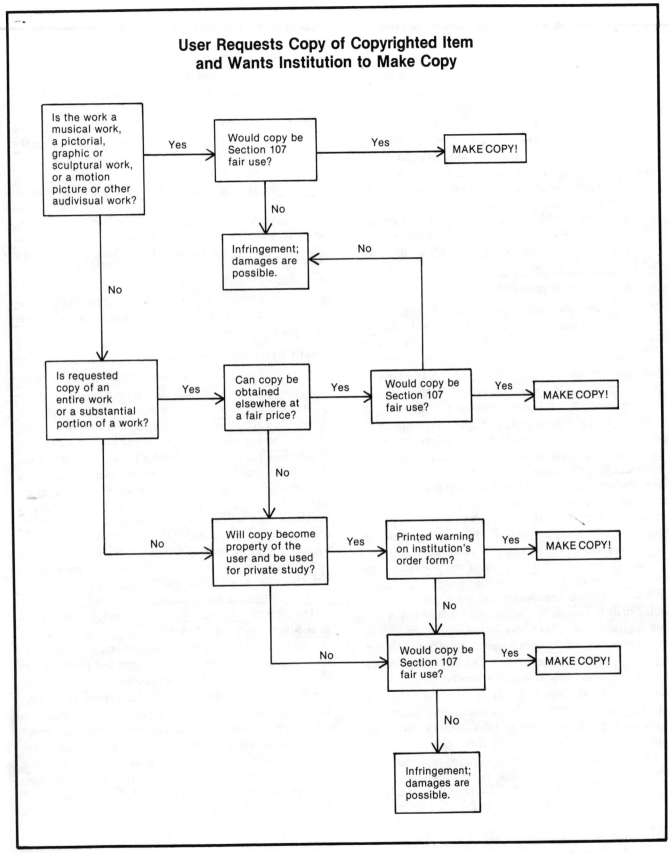

Figure 9

Copyright of Facts

The first question is whether facts can be copyrighted. Although there is a split in authority in cases addressing this issue, the better reasoned view is that one cannot copyright facts discovered in the course of research.[24] The reason for this is obvious when considered in the context of the copyright act. The purpose of the act is to provide financial incentives to those adding to the body of existing knowledge by creating an original work. The act does not force others to obtain the facts and do the research independently; the act instead allows a subsequent researcher to build upon the prior work without unnecessary duplication in order to create a new original work. The caveat is that the new work must be truly new and cannot be a mere paraphrase of the prior work.[25] Thus, the thrust of the act is that facts are freely available and cannot be copyrighted.

Copyright and Documentary Publication

Even though facts cannot be copyrighted, the organization of facts can. Furthermore, the organization of documents can be copyrighted as well. Take the case of a microfilm publication of documents in the public domain (such as documents created by the federal government or documents on which the copyright has expired). The organization of the documents on the film, if original, can be copyrighted, as can any accompanying pamphlets, notes, or editorial remarks. However, someone could take one or more of the documents and reproduce them because the documents themselves are in the public domain — the person could not just reproduce the entire work, for that would violate fair use. This means that if the archives is requested to prepare a microfilm of a body of records, filmed in the order in which the archives has arranged them for general public use, the archives can keep a copy of the microfilm and sell all or part of it to others — the arrangement is the archives' not the requester's. A more difficult case would arise if a researcher wants records filmed in a certain logical order. There may be enough originality in the arrangement of the documents that the requester can copyright the arrangement and the archives may not sell a copy of the uniquely arranged microfilm to others. Of course, if the archives is a private one and holds the copyright to the documents being microfilmed, it can require as a condition prior to microfilming that it be allowed to retain a copy and sell it to others.

The most common case of microfilm reproduction, however, does not involve all public domain or all private documents. Instead the microfilm normally is a mix of public domain documents and documents whose copyright is held by private citizens, or private documents produced by the institution of which the archives is a part and documents whose copyright is held by private citizens. Can the archives film and sell? Can a researcher uniquely arrange and copyright such mixed films? Here is where the archivist's loophole comes into play. Even if the archives does not hold copyright in the items filmed, it is likely that the items are not registered, making monetary penalties for the reproduction and sale of the film remote. It also means that so long as copyright is asserted in the organization of the items and the explanatory texts but not in the items themselves, copyright can be defended. So the answer remains that an archives can film and sell and, as long as it is not the National Archives, copyright its film. The answer to the researcher is that he can uniquely arrange and copyright the films made of a mix of public and private documents, so long as he does not attempt to copyright the documents themselves.

Oral History and Copyright

Oral history interviews are a unique copyright problem, since it is only through the intervention of the interviewer that the interviewee's words are recorded and it is only that capture of the exact sequence of words that makes the copyright possible. Oral history tapes and transcripts present a problem as to who has the copyright to an oral history interview: the interviewee or the interviewer? Generally, the interviewer and the interviewee each hold the copyright to their own words; a single oral history tape or transcript embodies two copyrights.[26] Of course, if either the interviewer or the interviewee is relating facts or words spoken by others, they cannot copyright that portion of their spoken words.[27] For this reason, when the interviewee is a public figure, most of his words may not be copyrighted.

The general rule on who holds the copyright to an oral history interview has some exceptions. As noted previously, the United States cannot copyright a work, so in the case of an oral history interview prepared for the United States, either by an employee or contractor, the interviewer's words can not be copyrighted. This may also be true for another public organization such as a state archives if the state legislation does not permit the archives to hold copyright or waives copyright generally; otherwise, state archives can copyright the words of interviewers. Private organizations can copyright the words of the interviewer if they wish to do so. Under what circumstances a federal employee being

---

[24] *Miller v. Universal City Studios, Inc.*, 650 F.2d 1365 (5th Cir. 1981); *Suid v. Newsweek Magazine*, 503 Fed. Supp. 146 (D.DC 1980).

[25] *Harper & Row Publishers, Inc. v. Nation Enterprises*, 723 F.2d 195, 205 (2d Cir. 1983).

[26] *Suid v. Newsweek.*

[27] *Harper & Row v. Nation.*

interviewed can claim copyright in his words is unclear, although it is the position of the Society for History in the Federal Government that an off-duty employee or one who is not in normal job status can retain copyright. In most cases the nonfederal interviewee will have copyright in his words and the archives should seek the transfer of his copyright to the archives. Remember that the transfer must be recorded; without recordation the archives could not bring a suit for infringement if some other institution or organization uses the words of the interview.

Conclusion

Copyright problems can be complicated. Archivists must learn to recognize copyright problems when they arise; however, because they can involve complex issues, self-diagnosis and medication is not recommended. Upon spotting a potential copyright problem, seek professional assistance from a lawyer. And do it promptly, especially if an infringement is suspected: copyright colds can quickly turn into pneumonia.

7 Special Problems

Archivists occasionally are faced with problems that are not uniquely archival in nature but are problems nonetheless. These problems relate to conflicts over the perceived necessity of having the original document rather than a copy. The first part of this chapter discusses continuous custody and whether a copy of a document is legally sufficient. The second part of the chapter addresses the issues surrounding the recovery of an original document that has strayed from the archives. Both parts ask the question, "Would a copy be sufficient?"

Custody and Authentication

In England, from about the thirteenth century on, nobles and laymen and even some peasants documented their transfers of property through use of written charters (essentially deeds). Curiously, England did not simultaneously develop the notarial system on the Roman model, where each document was precisely dated and written by an authorized scribe or notary who registered a copy of the document in a record kept by a public authority. Instead, as documents proliferated, questions about the authenticity of some of the charters arose and legal problems multiplied. English common law eventually developed a series of tests whereby the

existing documents could be authenticated. A key question in authenticating documents was in whose hands the documents had lain. For the royal government, the easiest demonstration that a governmental document was authentic was to show that it had been written by a government official and thereafter had been officially maintained by the government. This is the root of the English archival concept of continuous custody which argues that if a document is to be of archival quality it must have an unbroken chain of responsible custodians.[1]

The United States adopted the common law from England and with it the practice of authenticating documents for use in legal proceedings. A common law concept that directly affected questions of authenticity is the "best evidence rule," which basically says that the original document is the best evidence. The reason for the rule is that copies of documents were originally made by hand and there was a substantial question of the accuracy of a human-hand copy of an original. The advent of modern methods of making a copy and the introduction of modern rules of evidence changed the common law tests of authenticity. These new rules, adopted in 1975, now govern the admissibility of evidence in federal courts.[2]

The rules first make a bow to the best evidence rule and require that the original of the writing, recording, computer tape, or photograph be produced in legal proceedings.[3] What the rules first require they then take away by allowing the admission into evidence of a duplicate so long as there is no genuine question of the authenticity of the original or no unfairness in admitting a duplicate.[4] Thus carbon copies, microfilm copies, and electrostatic and photostatic copies of writings and recordings such as charge card receipts, purchase orders, checks, and passports are routinely admissible.[5] Most importantly, the original is never required if the original is lost or destroyed.[6] Thus originals can be microfilmed and destroyed and the microfilm copy would be admissible as if it were the destroyed original.

The practice of using a copy instead of an original is further bolstered by the rules on authentication.

---

[1]M.T. Clanchy, *From Memory to Written Record: England, 1066–1307* (Cambridge: Harvard University Press, 1979), pp. 38, 48-53, 120-125, 232-236.

[2]Most states have similar rules, but for ease of distinction only the federal rules will be discussed.

[3]§1002, Federal Rules of Evidence (hereafter Fed. R. Evid.)

[4]§1001(4) and 1003, Fed. R. Evid.

[5]*U.S.* v. *Rangel*, 585 F.2d 344 (8th Cir. 1978); *CTS Corp.* v. *Piher Intern. Corp.*, 527 F.2d 95 (6th Cir. 1975), cert. den. 424 U.S. 978; *Williams* v. *U.S.*, 404 F.2d 1372 (5th Cir. 1968), cert. den. 394 U.S. 992; *Myrick* v. *U.S.*, 332 F.2d 279 (5th Cir. 1964), cert. den. 377 U.S. 952; *U.S.* v. *Benedict*, 647 F.2d 928 (9th Cir. 1981), cert. den. 454 U.S. 1087.

[6]§1004(1), Fed. R. Evid.

Authentication is the process to determine whether the item sought to be introduced as evidence in a legal proceeding is authentic, i.e., it is what the party seeking to introduce it claims it is.[7] Perhaps the easiest way to authenticate an item is to have a witness state that it is what it is claimed to be.[8] Public records or reports that are recorded in a public office or kept in the public office where they should be kept will also meet the authentication test.[9] Further, a certified copy of a public record is presumed to be authentic.[10]

Of special importance to archivists is the ancient document rule. (Do not be thrown off by the word "ancient"; it means that the document has been in existence for more than twenty years.)[11] The requirements of the ancient document rule are that the document (1) is over twenty years old, (2) appears authentic, and (3) is found where it would be expected to be found.[12]

A document having been shown to be authentic is not necessarily admissible; the document must still be relevant and not be hearsay. Normally a document is introduced to get into evidence the contents of the document. A document is a classic example of hearsay, i.e., an out of court statement made by someone other than the witness that is introduced for the truth of the statement.[13] (A writing is considered a statement for the purposes of the hearsay rule.)[14] The reason for the hearsay rule is the principle of American jurisprudence that the witness must be in court so that the truth of his statements can be tested under cross-examination. With hearsay, one cannot examine the maker of the statement.

But just as there is a hearsay rule, there are also many exceptions to the rule; so many, in fact, that one may question whether there really is a hearsay rule at all. The exceptions most important to an archivist are those affecting records of businesses, public bodies, religious organizations, families, and ancient records (over twenty years old).[15] The reason for these exceptions is that years of experience have shown that all of these records have a high degree of reliability.

The records of a business are admissible even though they are hearsay if it is shown by one with knowledge that the record was made routinely as part of the practice of the business. The custodian of the documents or a knowledgeable person must testify as to the record-keeping practices of the business. The archivist may be called to testify as the custodian and if called must describe, to the best of his knowledge, how the business makes and keeps its records. Public records, reports, or data compilations are admissible if they show the activities of the agency or are required by law to be prepared. Regularly kept religious records of births, deaths, marriages, divorces, and similar personal or family history records are admissible as are marriage, baptismal, and other similar certificates. Similarly, family history in family Bibles, genealogies, or other like records are also admissible. Finally, properly authenticated ancient records are also an exception to the hearsay rule.

All of the above — continuous custody, the best evidence rule, hearsay — are important in determining the admissibility of a document as evidence in court. Obviously, if one can show continuous, unbroken custody any challenge to their authenticity would be difficult to sustain. The law, however, does not have such a strict requirement. Just like the modern archivist, the law is interested in the regularity of the process. The value of the records as evidence rests in the way in which the records were created and maintained. Records kept together, respecting provenance and in their original order, with a clear and demonstrable chain of custody are the best candidates for admission as evidence in court.

Replevin: Recovering the Missing Document

Every decade seems to have a major lawsuit in which the dispute is the possession of documents or books that have strayed from an institution into private hands. In the 1950s the case involved the Lewis and Clark expedition papers;[16] in the 1960s the case involved Spanish and Mexican documents from the seventeenth through nineteenth centuries;[17] in the 1970s the case involved indictments signed by a signer of the Declaration of Independence;[18] and the case of the 1980s most surely will be the one involving the auction of fifty-eight rare Hebrew books and manuscripts that had been spirited out of Nazi Germany.[19] The actions to recover these items have become lumped together under the heading

[7]§901(a), Fed. R. Evid.

[8]§901(b)(1), Fed. R. Evid.

[9]§901(b)(7), Fed. R. Evid.

[10]§902(4), Fed. R. Evid.

[11]§901(b)(1)(C), Fed. R. Evid.

[12]§901(b)(A) and (C), Fed. R. Evid. If an ancient document is found in another location it may have to be authenticated by means of expert testimony saying, "Yes, that is George Washington's signature."

[13]§801(c), Fed. R. Evid.

[14]§801(a), Fed. R. Evid.

[15]§803(6), (8), (11), (12), (13), and (16), Fed. R. Evid.

[16]*United States* v. *First Trust Company of Saint Paul*, 146 F.Supp. 652 (D.C. MN 1956), aff'd 251 F.2d 686 (8th Cir. 1958).

[17]*Sender* v. *Montoya*, 73 N. Mex. 287, P.2d 860 (1963); *Historical Society of New Mexico* v. *Montoya*, 74 N. Mex. 285, 393 P.2d 21 (1964); *United States* v. *Sender*, Civil No. 14965-2, United States District Court, Western District of Missouri.

[18]*State* v. *West*, 31 N.C. App. 431, 229 S.E.2d 826 (1976), aff'd 293 N.C. 18, 235 S.E.2d 150 (1977).

[19]*New York Times*, July 15, 1984: E9; August 16, 1984: C17; August 30, 1984: C17.

of "replevin," an important legal action, the elements of which must be understood by archivists.[20]

The Nature of Replevin

A number of actions developed in the common law to recover possession of or obtain damages for the loss of personal property. All property is either real property (real estate) or personal property (personalty). Those actions relating to the recovery of personal property were known as "replevin," "detinue," and "trover." Replevin is an action to recover personal property taken, while detinue is an action to recover personal property detained. An archives would have an action in replevin if a document was taken from the archives and the archives sued for its return. The archives would have an action in detinue if the archives loaned a document and the person to whom it was loaned refused to return it so the archives sued for its return. In either case the archives would also have the right to recover for any damages incurred by the temporary loss of possession. An action in trover, on the other hand, is for damages for the wrongful taking of personal property; in other words, the archives wants money and not the return of the property.

All states have some legal method for the recovery of personal property. Most states (and the United States) have replaced these common law remedies with some form of statutory ones. All of these remedies, whether common law or statutory, whether replevin, detinue, or trover, have come to be called replevin by archivists, and for the purposes of this discussion will be referred to as such even though the term is not technically correct.

In order to recover in a replevin action, the plaintiff must prove title in himself; he must recover on the strength of his title and right to possession of the document rather than on the weakness of his opponent's title and right to possession.[21] In other words, just because the person in possession of a document does not have good title to it does not mean that the archives can recover the item; the archives will have to show a right to title and possession. There have been very few reported cases involving replevin of documents; however, the few that there are fall into two categories: replevin of public documents and replevin of private documents.

Replevin of Public Documents

The issues in public document replevin cases revolve around whether or not the document is a public document and whether on its face it appears to be a public

document. One such case involved a letter signed by George Washington.[22] From the facts of this case it appears that one John Allan was a collector of rare manuscripts and that for at least thirty years before his death in 1863 he had in his possession a letter signed by George Washington and addressed to "Honble. The Mayor, Recorder, Alderman and Commonalty of the city of New York." His daughter, as executrix of his estate, had the letter sold at auction, where it was bought by DeWitt Lent in May of 1864 for $2,050. The City of New York sued to recover the letter, claiming ownership. Apparently in December of 1778 the Common Council of the City, "imbued with emotions of gratitude for the distinguished services of General Washington," voted an "address to him, together with the freedom of the city, in a gold box." General Washington's reply was read at the meeting of the council on May 2, 1785, transcribed into the minutes, and ordered to be published. No evidence was produced to show what had happened to the letter between 1785 and the date the letter appeared in John Allan's collection. The court awarded the letter to the city, finding that the style of the letter, its address, and the fact that it was in response to a legislative act gave notice at all times that the letter was property of the city. The court noted that other personal property may not have such distinctive notice as this particular letter.

A more recent case has confirmed this concept of notice on the face of the document as a test of ownership. In 1974, B.C. West, Jr., purchased at an auction conducted by Charles Hamilton Galleries two bills of indictment from 1767 and 1768 that were signed by William Hooper, Attorney for the King. (Hooper was subsequently one of the North Carolina signers of the Declaration of Independence.) North Carolina sued for the return of the documents. The court found that the records should be returned to the state of North Carolina because the documents on their face gave notice that they were court records of the colony of North Carolina and because of this notice, a purchaser could not be a bona fide purchaser of the items.[23]

As can be seen from both of these cases, the fact that the documents themselves put the purchaser on notice that they were public documents was important. The reason the notice is important is the "bona fide purchaser" or "innocent purchaser for value" rule. This rule states that one who has purchased personal property need not return it if he paid a fair price for the item, had a reasonable belief that the seller had a right to sell,

---

[20]James E. O'Neill, "Replevin: A Public Archivist's Perspective," *Prologue* 11 (Fall 1979): 200-4.

[21]66 *Am. Jur. 2d*, Replevin, sec. 16.

[22]*Mayor and City of New York* v. *Lent*, 51 Barb. 19 (N.Y. 1868). For an older case involving pueblo records, see *DeLaO* v. *Acoma*, 1 N.M. 226 (1857).

[23]*State* v. *West.*

and there was nothing about the transaction to put him on notice to inquire further into the title to the item. Both courts found that the purchaser was not a bona fide purchaser because the documents themselves should have put the purchaser on notice. The courts could have reached the same result if either buyer had paid only $1 — that is, if a fair price had not been paid.

Unfortunately, not all documents put the purchaser on notice that the document is a public one. This was the problem in *United States* v. *First Trust Company of Saint Paul*.[24] This case started in the Minnesota State District Court as a suit between some of the heirs of Mrs. Sophia V. H. Foster and the Minnesota Historical Society. The facts of the case are interesting. When Mrs. Foster died, one of her daughters found a desk that belonged to Mrs. Foster's father, General John Henry Hammond. In the desk were his Civil War diaries and other papers. Without realizing what the other documents were, she turned them over to the Minnesota Historical Society. The other documents turned out to be notes written in 1803 and 1804 by William Clark, the co-leader of the Lewis and Clark expedition. Some of the heirs of General Hammond were offered $20,000 for the papers and they sued the Historical Society in state court to recover them.[25]

The United States then entered the case and had it removed from state court to the federal district court. The United States claimed ownership of the items because they were prepared by an army officer during a military expedition financed by the United States. The United States asserted that it had superior title because General Hammond had probably obtained the papers when he closed a government office at which Clark had been Indian agent. The government also argued that the heirs of Clark had superior title to that of the Hammond heirs. The documents did not contain any evidence on their face that they were public records but appeared to be private diaries. The court found that they were private papers, there was no notice on the face of the documents that they were government records, and the government had failed to prove its title. The United States also lost on the argument that the Hammond heirs' title was not clear; it certainly was not, but, as previously stated, one cannot recover on the weakness of the other's title.

In the case of public records the government seeking replevin must establish that the records were made or received as part of the official function of the government and that the records, on their face, put a purchaser on notice that they are public documents.

Replevin of Private Documents

Private records present special problems. Records of corporations may appear on their faces to be records of the corporation, and self-identification may also be found in records of universities, churches and religious orders, eleemosynary and volunteer institutions. If they do have such notice on their faces, then the bona fide purchaser rule would apply.

But many institutional records, as well as most personal papers, give no such warning that they are documents that belong elsewhere. Title to them must be proved by other means, and if the documents were purchased by a bona fide purchaser, they may never be recovered. The Clark case has shown that if the documents are of private origin, only someone having a superior title, such as the Clark heirs would have had if they had claimed the documents, can be successful in a replevin action. Thus, replevin actions for private documents by necessity revolve around questions of superior title and innocence of the purchaser.[26]

Facing Replevin

With this background in replevin, it is obvious that an archives, whether public or private, is faced with a number of replevin problems. These issues include when to seek replevin of documents, how to prove the documents are from the archives, and how to avoid replevin actions for documents in archival custody.

Whether or not to seek replevin is a complex issue that will require the advice of a lawyer. If the archival institution is a private one, the choice may be to seek replevin only in order to protect the institution's collection and reputation. A public institution may have somewhat broader choices because a public institution should be interested in both access for the public and the integrity of the records to protect public rights and preserve government accountability. Some of the criteria a public institution could use to determine whether or not to seek replevin of public documents include:

(1) Every effort should be made to recover documents, regardless of value or significance, if the documents were clearly removed illegally.

(2) Significant documents that should be in public custody should always be sought.

(3) When the missing document is available to the public in a research facility, the government should insure that this will be so in perpetuity and may decide to seek a copy instead of the original.

(4) Privately held documents not available for public research should be made available for research. If this is

---

[24]*U.S.* v. *First Trust of Saint Paul*.

[25]"U.S. Presses Claim to 1804 Lewis Data," *New York Times*, November 19, 1957: 25.

[26]For a case involving church records, see *Sawyer* v. *Baldwin*, 11 Pick. 492, 28 Mass. Rpts. 492 (1831).

not possible, either a copy or the original should be sought to ensure public access.

The above, with modifications, might also be used by a private archives as tests of whether or not to bring a suit to recover a document.[27]

If the archives has the misfortune to become involved in a suit to recover possession of an item removed from the archives, there are a number of things the archivists can do to assist the lawyers. Among them are:

(1) Know the collection and be able to demonstrate that the item is most likely from the archives. One obvious way is to show that the document bears a stamp giving notice of the archives' ownership; in the absence of a stamp, another obvious way is to show that the document is a logical part of a series.[28]

(2) Come up with an argument as to why the document itself would have put a purchaser on notice that the item was stolen.

(3) Through the use of researcher records, demonstrate the opportunity that an identifiable person had to take the item.

(4) Describe in writing the security system in use at the archives.

(5) Decide whether a copy would serve researchers equally as well as the original; if the answer is that it would, consider settling for the copy if the archives does not have a strong case.

If the archives receives documents, either through purchase or donation, it should also be concerned about replevin actions *against* the archives. There are a few questions the archives should ask when accepting documents, especially if paying for them:

(1) Are these documents on their faces public documents?

(2) Has the archives had a long history of dealing with the party from whom it is receiving the documents, and has the party been reliable?

(3) Is there anything about the transaction that makes it suspicious?

(4) Should these documents properly belong elsewhere?

If the archives has problems answering the questions above, it should start asking questions. If the archives suspects that the document offered is part of the holdings of another institution, it might call the institution where the document may properly belong. If the document is of foreign origin, the archives should treat it with even greater suspicion, particularly if it appears to be part of the records of a foreign government or documents of cultural patrimony of another nation.[29]

Finally, archivists should remember that, as with all legal problems, litigation and replevin are a last resort. In other words, negotiate: half a loaf is nearly always better than none. Lawyers have a saying: "A bad settlement is better than a good trial." The legal remedy of replevin developed in the centuries when the only copies available were those made by hand transcription. Today a number of techniques are available to produce a facsimile copy suitable for research and legal uses. A good copy, like a bad settlement, may be better than no document at all.

---

[29]For examples of problems, see "A Stolen Relic is a Problem for Mexicans," *New York Times,* August 29, 1982: 11; "Sale of Che Diaries Blocked," *Washington Post*, July 10, 1984: C4; "Curbing the Antiquities Trade," *Science* 217 (Sept. 1982): 1230-31.

---

8 Working with the Lawyer

Many archivists may never have to cope with lawyers and the legal system; others will not be so fortunate. Archivists who are not among the fortunate will usually have contact with lawyers in one of three ways: (1) the archives is involved in a lawsuit either as plaintiff or defendant; (2) lawyers use the holdings of the archives for research; or (3) the archivist receives a subpoena to attend a deposition or trial and is directed to bring certain records. This chapter will discuss contacts between lawyers and archives and will suggest ways of making the relationship a successful one.

Who Is the Lawyer?

The relationship of an archives and its lawyer will vary according to the type of organization in which the archives is situated. If the archives is part of the federal government the first person to contact after events 1 or 3 above happen is the agency's general counsel. The general counsel, in turn, will contact the appropriate division of the Department of Justice or the pertinent United States Attorney's office. An archives that is a part of a state agency or a state university may follow the federal practice (i.e., agency counsel and then attorney general) or may be authorized to go directly to the attorney general's office. Finally, private sector archives may have an in-house counsel who either handles all legal problems or employs private attorneys on a

---

[27]These criteria have been adapted from those in an excellent draft opinion by Paul A. Barron, Assistant General Counsel, General Services Administration, to Acting Archivist of U.S., December 8, 1965, P&C Case 66-112, Record Group 64, Records of the National Archives.

[28]Stamping each document with some notice of the archives' ownership is the most desirable protection for the document in case of a replevin action; if the holdings are extensive, however, stamping is prohibitively expensive. The next best policy is to have a clear, comprehensive, strict security system for the archives. See the suggestions incorporated in Timothy Walch, *Archives and Manuscripts: Security* (Chicago: Society of American Archivists, 1977).

case-by-case basis. Another possibility in private archives is that the institution may not have a house
counsel but may have a private law firm on retainer to
handle all legal work.

Archivists in the public sector will have a very difficult time picking a lawyer because normally a lawyer is
simply assigned to the agency as the archives' lawyer for
that case, and the archives must live with that lawyer,
whether the individual is a good or bad attorney. If the
archives is not satisfied with the lawyer assigned, the archives can go to the lawyer's supervisor and privately
ask to have him replaced. Just because the archives is a
governmental entity does not mean that it must be
satisfied with poor or incompetent counsel. It does
mean, however, that the archives must have good, well-
documented reasons to present to the lawyer's superior
in support of the request for removal. All of the above is
true in the private sector as well, except that it may be
easier and quicker to discharge outside counsel. Getting
rid of an in-house counsel presents the same problems to
a private archives that getting rid of a government
counsel presents to a public one.

Finding the Lawyer

If the archives has no lawyer and the archivist is permitted to retain a private lawyer, finding the lawyer who
is particularly suited to represent the archives is no different than finding a doctor, dentist, or plumber: ask
around. The most obvious choice is to ask other archives who represents them. Local libraries, colleges
and universities, museums, hospitals, and charitable
organizations should also be questioned as to who is
their lawyer, whether they are satisfied with the
representation, and what was the nature of the problem
or case in which they used the lawyer. Finally, the
Martindale-Hubbell Directory, a listing of lawyers by
state and city, may also be consulted to ascertain
lawyers in the area.

After assembling a list of names, the archivist may
wish to ask members of the board of the archives (if
there is such) about the lawyers on the list. The board
members may also be a good source for additional
recommendations about lawyers with special competen-
cies.

With the list narrowed, an interview, carefully stated
as such, is in order. At the interview, be sure to ask
about the size and experience of the firm, important
cases the firm has handled, and the firm's schedule of
fees and expenses. Finally, weigh all of the information,
select the lawyer, and as his or her first duty have him or
her prepare a contract for the firm's legal services. By
all means also remember that if the archives' choice
turns out to be a regretable one, change lawyers at once.

Educating the Lawyer

Whether the archives is a public or a private one, archivists must get to know their lawyers very well and
familiarize him with archivists and archives. The first
thing an archives should do with a new lawyer assigned
to it is conduct a tour of the institution, going behind
the scenes, explaining the archives' functions, and
demonstrating how an archives works. This is important
because what the archives is trying to do is sell the
organization to the lawyer: have the lawyer understand
what it does, why it is important, and why the particular
litigation is important to the purposes of the institution.
The easiest way to do this is a tour. The archives wants
its lawyer to be its advocate and he will be the advocate
whether he believes in archival goals or not, but how
well the lawyer does that depends in part on how well he
has been convinced by the archives of the importance of
the archival program. A tour is only part of what the archives must do. The archives must also be a good
teacher: the archives' counsel needs a basic archival
education. The lawyer must understand archives and archivists, know archival theory and terminology, and
think like an archivist: all the better to represent the archives.

The Lawyer as Researcher

Problems arise when lawyers use records (in other
words, when the lawyer is a researcher). This lawyer-
researcher may be your own lawyer, the opposition's
lawyer, or a third party's lawyer. The first thing an archives will have to explain is that archivists don't do research. Most lawyers will think that going to an archives
is like going to the library: you ask for a particular book
and it is handed to you. When a lawyer appears in an archives to do research, the archivist had better quickly
explain the ground rules on research. Furthermore, if
the archivist learns that the lawyer is going to attempt a
massive research effort, the archivist should suggest that
the lawyer hire an expert researcher. The archivist
should be sure to use the word "expert," because
lawyers like to use experts. The reason for this is that an
expert can testify to hearsay (something no other
witness can do) so long as the hearsay is of the type the
expert would normally rely upon to formulate his opinion. Because of this, lawyers love experts and archivists
should, too.

Archives and Subpoenas

Another example of an archivist's involvement with a
lawyer is the subpoena. A subpoena is nothing more
than a piece of paper issued by the clerk of court that
commands a person, or a person along with certain

specified documents, to appear to give testimony at a stated location either for a deposition or a trial. (If the person is asked to appear with documents it is called a subpoena duces tecum.) Everyone knows what a trial is; a deposition is slightly different in that only the lawyers for all sides and a court reporter are present — there is no judge or jury. The purpose of a deposition is to discover evidence; a trial presents the discovered evidence to the court and jury. You could look at the deposition as a rehearsal and the trial as the concert. If a subpoena is tendered to the archives, it should also include a check for mileage to attend the deposition or trial. The United States does not have to tender a check; however, if the archives presents the subpoena to the U.S. Marshal, the mileage will be paid. States handle the payment in various ways, and local rules may vary.

The first thing an archives should do when it receives a subpoena is to try and identify any documents that are requested. Usually the subpoena has been so broadly drafted that the archives would have to produce the entire holdings in order to comply with the subpoena. If that happens, the archives or its lawyer can call the lawyer that signed the subpoena and explain that it is too broad and that the archives is not sure what to bring, ask if the request can be narrowed, determine what is really wanted. If agreement to limit the subpoena is reached, confirm this agreement in writing. If not, attempt to spread out the time of delivery (e.g., 25 percent the first week, 25 percent the second, and so on).

The second thing an archives must do in response to a subpoena is determine what restrictions, if any, there are on the documents subpoenaed: are they classified, restricted under the terms of a donor's deed of gift, or open. If there are restrictions on donated material that is subpoenaed, the archives should notify the donor or the donor's representative because they may want to appear in court and object (through a motion for a protective order) to the subpoena. The restrictions themselves are no bar to the subpoena. The archives has no obligation to represent the donor in court unless the deed of gift requires it; the archives is the custodian of the documents and the archivist must present them pursuant to the subpoena. In any event, the archives should always notify its own lawyer whenever a subpoena is received, and the archives should also insure that whomever the archives received the documents from, whether a public or private source, is also notified. The notification gives the lawyers time to quash (prevent the fulfillment of) the subpoena.

Finally, archivists and their lawyers can negotiate to prevent the issuance of a subpoena. Sometimes an archives has advance notice that a subpoena may be in the offing (this is most likely if the lawyer has come in to do research in the archives). If the lawyer-researcher requests restricted records and is refused, his instinctive reaction may be to subpoena them. Similarly, lawyers confronted with a large volume of material to review may want it subpoenaed so they can go through it at their convenience, not having to work in an archives search room under archives rules. Archivists can try to explain the reasons for the restrictions and rules and can try to accommodate the lawyers' legitimate needs for access to the materials. In particular, archivists should try to persuade lawyers to accept copies of documents instead of subpoenaing the originals (see Chapter 7 on admissibility of copies).

If negotiation fails and the originals are subpoenaed, the archives should keep a careful record of all documents out of custody because of subpoenas and should require signed receipts from the lawyers receiving the items. The lawyers for the archives should ensure that at the conclusion of the legal proceedings the subpoenaed documents are returned to archival custody. Although on occasion an archivist may actually carry the documents to the legal proceeding, remain with them, and take them back to the archives at its conclusion, this is quite unusual. There are several reasons for this. First, many subpoenas for documents are not directed to the archives itself but to a different part of the same institution (the president of the corporation, for example), and the lawyers for the institution will require the archives to locate and turn over to them the requested documents, which they will retain until the proceeding is completed. Second, if the documents are subpoenaed for presentation at trial, the court will take custody until the trial is complete.

What to Expect from the Lawyer during Litigation

In all lawsuits involving an archives, whether public or private, the archives has several rights that it should demand from its lawyer. First, the archives has a right to know at all times the status of the litigation. Second, the archives should receive a copy of all pleadings (documents) filed in court or sent to or received from other parties. Third, if the archives has a private counsel, it has a right to know in advance of hiring the lawyer what the services will cost. In other words, the archives should have a written contract stating the services to be provided and the fee to be charged. In any event, both public and private archives should expect, demand, and receive information about the case at all times. If the archives does not, it should get worried.

The Stages of Civil Litigation

If the archives is involved in a civil lawsuit either as plaintiff or defendant and if the lawyer representing the archives is doing a proper job, the archives should receive numerous copies of pleadings. Pleadings are documents filed in the case. In order to follow the litigation and to better assist the lawyer, an archivist needs a basic understanding of what pleadings are and the stages in litigation in which pleadings are usually found. Since civil procedure varies from state to state, federal procedure will be used as the basis for this discussion. Most states follow federal civil procedure after a fashion, but there are usually some differences. In all cases, however, a civil lawsuit has three logical stages and an optional fourth stage. The three stages are (1) the initial pleadings, (2) the pretrial motions and preparations, and (3) the trial. The optional fourth stage is, of course, the appeal.

Initial Pleadings

The purpose of the initial pleadings is to set the stage and identify the players. This is done by the plaintiff paying a fee and filing a complaint in court (this is done in the clerk of court's office). The complaint is a document that identifies the plaintiff and defendant, states the authority for the court to hear the case (jurisdiction), states the facts that have resulted in the filing of the case, and asks for the appropriate remedy (money damages, some other relief, or both). Filed with the complaint is a summons (or notice), which is served upon the defendant to give him notice that the suit has commenced. Depending on the jurisdiction, the summons may be served in person or by mail.

Upon being served, the defendant has a specified period of time in which to appear and file an answer, usually between twenty and thirty days. In the answer the defendant will admit or deny some or all of the facts asserted in the complaint, may assert some affirmative defenses to the suit (such as a prior decision on the matter, duress, etc.), and may assert a counterclaim against the plaintiff for money damages or other relief. If there are multiple defendants they may also in their answers assert claims against each other as well as against the plaintiff; these claims between defendants are known as cross-claims. At this point the parties are all present and the stage is set.

Pretrial Motions and Preparations

In this stage of the litigation the lawyers have many different options on how to proceed. The order will vary according to the various strategies worked out by the respective lawyers and their clients. One of the options almost always pursued is that of discovery. The purpose of discovery is to ascertain facts about the case in the possession of others and to learn the opponent's facts so that the lawyers may properly prepare for trial. Discovery is accomplished in a number of ways:

(1) Interrogatories: written questions submitted to the other party and answered under oath;

(2) Depositions: discussed above in the section on subpoenas;

(3) Requests for admissions: written requests to the other party asking him to admit that a certain statement is true;

(4) Production of documents: asking the other party to produce for inspection and copying documents relevant to the lawsuit.

In addition to discovery, a motion for summary judgment may be filed. This motion often is a way to avoid a long trial. It is used to dispose of either the entire case or certain issues in the case and is based upon the facts learned in discovery. The motion claims that there are no disputes as to certain facts and, based on those undisputed facts, asks that judgment be entered against the other party (either plaintiff or defendant can file this motion).

If there are disputed facts there has to be a trial because the fact-finder must hear the testimony and determine the true facts. As part of all motions, memorandums of law (sometimes called briefs) are submitted to the court, stating the facts and arguing the law as it relates to the facts. If the motion for summary judgment is not granted or only granted in part and there has not been a settlement of the case, a trial must be held.

The Trial and Post-trial Motions

The trial is the final production; all that has gone before has been the writing of the play and the rehearsal. Now comes opening night with all its jitters. The trial is conducted by a judge and may be with or without a jury. Although one always has a constitutional right to a jury trial in a criminal case, this is not always so in a civil case; also, the parties may decide to waive a jury. If the case is tried to the jury, the jury's function is to decide the disputed facts in the case based on the instructions of law given to them by the judge.

The first step in a jury trial is to pick a jury. This is done by bringing in a number of prospective jurors and asking them questions (a proceeding known as voir dire) to establish that they are unbiased and can fairly decide the case. The questions can, depending on local practice, be asked by either the judge, the lawyers, or both the judge and the lawyers. Each side is given the right to strike (throw out) a number of prospective jurors and thereafter a panel is selected. Jury selection is one of the least standardized procedures in a court proceeding and varies not only from courthouse to courthouse but from judge to judge within the same courthouse. The number of jurors also varies, usually from a minimum of six to a maximum of twelve, and the number of alternate jurors varies as well. Alternates are picked to replace any of the regular jurors who may not be able to continue the trial.

Whether the trial is to a judge or a judge and jury, the order of the trial is the same:

(1) Opening statements. The purpose of an opening statement is to explain the respective parties' theory of the case and to familiarize the fact-finder with the issues in the case.

(2) Presenting the evidence. Usually the plaintiff goes first, followed by the defendant. The plaintiff then can put on rebuttal evidence to rebut any of the defendant's witnesses.

(3) Final argument. The lawyers can argue how the evidence supports their theory of the case. Usually the plaintiff argues first and last and the defendant argues in the middle; however, the plaintiff cannot save all of his arguments for the last period because at that stage he can only comment on what the defendant has argued.

(4) Instructing the jury. The judge tells the jury the law to which they must apply the facts as they find them. If the trial is to a judge only, this step is omitted, as is the next one.

(5) Jury deliberations. The jury decides the facts in the case, applies them to the law, and renders its verdict. In a judge-tried case the judge issues a written opinion giving his findings of fact and conclusions of law.

After the jury verdict or after the judge has written his findings, a final judgment is entered by the judge. It is at this point that the parties may wish to consider the possibility of an appeal.

The Appeal

During a set period of time, usually from thirty to sixty days after the judgment is entered, either party can file an appeal. If no appeal is filed during that time, the right to appeal is waived and the case is closed. The federal system and many state systems have an intermediate appeals court that one must appeal to before reaching the highest appeals court in the system. Also, as with the U.S. Supreme Court, some of the highest courts do not have to hear every appeal made to them but can pick the appeals they wish to hear. In the case of an appeal to the U.S. Supreme Court, one files a peti-

tion for a writ of certiorari with the Court, explaining the importance of the case. The Court then decides whether or not to hear the case (most petitions are not granted). All appeals, whether to an intermediate or the highest court, cannot reargue the facts. The facts have been fixed for all time by the finder of fact (judge or jury) in the original trial. Instead, the appeal must be based on some error in law committed by the court. Most appeals are not successful; however, if successful a retrial may be necessary and the whole procedure starts over again.

The Lawyer Adviser

Involvement of an archives with lawyers will usually not be related to litigation. Most likely the archives will find itself working with a lawyer because the archives has become aware of a legal issue and wants a legal opinion. The archives should be careful when requesting a legal opinion because a lawyer, if the archives permits, will run the institution and tell the archives how to do things; a lawyer is an expert on everything. The archives should instead present the lawyer with options and ask what the legal ramifications are for each option. Based on the lawyer's advice the archives can then make an informed business decision. As a manager, the archivist wants advice on what will happen if a certain action is taken, the archivist doesn't want to be told what to do. The archivist wants to weigh the risks. Getting the archives' lawyer involved in the basics, such as deeds, access agreements, publications, and reviews of procedures is a good idea. But the archives should have the last word, making clear to the lawyer and to itself that it is only soliciting the lawyer's professional advice.

Finally, just as the archives can expect certain things from its lawyer, the lawyer demands that the archives conceal nothing. To receive and to provide effective legal services, there must be no surprises for either archives or lawyer. Do not procrastinate when legal problems seem to be arising. Tell the lawyer about the subpoena, and inform him that the archives did not obtain a deed of gift. Law, like archives, is a service profession. Lawyers can serve the archives best if the archives works openly and honestly and closely with them.

Appendix 1
ALA–SAA Joint Statement on Access to Original Research Materials in Libraries, Archives, and Manuscript Repositories

1. It is the responsibility of a library, archives, or manuscript repository to make available original research materials in its possession on equal terms of access. Since the accessibility of material depends on knowing of its existence, it is the responsibility of a repository to inform researchers of the collections and archival groups in its custody. This may be accomplished through a card catalog, inventories and other internal finding aids, published guides or reports to the National Union Catalog of Manuscript Collections where appropriate, and the freely offered assistance of staff members, who, however, should not be expected to engage in extended research.

2. To protect and insure the continued accessibility of the material in its custody, the repository may impose several conditions which it should publish or otherwise make known to users.

    a. The repository may limit the use of fragile or unusually valuable materials, so long as suitable reproductions are made available for the use of all researchers.

    b. All materials must be used in accordance with the rules of and under the supervision of the repository. Each repository should publish and furnish to potential researchers it rules governing access and use. Such rules must be equally applied and enforced.

    c. The repository may refuse access to unprocessed materials, so long as such refusal is applied to all researchers.

    d. Normally, a repository will not send research materials for use outside its building or jurisdiction. Under special circumstances a collection or a portion of it may be loaned or placed on deposit with another institution.

    e. The repository may refuse access to an individual researcher who has demonstrated such carelessness or deliberate destructiveness as to endanger the safety of the material.

    f. As a protection to its holdings, a repository may reasonably require acceptable identification of persons wishing to use its materials, as well as a signature indicating they have read a statement defining the policies and regulations of the repository.

3. Each repository should publish or otherwise make available to researchers a suggested form of citation crediting the repository and identifying items within its holdings for later reference. Citations to copies of materials in other repositories should include the location of the originals, if known.

4. Whenever possible a repository should inform a researcher about known copyrighted material, the owner or owners of the copyrights, and the researcher's obligations with regard to such material.

5. A repository should not deny access to materials to any person or persons, nor grant privileged or exclusive use of materials to any person or persons, nor conceal the existence of any body of material from any researcher, unless required to do so by law, donor, or purchase stipulations.

6. A repository should, whenever possible, inform a researcher of parallel research by other individuals using the same materials. With the written acquiescence of those other individuals, a repository may supply their names upon request.

7. Repositories are committed to preserving manuscript and archival materials and to making them available for research as soon as possible. At the same time, it is recognized that every repository has certain obligations to guard against unwarranted invasion of personal privacy and to protect confidentiality in its holdings in accordance with the law and that every private donor has the right to impose reasonable restrictions upon his papers to protect privacy or confidentiality for a reasonable period of time.

    a. It is the responsibility of the repository to inform researchers of the restrictions which apply to individual collections or archival groups.

    b. The repository should discourage donors from imposing unreasonable restrictions and should encourage a specific time limitation on such restrictions as are imposed.

    c. The repository should periodically reevaluate restricted material and work toward the removal of restrictions when they are no longer required.

8. A repository should not charge fees for making available the materials in its holdings. However, reasonable fees may be charged for the copying of material or for the provision of special services or facilities not provided to all researchers.

Appendix 2

Code Citations to State Open Records and Privacy Laws

Some of the open records laws listed below closely follow the federal Freedom of Information Act, others do not. Some of these laws are very general and have received extensive judicial interpretation; others are equally general but have had no judicial interpretation. Some of the laws listed merely state that a citizen can obtain a copy of a public document from a public official, defining neither "public document" nor "public official." Some of the laws date from the last century; others are brand new.

Like the state open records laws, the state privacy laws vary greatly. The privacy laws listed are those laws that broadly protect information found in government records about an individual. Not listed are those laws that close only a specific body of records, such as separate statutes on hospital records, adoption records, and so forth. Some states have a number of such specific laws, and state archivists should consult both the state legal code and the archives' lawyer to find them.

Because the state laws can be very general and also because there has not been much litigation in state courts on either open records or privacy, a state archives should consult with its lawyer before drawing any conclusions just from reading the code sections listed here. The lawyer will examine the code, the cases, and any relevant state attorney general opinions before providing the archives with a definitive position. The archives should suggest that the lawyer look for any federal precedents as well, especially if there has been little state litigation.

State	Code	Open Records	Privacy
ALABAMA	ALA. CODE (1975)	36-12-40	None
ALASKA	ALASKA STAT.	09.25.110-.125 (1983)	None
ARIZONA	ARIZ. REV. STAT. (1974 & Supp. 1983)	39-121 to 121.03	None
ARKANSAS	ARK. STAT. ANN. (1979 & Supp. 1983)	12-2801 to 2807	None
CALIFORNIA	CAL. GOV'T CODE (1980 & Supp. 1984)	6250-6265	1798-1798.70 (Civil Code)
COLORADO	COLO. REV. STAT. (1982 & Supp. 1983)	24-72-201 to 402	None
CONNECTICUT	CONN. GEN. STAT. ANN. (West 1969 & Supp. 1984)	1-15 to -21k	4-190 to 197 & 31-128a to 128h
DELAWARE	DEL. CODE ANN. (1983)	29: 10001-10112	None
DISTRICT OF COLUMBIA	D.C. CODE ANN. (1982)	1-1521 to 1529	None
FLORIDA	FLA. STAT. ANN. (1982 & Supp. 1984)	119.01-.12	None
GEORGIA	GA. CODE (1984)	50-18-70 to 74	None
HAWAII	HAWAII REV. STAT. (1976)	92-21, 92-50 to 52	92E-1 to 13
IDAHO	IDAHO CODE (1976 & Supp. 1983)	9-301 to 302 (1979); 59-1009 (1976)	None
ILLINOIS	ILL. REV. STAT. (1954 & Supp. 1984)	116: 43.4-.29, .101-.103a, .113; .201-.211	None
INDIANA	IND. STAT. ANN. (1983 & Supp. 1984)	5-14-3-1 to -10	4-1-6-1 to -9
IOWA	IOWA CODE ANN. (1973 & Supp. 1984)	68A.1-.9	None
KANSAS	KAN. STAT. ANN. (1981 & Supp. 1983)	45-205 to 214	None
KENTUCKY	KY. REV. STAT. (1980 & Supp. 1984)	61.870-.884	None
LOUISIANA	LA. STAT. ANN. (1982 & Supp. 1984)	44:1-:13, :31-:44	None
MAINE	ME. REV. STAT. ANN. (1979 & Supp. 1983)	1: 401-410	None

MARYLAND	MD. ANN. CODE (1980 & Supp. 1983)	76A: 1-6	None
MASSACHUSETTS	MASS. ANN. LAWS (1980 & Supp. 1983)	4:7, cl. 26; 66:10	66A: 1-3
MICHIGAN	MICH. STAT. ANN. (1977 & Supp. 1984)	4.1801(1) to (16)	None
MINNESOTA	MINN. STAT. ANN. (1977 & Supp. 1984)	13.01-13.86	Same
MISSISSIPPI	MISS. CODE ANN. (1972)	25-61-1 to 17	25-53-53
MISSOURI	MO. REV. STAT. (1978)	109.180-.190	None
MONTANA	MONT. CODE ANN. (1983)	2-6-101 to 111	None
NEBRASKA	REV. STAT. NEB. (1981)	84-712 to -712.09	None
NEVADA	NEV. REV. STAT. (1979)	239.010, .020, .030	None
NEW HAMPSHIRE	N.H. REV. STAT. ANN. (1977 & Supp. 1983)	91-A:1 to :8	None
NEW JERSEY	N.J. STAT. ANN. (West Supp. 1984)	47:1A-1 to -4	None
NEW MEXICO	N.M. STAT. ANN. (1978 & Supp. 1984)	14-2-1 to -3	None
NEW YORK	N.Y. PUB. OFF. LAW (McKinney Supp. 1984)	84 to 90	91 to 99
NORTH CAROLINA	N.C. GEN. STAT. (1981)	132-1 to -9	None
NORTH DAKOTA	N.D. CENT. CODE (1978)	44-04-18	None
OHIO	OHIO REV. CODE ANN. (1984)	149.43	1347.01
OKLAHOMA	OKLA. STAT. ANN. (1962 & Supp. 1984)	51: 24	None
OREGON	OR. REV. STAT. (1981)	192.410-.500	None
PENNSYLVANIA	PA. STAT. ANN. (Purdon 1959 & Supp. 1984)	65: 66.1-.4	None
RHODE ISLAND	R.I. GEN. LAWS (Supp. 1980)	38-2-1 to -12	38-2-1
SOUTH CAROLINA	S.C. CODE (1976 & Supp. 1980)	30-4-10 to -110	None
SOUTH DAKOTA	S.D. CODIFIED LAWS (1980 & Supp. 1984)	1-27-1, -3	None
TENNESSEE	TENN. CODE ANN. (1980 & Supp. 1984)	10-7-503 to 507	10-7-504
TEXAS	TEX. REV. CIV. STAT. ANN. (Vernon Supp. 1985)	6252-17(a)	None
UTAH	UTAH CODE ANN. (1977)	78-26-1 to -3	63-2-59 to -89
VERMONT	VT. STAT. ANN. (1972 & Supp. 1983)	Title 1: 315-320	None
VIRGINIA	VA. CODE (1979 & Supp. 1984)	2.1-340 to -346.1	2.1-377 to -386
WASHINGTON	WASH. REV. CODE ANN. (1972 & Supp. 1985)	42.17.250 to .340	50.13.010 to .910
WEST VIRGINIA	W. VA. CODE (1980 & Supp. 1984)	29B-1-1 to -6	None
WISCONSIN	WIS. STAT. ANN. (1972 & Supp. 1984)	19.21-.37	None
WYOMING	WYO. STAT. (1977 & Supp. 1984)	9-9-101 to -105	None

Appendix 3

Requirements for the Loan of Original Records from the National Archives

In accordance with Title 41 U.S. Code of Federal Regulations Chapter 105-61-101-1 (f) the loan of original records from the National Archives is subject to the following conditions:

1. All loans must be authorized by the Deputy Archivist of the United States or Director of a Presidential Library. Requests must be made in writing at least 120 days before the documents are to leave the National Archives.

2. Records shall be stored or displayed in a fire-proof building and protected by fire alarms, smoke alarms, and a direct alarm tie-in with a fire department.

3. All records on display or in storage must be under 24-hour guard surveillance. Electronic systems to indicate if and when exhibition areas are breached after hours are required.

4. A temperature of $70° \pm 4°$ F and a relative humidity of $50\% \pm 4\%$ without rapid fluctuations must be maintained in the exhibit and storage area. If a case in which a record is displayed is internally lighted, proper ventilation or air-conditioning must be provided to maintain the prescribed temperature and humidity inside the case.

5. a. Incandescent lighting is desirable, but if it is unavailable fluorescent lighting is acceptable. Filters must be used to protect records against the ultraviolet light rays produced by fluorescent lighting. Only filters that exclude light below a wave length of 460 micrometers are acceptable. Examples of such filters are yellow plexiglass number 2208 and yellow polycast number 2208.

    b. Records with color such as prints or lithographs must also be protected against ultraviolet light produced by fluorescent lighting. Filters that exclude light below a wave lengh of 390 micrometers are acceptable. Plexiglas UF-3 and polycase UF-3 are two products that satisfy this requirement. Filters such as those described in 5.a. do not allow true color rendition.

    c. Lighting of records may not exceed (10)-foot candles for black and white documents or (5)-foot candles for displaying documents with color. Photographs may not be taken using photoflood lights or photoflash.

6. The records must be displayed in locked exhibit cases. The cases must be dust and dirt proof.

7. The records are not to be moved from the approved exhibit area or storage vault, or shown in any other location.

8. Original records must be handled only by the curator, registrar, or equivalent museum professional of the borrowing institution. No records may be altered, cleaned, or repaired without written permission from the Archives. No plexiglas frame (sandwich) shall be opened without the Archives' approval.

9. No adhesive used in mounting the records on exhibit may contact the records directly.

10. Provisions must be made to prevent the public from touching wall hung objects. Such provisions could involve an appropriate hanging system, the use of stanchions, or a combination of any of these.

11. In display and publicity the National Archives must receive clear and prominent credit. The credit line should normally read:

The National Archives
Washington, DC

Copies of all press clippings must be sent to the National Archives.

12. A member of the staff of the National Archives and Records Service (NARS) may inspect the exhibit area before the records are placed on display. If, in his or her judgment, the above conditions have not been met, the loan will not be made. Staff members or personnel designated by the National Archives may also make additional unannounced inspection trips once every three months during the period of the loan. Travel expenses of NARS staff will be borne by the borrower.

13. Original records are normally hand-carried by a NARS staff member. A member of the requesting institution's staff or their designee may hand-carry the documents subject to approval by the National Archives. Under special circumstances alternative means of transportation may be approved. The expenses of transportation to and from the borrowing institution will be borne by the borrower.

14. The borrowing institution must, at its own expense, cover the documents involved with an all-risk fine arts insurance policy from the time the documents leave the Archives until the time they are returned. An evaluation for insurance purposes will be made by the National Archives and must be kept confidential. Evidence that insurance coverage is in full force and effect must be given to the National Archives before the documents may leave the building.

15. Loans will be made for a period not to exceed one year.

16. The National Archives must approve any arrangements to include loaned records in related publications.

17. The National Archives reserves the right to require other safeguards and to withdraw records from exhibit at any time.

Any departure from these requirements must be approved in writing by the Deputy Archivist of the United States.

OUTGOING LOAN AGREEMENT

TO	FROM

in accordance with the conditions printed on the reverse, the objects listed below are borrowed for the following purpose only

PERIOD	LOCATIONS OF OBJECTS
FROM TO	

DESCRIPTION OF ITEMS

INSURANCE

☐ TO BE CARRIED BY NATIONAL ARCHIVES AND PREMIUM BILLED TO BORROWER

☐ TO BE CARRIED BY BORROWER

☐ INSURANCE WAIVED

☐ TO BE CARRIED BY NATIONAL ARCHIVES WITHOUT REIMBURSEMENT

INSURANCE VALUE

SHIPPING AND PACKING

OBJECTS PACKED BY

CHARGES TO BORROWER
☐ YES   ☐ NO

OBJECTS RETURNED (Date)

OBJECTS SHIPPED TO

OBJECTS SHIPPED FROM
☐ NARS
☐ OTHER (Specify)

SHIPMENT TO BE VIA

OUTGOING

RETURN

CREDIT LINE (For exhibition label and catalogue)

SPECIAL REQUIREMENTS (For installation and handling)

GENERAL SERVICES ADMINISTRATION   3. INSURANCE   **GSA** FORM **7251** (10-77)

LOAN AGREEMENT

The Borrower agrees to the following conditions of loan:

PROTECTION

Each object, which term includes documentary material, is loaned for the benefit of the borrower, and shall be given special care at all times to insure against loss, damage, or deterioration. The borrower agrees to meet the special requirements for installation and handling as noted on the face of this agreement form. Furthermore, the National Archives may require an inspection and approval at the actual installation by a member of its staff as a condition of the loan at the expense of the borrower. The National Archives further reserves the right to enter on the premises where the object may be located for the purpose of inspecting it or observing its use. Upon receipt and prior to return of the objects, the borrower must make a written record of condition. Unless the borrower gives written notice specifying any defect in or other proper objection to the object upon receipt thereof, the borrower agrees that it shall be conclusively presumed, as between the borrower and the National Archives, that the borrower has fully inspected and acknowledged that the object is in good condition and repair. The Archives is to be notified immediately, followed by a full written report, including photographs, if damage or loss is discovered. No object may be altered, cleaned, or repaired without the prior written permission of the Archives. Objects borrowed must be maintained in a fireproof building under 24-hour security and protected from unusual temperatures and humidity, excessive light, and from insects, vermin, or dirt. Objects must be handled only by experienced personnel and be secured from damage and theft by appropriate brackets, railings, display cases, and other responsible means. Without prior written consent of the Archives, the borrower shall not (a) assign, transfer, pledge, or hypothecate this agreement, the objects or any part thereof or any interest therein; (b) sublet or lend the objects or any part thereof; (c) permit the objects or any part thereof to be used by anyone other than the borrower or the borrower's employees; or (d) permit the object to be removed from the location specified upon the face of this agreement. The object shall be used only for the purposes specified on the face of this agreement. The property is and shall at all times remain the sole property of the Archives, and the borrower shall have no right, title, or interest therein except as expressly set forth in this agreement. Finally, the borrower shall give the Archives immediate notice of any attachment or other judicial process affecting any object borrowed and shall, whenever requested by the Archives, advise the Archives of the exact location of the objects.

INSURANCE

Documents and objects shall be insured during the period of this loan under an all-risk, wall-to-wall policy subject to the standard exclusions. In the case of long-term loans, insurance premiums may be reviewed periodically, and the Archives reserves the right to increase coverage and/or premiums, if necessary. If the borrower is insuring the object, the Archives must be furnished with a certificate of insurance or a copy of the policy made out in favor of the National Archives prior to shipment of the objects. The Archives must be notified in writing at least 20 days prior to any cancellation or meaningful change in the borrower's policy. Any lapses in this coverage will not release the borrower from liability for loss or damage. If insurance is waived, the borrower agrees to indemnify the Archives for any and all loss or damage to the objects occurring during the course of the loan, except for loss or damage resulting from wear and tear, gradual deterioration, inherent vice, war and nuclear risk. In the event of loss or damage, the maximum liability of the borrower will be limited to the dollar value as stated under "Insurance value" on the face of this agreement.

Borrower shall indemnify the Archives against all claims, actions, proceedings, costs, damages, and liabilities, including attorney's fees, arising out of, connected with, or resulting from use of or borrowing of the objects.

PACKING AND TRANSPORTATION

Packing and transportation shall be by safe methods approved in advance by the National Archives. Unpacking and repacking must be done by experienced personnel under competent supervision. Repacking must be done with the same or similar materials and boxes, and by the same methods as the objects were received. Any additional instructions will be followed.

CREDIT

Each object shall be labeled and credited in any publication to the National Archives, Washington, DC or_____ Unless otherwise agreed to in writing, no reproductions are permitted by the borrower or its viewing public except photographic copies for catalog and publicity uses related to the stated purpose of this loan.

COSTS

Unless otherwise noted, all costs of packing, transportation and insurance shall be borne by the borrower.

RETURN/EXTENSIONS/CANCELLATION

Objects lent must be returned to the Archives in satisfactory condition by the stated termination date unless because of damage or loss to the objects the Archives receives the "Insurance value" thereof instead. Furthermore, the borrower has the duty to repair the objects or reimburse the Archives for repairs made subsequent to notification of the damage as required above. Any extension of the loan period must be approved in writing by the Archivist of the United States or his designate and covered by parallel extension of the insurance coverage. The Archives reserves the right to recall the object from loan on short notice, if necessary. Furthermore, the Archives reserves the right to cancel this loan for good cause at any time, and will make every effort to give reasonable notice thereof. The Archives can require the borrower to return the object to a location other than the Archives; however, the borrower shall not be responsible for any excess transportation costs as a result of such transfer.

In the event of any conflict between this agreement and any forms of the borrower, the terms of this agreement shall be controlling. No modification of this agreement shall be effective unless it is in writing.

I have read and agree to the above conditions and certify that I am authorized to agree thereto:

SIGNATURE (Borrower or authorized agent)	TITLE	DATE
SIGNATURE (Approved for the National Archives)	TITLE	DATE

Appendix 4
Copyright Act, Title 17 of the United States Code

Sections 106, 107, and 108

§ 106. Exclusive rights in copyrighted works

Subject to sections 107 through 118, the owner of copyright under this title has the exclusive rights to do and to authorize any of the following:

(1) to reproduce the copyrighted work in copies or phonorecords;

(2) to prepare derivative works based upon the copyrighted work;

(3) to distribute copies or phonorecords of the copyrighted work to the public by sale or other transfer of ownership, or by rental, lease, or lending;

(4) in the case of literary, musical, dramatic, and choreographic works, pantomimes, and motion pictures and other audiovisual works, to perform the copyrighted work publicly; and

(5) in the case of literary, musical, dramatic, and choreographic works, pantomimes, and pictorial, graphic, or sculptural works, including the individual images of a motion picture or other audiovisual work, to display the copyrighted work publicly.

§ 107. Limitations on exclusive rights: Fair use

Notwithstanding the provisions of section 106, the fair use of a copyrighted work, including such use by reproduction in copies or phonorecords or by any other means specified by that section, for purposes such as criticism, comment, news reporting, teaching (including multiple copies for classroom use), scholarship, or research, is not an infringement of copyright. In determining whether the use made of a work in any particular case is a fair use the factors to be considered shall include—

(1) the purpose and character of the use, including whether such use is of a commercial nature or is for nonprofit educational purposes;

(2) the nature of the copyrighted work;

(3) the amount and substantiality of the portion used in relation to the copyrighted work as a whole; and

(4) the effect of the use upon the potential market for or value of the copyrighted work.

§ 108. Limitations on exclusive rights: Reproduction by libraries and archives

(a) Notwithstanding the provisions of section 106, it is not an infringement of copyright for a library or archives, or any of its employees acting within the scope of their employment, to reproduce no more than one copy or phonorecord of a work, or to distribute such copy or phonorecord, under the conditions specified by this section, if—

(1) the reproduction or distribution is made without any purpose of direct or indirect commercial advantage;

(2) the collections of the library or archives are (i) open to the public, or (ii) available not only to researchers affiliated with the library or archives or with the institution of which it is a part, but also to other persons doing research in a specialized field; and

(3) the reproduction or distribution of the work includes a notice of copyright.

106   LAW

(b) The rights of reproduction and distribution under this section apply to a copy or phonorecord of an unpublished work duplicated in facsimile form solely for purposes of preservation and security or for deposit for research use in another library or archives of the type described by clause (2) of subsection (a), if the copy or phonorecord reproduced is currently in the collections of the library or archives.

(c) The right of reproduction under this section applies to a copy or phonorecord of a published work duplicated in facsimile form solely for the purpose of replacement of a copy or phonorecord that is damaged, deteriorating, lost, or stolen, if the library or archives has, after a reasonable effort, determined that an unused replacement cannot be obtained at a fair price.

(d) The rights of reproduction and distribution under this section apply to a copy, made from the collection of a library or archives where the user makes his or her request or from that of another library or archives, of no more than one article or other contribution to a copyrighted collection or periodical issue, or to a copy or phonorecord of a small part of any other copyrighted work, if—

(1) the copy or phonorecord becomes the property of the user, and the library or archives has had no notice that the copy or phonorecord would be used for any purpose other than private study, scholarship, or research; and

(2) the library or archives displays prominently, at the place where orders are accepted, and includes on its order form, a warning of copyright in accordance with requirements that the Register of Copyrights shall prescribe by regulation.

(e) The rights of reproduction and distribution under this section apply to the entire work, or to a substantial part of it, made from the collection of a library or archives where the user makes his or her request or from that of another library or archives, if the library or archives has first determined, on the basis of a reasonable investigation, that a copy or phonorecord of the copyrighted work cannot be obtained at a pair price, if—

(1) the copy or phonorecord becomes the property of the user, and the library or archives has had no notice that the copy or phonorecord would be used for any purpose other than private study, scholarship, or research; and

(2) the library or archives displays prominently, at the place where orders are accepted, and includes on its order form, a warning of copyright in accordance with requirements that the Register of Copyrights shall prescribe by regulation.

(f) Nothing in this section—

(1) shall be construed to impose liability for copyright infringement upon a library or archives or its employees for the unsupervised use of reproducing equipment located on its premises: *Provided*, That such equipment displays a notice that the making of a copy may be subject to the copyright law;

(2) excuses a person who uses such reproducing equipment or who requests a copy or phonorecord under subsection (d) from liability for copyright infringement for any such act, or for any later use of such copy or phonorecord, if it exceeds fair use as provided by section 107;

(3) shall be construed to limit the reproduction and distribution by lending of a limited number of copies and excerpts by a library or archives of an audiovisual news program, subject to clauses (1), (2), and (3) of subsection (a); or

(4) in any way affects the right of fair use as provided by section 107, or any contractual obligations assumed at any time by the library or archives when it obtained a copy or phonorecord of a work in its collections.

(g) The rights of reproduction and distribution under this section extend to the isolated and unrelated reproduction or distribution of a single copy or phonorecord of the same material on separate occasions, but do not extend to cases where the library or archives, or its employee—

(1) is aware or has substantial reason to believe that it is engaging in the related or concerted reproduction or distribution of multiple copies or phonorecords of the same material, whether made on one occasion or over a period of time, and whether intended for aggregate use by one or more individuals or for separate use by the individual members of a group; or

(2) engages in the systematic reproduction or distribution of single or multiple copies or phonorecords of material described in subsection (d) : *Provided*, That nothing in this clause prevents a library or archives from participating in interlibrary arrangements that do not have, as their purpose or effect, that the library or archives receiving such copies or phonorecords for distribution does so in such aggregate quantities as to substitute for a subscription to or purchase of such work.

(h) The rights of reproduction and distribution under this section do not apply to a musical work, a pictorial, graphic or sculptural work, or a motion picture or other audiovisual work other than an audiovisual work dealing with news, except that no such limitation shall apply with respect to rights granted by subsections (b) and (c), or with respect to pictorial or graphic works published as illustrations, diagrams, or similar adjuncts to works of which copies are reproduced or distributed in accordance with subsections (d) and (e).

(i) Five years from the effective date of this Act, and at five-year intervals thereafter, the Register of Copyrights, after consulting with representatives of authors, book and periodical publishers, and other owners of copyrighted materials, and with representatives of library users and librarians, shall submit to the Congress a report setting forth the extent to which this section has achieved the intended statutory balancing of the rights of creators, and the needs of users. The report should also describe any problems that may have arisen, and present legislative or other recommendations, if warranted.

Glossary of Selected Legal Terms

Affidavit. A written statement of facts, made voluntarily, and sworn to before an officer, such as a notary public, who has authority to administer an oath or affirmation.

Amicus. Literally, a friend; usually used in the context of an amicus brief, which is a brief filed by a person who has no right to appear in a suit (that is, the person is not a party to the suit) but who is allowed to introduce argument, authority, or evidence to protect his interests.

Brief. A written document, prepared by an attorney to serve as the basis for an argument in court, embodying the points of law which the lawyer seeks to establish, together with the arguments and authorities upon which he rests his contention. Sometimes called a Memorandum of Law.

Condition Precedent. An event which must happen before an agreement becomes effective; for example, a donor signs a deed with the archives to give the archives some personal papers but only if the papers are first successfully appraised for tax purposes.

Condition Subsequent. An event which follows the agreement but which must happen if the agreement is to be kept and continued; for example, a donor deeds the archives some papers with the condition that the archives will subsequently review them for restricted items and isolate those items before making the papers available for research use.

Confidential. Intrusted with the confidence of another or with his secret affairs or purposes; intended to be held in confidence or kept secret. Confidential communications are certain classes of communications, passing between persons who stand in a confidential or fiduciary relation to each other (or who, on account of their relative situation, are under a special duty of secrecy and fidelity), which the law will not permit to be divulged, or allow them to be inquired into in a court of justice, for the sake of public policy and the good order of society. Examples of such privileged relations are those of husband and wife and attorney and client.

Contract. A promissory agreement between two or more persons that creates, modifies, or destroys a legal relation. A deed of gift is a contract.

Copyright. A right granted by statute to the author or originator of certain literary or artistic productions, whereby he is invested, for a limited period, with the sole and exclusive privilege of multiplying copies of the same and publishing and selling them.

Custody. The care and keeping of a thing, carrying with it the idea of the thing being within the immediate personal care and control of the person to whose custody it is subjected; charge; immediate charge and control, and not the final, absolute control of ownership, implying responsibility for the protection and preservation of the thing in custody.

Deed. A written instrument, signed, sealed, and delivered, by which one person conveys land, tenements, or hereditaments (things capable of being inherited) to another. A deed of gift is a deed executed and delivered without consideration (that is, without receiving something in return). The essential difference between a deed and a will is that the deed passes a present interest in something and the will passes no interest until after the death of the maker.

Defendant. The party against whom relief or recovery is sought in an action or suit; the person defending or denying.

Deposition. The testimony under oath of a witness taken upon interrogatories, not in open court, but in pursuance of a commission to take testimony issued by a court, and reduced to writing and duly authenticated, and intended to be used upon the trial of an action in court.

Detinue. A form of action for the recovery of personal chattels (that is, personal items, not real property) from one who acquired possession of them lawfully, but retains them without right, together with damages for the detention.

Dominion. Ownership, or right to property or perfect and complete property or ownership.

Donation. A gift.

Fair Market Value. Price which a seller, willing but not compelled to sell, would take, and a purchaser, willing but not compelled to buy, would pay.

Gift. A voluntary transfer of property without consideration. In popular language, a voluntary conveyance or assignment is called a deed of gift. Essential requisites of a gift are capacity of donor, intention of donor to make gift, completed delivery to or for donee, and acceptance of gift by donee.

Hearing. Proceeding of relative formality, generally public, with definite issue of fact or of law to be tried, in which parties proceeded against have right to be heard, and is much the same as a trial and may terminate in final order.

Hearsay. Second-hand evidence, as distinguished from original evidence; it is the repetition at second-hand of what would be original evidence if given by the person who originally made the statement. Literally, it is what the witness says he heard another person say.

Heir. One who inherits property, whether real or personal. The person can be either a nonrelative or a relative, and in the latter case, can be from the same, a previous, or a subsequent generation.

Injunction. A judicial process that requires a person to whom it is directed either to do or to refrain from doing a particular thing. Injunctions may be temporary (pending the final resolution of a lawsuit) or permanent (that is, final, after the rights of the parties in the suit are determined).

Interrogatory. Written questions propounded by one party and served on an adversary, who must provide written answers to them under oath.

Jurisdiction. The authority by which courts decide cases.

Libel. A method of defamation expressed by print, writing, pictures, or signs; in the most general sense, any publication that is injurious to the reputation of another.

Parties. The persons who are actively concerned in the prosecution and defense of any legal proceeding; more generally, the persons who take part in the performance of any act or who are directly interested in any affair, contract, or conveyance.

Plaintiff. A person who brings an action; the party who complains or sues.

Pleadings. The formal allegations by the parties of their respective claims and defenses, for the judgment of the court.

Privacy. The right to be let alone; the right of an individual (or corporation) to withhold himself and his property from public scrutiny if he so chooses.

Pro Bono. Literally, for good or for welfare; in common usage, it means that a lawyer handles a legal action without expectation of payment.

Property. That which is peculiar or proper to any person; that which belongs exclusively to one. The word is also commonly used to denote everything which is the subject of ownership, corporeal or incorporeal, tangible or intangible, visible or invisible, real or personal; everything that has an exchangeable value or which goes to make up wealth or estate.

Pro Se. For himself; in his own behalf; in person.

Publish (a libel). To make a libel known to any person other than the person libeled.

Quiet Title. To pacify; to render secure or unassailable by the removal of disquieting causes or disputes. This is the meaning of the word in the phrase "action to quiet title," which is a proceeding to establish the plaintiff's title to land by bringing into court an adverse claimant and there compelling him either to establish his claim or be forever after estopped from asserting it.

Replevin. A personal action brought to recover possession of goods unlawfully taken.

Res. A thing, an object.

Slander. The speaking of base and defamatory words tending to prejudice another in his reputation, office, trade, business, or means of livelihood; oral defamation; the speaking of false and malicious words concerning another, whereby injury results to his reputation.

Statute of Limitations. A statute prescribing limitations to the right of action on certain described causes of action; that is, declaring that no suit shall be maintained on such causes of action unless brought within a specified period of time after the right accrued.

Subpoena. A written process to cause a witness to appear before a court or magistrate therein named at a time therein mentioned to testify for the party named under a penalty therein mentioned.

Subpoena duces tecum. A process by which the court, at the instance of a party, commands a witness who has in his possession or control some document or paper that is pertinent to the issues of a pending controversy, to produce the paper or document at a legal proceeding.

Trover. An action to recover the value of personal chattels wrongfully converted by another to his own use.

Venue. The geographical division in which an action is brought for trial.

Bibliographical Essay

Research into a topic like archives and the law requires a review of literature in a wide variety of sources. Rather than attempt a comprehensive list of pertinent books and articles, it seemed more useful to direct the reader to bibliographies, periodicals, and recurrent government publications that provide leads to sources of information. Publications cited in footnotes are normally not repeated in this essay, and none of the legal cases cited are also listed here. Instead we hope to point towards additional and general sources.

For literature through the early 1970s, there is no better place to begin than *Modern Archives and Manuscripts: A Select Bibliography* compiled by Frank B. Evans and published by the Society of American Archivists in 1975. A second stop might be the manuals that the Society has published, especially those on security (written by Timothy Walch) and reference service (Sue Holbert). For anyone handling public records, the pamphlet published by the National Association of State Archives and Records Administrators, "Principles for Management of Local Government Records," contains excellent brief advice. George W. Bain's "State Archival Law: A Content Analysis" (*American Archivist*, Spring 1983) looks very narrowly at state archival statutes and, consequently, misses a number of laws that have direct impact on archives (such as general property statutes). For an international perspective on the rights of researchers and governments to national records, the Spring and Fall 1982 *Newsletters* of IASSIST (International Association for Social Science Information, Service, and Technology) contain interesting articles by scholars from a number of nations.

In the area of access and privacy, there are two key periodicals and innumerable other articles. The indispensable reading for anyone interested in the Freedom of Information Act is the biweekly newsletter *Access Reports: Freedom of Information* (The Washington Monitor, Inc., 1301 Pennsylvania Avenue N.W., Washington, DC 20004). All issues provide information on federal access questions, principally recently decided lawsuits; most issues also cover state legislation or court cases; news from Canada also appears in each newsletter. Another biweekly is *Privacy Times* (2354 Champlain St. N.W., Washington, DC 20009). Similar to *Access Reports* in coverage, it focuses on federal and state privacy acts, privacy portions of federal and state FOIAs, and similar statutes. If one is going to read only one article on state FOI issues, it must be "A Practical Review of State Open Records Laws," by Burt A. Braverman and Wesley R. Heppler (*George Washington Law Review*, May 1981).

One major federal publication on access is the quarterly *FOIA Update*, published by the Department of Justice (Superintendent of Documents, GPO, Washington, DC 20402, Stock No. 027-000-80002-5). Each issue has a few articles, a legislative update on federal laws, a question-and-answer column on access questions, and synopses of a few significant new court decisions on federal FOIA cases. The annual volume, *Freedom of Information Case List* (GPO Stock No. 027-000-01201-9), is a major resource for a variety of reasons. It includes the single most comprehensive list of federal Freedom of Information Act, Privacy Act, "Reverse" FOIA, Government in the Sunshine Act, and Federal Advisory Committee Act cases. In addition it prints the government's official interpretation of the current status of each of the FOIA provisions ("Short Guide to the Freedom of Information Act") and a 26-page bibliography of law review articles on all the acts listed. A final government publication, directed toward the user of the federal FOI and Privacy Acts but containing useful information for archivists as well, is "A Citizen's Guide on How to Use the Freedom of Information Act and the Privacy Act in Requesting Government Documents" (Thirteenth Report by the Committee on Government Operations, U.S. House of Representatives, for sale by GPO, Stock No. 052-071-00540-4).

A recently published bibliography gives a useful international perspective on access issues. Compiled by David Flaherty, a Canadian professor of history and law, it is titled *Privacy and Data Protection: An International Bibliography* (Knowledge Industry Publications, Inc., 701 Westchester Ave., White Plains, NY 10604).

Although we do not think it useful to list many individual articles, *The Wilson Quarterly* (Spring 1978) had two extremely helpful articles on the concepts of autonomy and privacy: "The Supreme Court and Modern Lifestyles" by A.E. Dick Howard and "Personal Privacy and the Law" by Kent Greenawalt. At the conclusion of these two articles there is a brief bibliography. Another thoughtful article on the problem of privacy is Philip B. Kurland's "The private I: Some reflections on privacy and the Constitution" (*The University of Chicago Magazine*, Autumn 1976).

Like the topics of access and privacy, copyright is the subject of an ever-expanding bibliography. The official source of information is the Copyright Office of the Library of Congress, which publishes a large number of pamphlets and informative brochures. One of particular interest to archivists is *Report of the Register: Library*

Reproduction of Copyrighted Works (17 U.S.C. 108) (1983). A useful private publication is Jerome K. Miller's *U.S. Copyright Documents: An Annotated Collection for Use by Educators and Librarians* (Littleton, CO: Libraries Unlimited Inc., 1981).

Five articles on copyright should be familiar to all archivists. They are "Archivists and the New Copyright Law," by Carolyn Wallace (*Georgia Archive*, Fall 1978); "Copyright and the Duplication of Personal Papers," by Linda Matthews (*Library Trends*, Fall 1983); "Copyright, Unpublished Manuscript Records, and the Archivist," by Michael J. Crawford (*American Archivist*, Spring 1983); "Decoding the Copyright Act," by Jon A. Baumgarten (*District Lawyer*, November/December 1981); and "Copyright in the 1980s: Fifth Anniversary of the Revised Law," by Victor Marton (*Federal Bar News and Journal*, January 1983). For archivists working with oral histories, the best article is "Oral History and Copyright: An Uncertain Relationship" by John A. Neuenschwander (*Journal of College and University Law*, Fall 1983-84).

In addition to the specialty articles mentioned in the footnotes, two additional ones are recommended. Kenneth Rendell's "Tax Appraisals of Manuscript Collections" (*American Archivist*, Summer 1983) is a good review of appraisal from the point of view of a manuscript dealer. Charles B. Elston's "University Student Records: Research Use, Privacy Rights and the Buckley Law," though written soon after the law was passed and before any litigation had taken place (*The Midwestern Archivist*, 1976), still is a good guide to the archival problems inherent in the Buckley Amendment.

Finally, the entire Summer 1984 issue of *Archivaria* is devoted to archives and the law in Canada, with some interesting comparisons with practices across the border. And the American Association for State and Local History, as part of their museum management series, has published *Museums and the Law* by Marilyn Phelan, which provides some basic legal advice that can be used by historical agencies generally.

The Legal Citation

Throughout this manual various citations to laws and legal cases have been given in the footnotes. If you want to look up any of them, you will have to decipher the legal citations. A complete explanation of the format for legal citations requires an entire treatise, but this appendix explains some of the fundamentals.

A typical citation is *United States* v. *First Trust Company of Saint Paul*, 146 F.Supp. 652 (D.C. MN 1956), aff'd 251 F.2d 686 (8th Cir. 1958). The italicized portion of the citation is the short title of the case; the actual title (or style) may be much longer and include many more names.

The next part of the citation, "146 F.Supp. 652 (D.C. MN 1956)," indicates that a decision made by the U.S. District Court in Minnesota in 1956 ("D.C. MN 1956") can be found in volume 146 of the *Federal Supplement* at page 652. (The *Federal Supplement* is the name of a publication series by a private publisher, West Publishing Company, that publishes selected opinions of all federal district courts. Oddly, perhaps, not all opinions are published; West publishes only those that the courts choose to submit to it for publication.) There are 96 federal judicial districts in the United States and the particular district court is always noted. For example, "S.D. NY 1972" would mean that in 1972 the U.S. District Court in the Southern District of New York issued an opinion.

The final part of the citation, "aff'd 251 F.2d 686 (8th Cir. 1958)" indicates that the lower court decision was affirmed in an appeal to the 8th Circuit Court of Appeals. The decision of the Court of Appeals was in 1958 and can be found in volume 251 of the *Federal Reporter Second* (again a series published by West Publishing Company) at page 686. There are 12 Circuit Courts of Appeals and the particular court is always indicated in the citation.

An example of a citation to a state decision is *Sender* v. *Montoya*, 73 N. Mex. 287, 387 P.2d 860 (1963). The italicized portion, as in citations to federal cases, is the short title of the case. The next part, "73 N.Mex. 287," shows that the report of the New Mexico Supreme Court can be found in volume 73 at page 287 of the series *New Mexico Reports*. The final portion, "387 P.2d 860," indicates that the same decision can also be found in volume 387 at page 860 of the series *Pacific Reporter Second*, part of a regional reporting system published by West Publishing Company. The system reports state high court opinions in volumes organized on a regional basis (e.g., Atlantic, Southern). Finally, the date "(1963)" is the date the opinion was issued.

Understanding the citation pattern described above allows you to deduce that *Kissinger* v. *Reporters Committee for Freedom of the Press*, 445 U.S. 136 (1980), is a 1980 decision of the U.S. Supreme Court found in volume 445 at page 136 of the *U.S. Supreme Court Reports*. This is the official series of opinions of the Supreme Court of the United States, it is comprehensive, and it is a publication of the Government Printing Office.

Sometimes you will see a citation that looks like *Penny A. Ricchio* v. *Gerald P. Carmen*, Civil Action No. 80-0773, U.S. Dist. Ct., D.C., June 8, 1984. Citations in this format are to unpublished cases, either very recent ones that have not yet appeared in the published series or cases that for some reason have never been published. In the former instance, after a little time you can go to the *Federal Supplement* or, if the case is from a circuit court of appeals, to the *Federal Reporter Second* and look up the case and get the final, permanent citation. In the latter instance, because the case remains unpublished, the only access to it is through the records of the courts.

A final example of a legal citation is 17 U.S.C. 301 *et. seq.* This citation refers to a law that has been codified and published in the *United States Code* (U.S.C.). The law can be found in Title 17 (the Code is organized in chapters known as "Titles," each of which contains laws on a particular topic), at section 301 and, by "et. seq.," the sections following 301.

This brief review should help demystify the majority of legal citations. There are other kinds of published cases from specialized courts, such as tax courts, military courts, and so on, but the citations to them usually follow the pattern described above. If you try to find some of the cases cited in this manual and have problems, you can always ask a law librarian for help.